Music on the
Beautiful Mountain:

A History of Music at Belmont

*For Keith Guyton who represents
the very best of Belmont
Warmly,*

By Richard C. Shadinger

*Richard C. Shadinger
March 12, 2007*

FIELDS PUBLISHING

NASHVILLE, TENNESSEE

December 2016

Printed in the United States of America
Library of Congress Number 2016954497
ISBN 978-1-57843-160-1

Published by

Fields Publishing
6545 Chessington Drive
Nashville, Tennessee 37221
615-972-8402
e-mail: tfields6545@gmail.com

Dedication

This book is dedicated to the more than 3500 graduates of the
Belmont University School of Music
in appreciation for the beauty you bring to the world
through your work in churches, the classroom,
the teaching studio, rehearsal room, the recording studio,
on the concert, Broadway and operatic stage.
After all, this story is your story,
and there are many chapters yet to be written.

Table of Contents

Foreword

When I first arrived on the Belmont campus as a young faculty member in 1974, I was vaguely aware of the unusual and interesting history of the campus and the institutions connected with it. As time went on I became more knowledgeable about the history and more fascinated by it. As the School of Music grew and matured, gaining a national reputation, it became clear that something remarkable was happening at this historic place. It seemed the right time to document the development of the Belmont University School of Music. Yet I felt that such a history needed to begin with Adelicia Acklen who set the stage for what was to follow. The musical history of Belmont College for Young Women and Ward-Belmont College had not been told as well, and serves as a precursor to the musical life of Belmont College and University. In a number of ways the histories are woven together in the same fabric. Not a day goes by that the influence of Adelicia Acklen is not seen or felt in this place. In subtle ways the ideals and tradition of excellence of the Ward-Belmont Conservatory of Music are lived out in the music programs of Belmont University.

This history does not claim to be a complete account of the Adelicia Acklen's life or a complete story of the institutions residing here. Instead, I have tried to show how Adelicia made Belmont a place of culture and beauty through involvement with art and music. In writing about Ward-Belmont and Belmont I focused on the history of the music schools in those institutions, but of necessity placed that history within the context of the larger institution.

Any written history is viewed and evaluated through the eyes of the author. At certain points I have tried to give analysis of what seemed to be happening amid the flurry of facts and documents. In writing about more recent decades (the story of which I am a part) it has been difficult to be objective, even while trying to do so. Where I have misunderstood or misstated, I ask for forgiveness. It has been a pleasure to research the beauty that Belmont has given Nashville and the world beyond since 1850 when Adelicia looked at the hill and thought "Let's build something beautiful here."

6

Acknowledgements

Special appreciation goes to Dr. Cynthia Curtis, Dean of the School of Music (1991-2016), for her support and invaluable insight. Dr. Jerry Warren, Dean of the School of Music from 1969-1991, was patient with my constant calls for clarification and insights. In addition, Dr. Stephen Eaves, Dean of the College of Visual and Performing Arts beginning in 2016, provided strong support for this project. Judy Williams, Director of the Belmont Archives in the Lila Bunch Library, was most gracious in allowing me to invade the archives for days at a time. Mark Brown, Director of the Belmont Mansion, gave me full access to the Mansion Archives for information on Adelicia Acklen and the Belmont Mansion. Dr. Mary Ellen Pethel, Archivist for Harpeth Hall School, was generous in allowing me to use the school archives for access to Ward-Belmont documents. In addition, the on-line archives from Harpeth Hall School were most useful in researching documents from Ward-Belmont College. The Wesleyan College (Macon, Georgia) Archives was helpful in researching Edouard Hesselberg. Many faculty members of the School of Music were helpful in giving interviews, information and clarification. Finally, appreciation is expressed to my wife, Marilyn, who was always there to provide advice and encouragement.

Prelude

Spoken at Portia's Belmont

Within the house your mistress is
And bring your music forth into the air.
How sweet the moonlight sleeps upon this bank!
Here we will sit and let the sounds of music
Creep in our ears; soft stillness and the night
Become the touches of sweet harmony.
. . . Look how the floor of heaven
Is thick laid with patines of bright gold;
There's not the smallest orb that thou behold'st
But in this motion like an angel sings,
Still quiring to the young-eyed cherubins;
Such harmony is in immortal souls;
But while the muddy vesture of decay
Doth grossly close it in, we cannot hear it.
Come, ho! And wake Diana with a hymn;
And draw her home with sweet music.
. . . Music! Hark! It is the music of the house.
Methinks it sounds much sweeter than by day.
Silence bestows that virtue on it . . .
How many things by season seasoned are
To their right praise and true perfection!
Peace, ho! The moon sleeps with Endymion,
And would not be awak'd!

From Shakepeare's *Merchant of Venice*, Act V, Scene 1

PART I
THE CULTURAL LEGACY OF ADELICIA ACKLEN AND THE BELMONT MANSION

*Portrait of Adelicia Acklen (c.1860)
with her horse Bucephalus*

Belmont Mansion, 1892

Beginnings

Today as one drives or walks south on 18th Avenue (Music Row) in Nashville, it becomes clear as one nears what is now Wedgewood Avenue that the terrain is gradually rising. A view to the left at Wedgewood confirms that indeed a major hill has risen south of downtown Nashville. Today's view of this hill reveals one of the most impressive views of an academic institution in America. A row of six magnificent academic buildings in impressive classical style face Wedgewood. With columns, impressive balustrades, turrets and fountains, these buildings range in construction dates from 1890 to 2014. Passersby sometime mistake Freeman Hall as the Belmont Mansion, but the north view of the Acklen Mansion has been obliterated since 1890 when Belmont College began to add buildings to the Acklen estate for a new girl's school. However, it is not difficult to imagine why the Acklens chose this lovely hill for their home to be called "Belle Monte" (Beautiful Mountain).

Many speculate that Adelicia Acklen named her Nashville home "Belmont" as a reference to Portia's grand estate outside of Venice in Shakespeare's *Merchant of Venice*. As a well-educated young woman, Adelicia possibly knew *Merchant of Venice* and took the name from Portia's beautiful home. There is even a legend that Adelicia and Joseph Acklen spent their honeymoon in Italy and were entranced by Venetian architecture. Mark Brown, Director of the Belmont Mansion, confirms that Joseph and Adelicia did not tour Europe after their wedding, and that Adelicia visited Europe for the first time after the end of the Civil War, years after Belmont had been completed in the 1850s. Whatever influenced Adelicia Acklen to name her estate "Belmont," it certainly has an Italian flair which invokes Venetian homes of centuries past.

Before there was a place called Belmont there was music on the hill. The beautiful mountain was a sacred place. It was the highest wooded place in a land of gently rolling hills where birds sang freely. The Native Americans who lived in the land prior to the settlement of Nashville would have celebrated the beauty of the place in word and song, leaving the space unmolested by human hands.

As Nashville grew to be the most prominent town in the region by the early 1800s, it is not surprising that someone would notice the beautiful mountain, which rose gradually from the town to the north and looked across a grand expanse to the south toward the Harpeth Hills, and decide to build a home there.

10

CHAPTER ONE

Adelicia Hayes Acklen - The Early Years (1817–1859)

It is into this setting that Adelicia Hayes Franklin Acklen Cheatham (1817-1889), one of Nashville's most interesting and important figures of the 19th century, enters. Adelicia Hayes was born on March 15, 1817 into a prominent Nashville family. In her later childhood the family built its home called Rokeby not far from the hill she would one day claim for her palatial home. Her upbringing was remarkable for a young girl of her time. She was well versed in literature, art, language and music, graduating from the Nashville Female Academy at the age of 16 "with highest honours."[1]

Evidence suggests that she was a gifted singer and a proficient pianist. These skills were quite common among cultured ladies of the day, but it seems that, as in most aspects of her life, she excelled beyond the norm. She certainly was capable of singing and playing standard parlor music and some of the classics of her era.

In 1834, at the age of 17 she was engaged to Nashvillian Alphonso Gibbs (1813-1834), a Harvard Law School graduate and the son of a leading banker of Nashville. He died of typhoid before the wedding took place. In response to his death she went into mourning (a portrait from the time shows her as a beautiful youth in a black dress). A poem she wrote at the time of Alphonso's death shows something of her grief, but also reveals a young woman with considerable writing skills:

> That eye is closed and deaf that ear,
> That lip and voice are mute forever;
> And cold that heart of faithful love,
> Which death alone from mine could sever.[2]

11

It would be five years before Adelicia Hayes would consider marriage again, this time to a wealthy (and older) planter, Isaac Franklin, owner of Fairvue Plantation in Gallatin, Tennessee. Several accounts describe how Franklin and Adelicia became acquainted. One of the accounts tells that Adelicia and a group of friends were on a picnic at Fairvue and were invited by Franklin into his home. When he requested a song, Adelicia sang a popular ballad "Buds and Roses." Whether this story is true or not, they were married on July 2, 1839 when she was 22 and he was 50. Adelicia had married one of the wealthiest men in Tennessee and Franklin had gained a lovely, cultured and well-educated wife. The union resulted in four children, but the second (Julius Caesar) died soon after birth in 1844. In 1846, after only seven years of marriage, Franklin died of a heart attack while in Louisiana, and soon after, the two older children (Victoria and Adelicia) died within three days of each other. Adelicia Franklin was now a wealthy widow with one child (Emma) and vast holdings in Tennessee, as well as Louisiana and Texas. Her shrewd business sense helped her increase the wealth and purchase large tracts of property in Nashville. In 1849 she purchased several tracts of land which included the Belmont property and an adjoining farm called Montvale.[3]

During her growing up years and later as Mrs. Isaac Franklin, Adelicia bought numerous copies of sheet music which she bound into a folio (now in the collection of the Belmont Mansion). The front of the book is engraved with the name: Adelicia Franklin. This remarkable collection contains 35 piano and vocal compositions, a cross-section of pieces popular in the 1830s and 40s. It is clear that Adelicia played and sang these works. The music has a used appearance and contains markings in the music (perhaps written by a teacher) indicating fingerings, phrasing and dynamics. The pieces fall into several categories: 1. Vocal songs and ballads, 2. Piano pieces by well-known composers such as Weber and Herz, 3. Popular dances of the day such as Quadrilles, Polkas and Waltzes, 4. Picturesque and sentimental parlor music, and 5. Works by American composers such as Richard Willis, Robert Sinclair and Mrs. Nixon (composers now mostly forgotten). Adelicia's music collection shows that she was a capable pianist and singer with interest in a wide range of styles.[4] Her early exposure to music study and performance would no doubt influence her support for music in the future as she became an advocate for the arts in Nashville.

The Beginning of Belmont

On May 7, 1849, after signing a pre-nuptial agreement which gave her control over her wealth, Adelicia Franklin married Joseph Acklen, the grandson of the founder of Huntsville, Alabama and an experienced plantation manager. The marriage seemed to be an advantageous one, because Joseph brought strength to the partnership through the careful running of Adelicia's plantations in Tennessee and Louisiana, adding considerably to the family wealth. Six children were born to the couple and all but the twins, Laura and Corinne, lived to maturity.

In the early 1850s Adelicia and Joseph began the building of their summer home, Belle Monte, which they would enlarge in 1859 by adding the "Grand Salon." The renowned German architect, Adolphus Heiman, seemed to have been engaged for the design of the villa which adopted an Italian style. Heiman, born in 1809, was the son of the superintendant of Sans Souci, the palace of the Prussian monarchs. An emigrant to America, he had been active in Nashville and Huntsville. While the Acklen mansion was strongly Italian, it also had Classical elements in the Corinthian columns. A Renaissance feature was the placement of statues along the top of the façade; the extensive iron grillwork on the side porches gave a New Orleans touch to the building. The grounds added to the grandeur of the house through gazebos of New Orleans ironwork, statues, elaborate gardens, extensive garden statuary and, to top it off, a water tower of brick, which provided a wonderful view of the entire estate. Eventually, the 180 acre estate would include an art gallery, a bowling alley, a bear house, a lake with alligators from Louisiana, a conservatory with exotic plants, a zoo, a deer park, and an aviary, all of which complemented the extensive gardens. The Mansion's Grand Salon would come to be known as the most elaborate domestic space built in Tennessee prior to the beginning of the Civil War.[5]

With the establishment of Belmont and the partnership of Adelicia and Joseph, Belmont became a center for musical and artistic culture. By 1855 the Acklens had purchased a Dunham Square Grand piano that was played and displayed prominently in the home. (Belmont records indicate payment on August 29, 1855 to Nashville piano technician G.W. Kibble for tuning the piano.)[6] The Acklens began to acquire an extensive collection of paintings and statuary, as well as fine furnishings for the home.

During the winter months the Acklens travelled to the warmer Louisiana plantations and often visited New Orleans during the season prior to Lent when balls, parties and concerts were in abundance. Acklen records indicate that these extensive visits to New Orleans took place in 1857, 1858 and 1859, and included attendance at opera performances and the "grand ball" at the St. Charles Hotel (February 10, 1858). On March 20, 1859 the Acklens even attended the opera to hear Piccolomini.[7] The journeys to New Orleans were important social events for the Acklen family, and also provided opportunities to shop and buy items for Belmont unavailable in provincial Nashville.

CHAPTER TWO

War Comes to Belmont (1860–1865)

By 1860 the Acklens had built an art gallery building to the west of the Mansion to hold their growing collection, concluding several years of building, collecting and expansion. Circumstances changed with the beginning of the Civil War. Nashville became an occupied city on February 25, 1862 when the Federal troops entered the city. As a wealthy prominent family and supporters of the Confederacy, the Acklens were closely watched, causing Joseph to flee south to Louisiana for his safety. Joseph died of malaria on September 11, 1863. Not long after his death, Adelicia began one of the most adventurous endeavors of her eventful life, as she headed to Louisiana with her cousin Mrs. Sarah Ewing Sims Carter to save the Acklen cotton crop from destruction by the Confederate forces. Through some tough negotiations with both Union and Confederate officers, she was able to commandeer wagons and move the cotton to New Orleans where she sold the 2000 bales of cotton for $960,000 and had it shipped to Liverpool.[8]

Adelicia returned to Nashville by way of New York City to find that her beloved Belmont had been occupied by federal troops and the house used as headquarters by officers. Shrewdly, before the battle began, she had moved her valuables (paintings, jewelry and silver) to the home of the widow of President James K. Polk in downtown Nashville. Mrs. Polk's home, safe from molestation by the Union troops, provided the perfect place for Adelicia Acklen to preserve many of her most precious belongings. The Battle of Nashville began on December 3, 1864 and major skirmishes in the battle were fought around the Belmont property, especially to the south. Prior to the battle, trees on the Belmont property were felled for firewood and many of the outbuildings were destroyed. The Belmont water tower served as an observation post and a signal tower for

15

the Union army during the fighting. Adelicia took her entire family to the Polk residence for the duration of the fighting since the battle lines were near Belmont. Although the sound of shells shook Belmont's foundation, the Mansion survived intact.[9]

The Battle of Nashville was one of the last major skirmishes in the Civil War, and it was not long before Adelicia had restored the property to its former grandeur. On April 12, 1865 (two days prior to the assassination of Abraham Lincoln) Adelicia hosted a large ball, indicating that life was in the process of returning to its pre-war status at Belmont. In the post-war years Belmont became a sort of park for the residents of Nashville before the establishment of the city parks system. The grounds were often open to the public, and there are many references to picnics, dances and sports being held on the grounds.[10]

CHAPTER THREE

The Post-War Years (1866–1889)

Adelicia's Grand Tour of Europe

On June 1, 1865 Adelicia and her children left Nashville for a grand tour of Europe, a journey which was to usher in the most glittering period of Adelicia's interesting life. From New York, they travelled to London, staying at the Langham Hotel, London's finest, and taking in sights such as Westminster Abbey, St. Paul's Cathedral and the Tower of London. On July 31 while sailing across the English Channel on the way to Paris, they met the famous opera singer Adelina Patti.

The family enjoyed a lengthy stay in Paris, which Adelicia deemed to be the most beautiful city of all. The children were tutored by French teachers and were speaking French as the stay in Paris lengthened. On January 17, 1866 Adelicia was presented to Napolean III and his wife, the Empress Eugenie, at the first presentation ball of the year held at the Tuileries Palace.[11]

In February, 1866 the Acklens travelled on to Rome where they visited St. Peter's Basilica, the Villa Borghese and the Roman ruins. By chance they even saw the Pope travelling in his carriage. In Rome Adelicia made some of her most important purchases of sculpture. On February 23 she visited the workshop of American sculptors Randolph Rogers, C.B. Ives and Joseph Mozier. She purchased Randolph Rogers' "Ruth," a statue portraying Ruth gleaning wheat. This impressive over-life-size work would eventually be placed in the Grand Salon upon its arrival in Nashville. "Rebecca at the Well" by C.B. Ives is less impressive in both size and workmanship, but it shows Adelicia's interest in art which portrayed religious themes. Another

17

statue purchased by Mrs. Acklen is the angel "Peri" mentioned in Moore's "Paradise and the Peri." "The Peri," sculpted by Joseph Mozier, was first displayed in the Grand Salon of the Belmont Mansion, but was later moved to the Acklen mausoleum at Mount Olivet Cemetery where it remains today.[12]

On February 26, 1866 Adelicia made one final purchase from William Henry Rinehart, his popular "Sleeping Children." While this sculpture, with its deep sentimentality, does not have an immediate appeal to modern viewers, it is technically a fine work with remarkable lifelike figures of two children in repose. The lifelike images of the two children, the folds of the bed clothes and the soft appearance of the pillows show the skill of Rinehart. The subject must have had a special attraction to Adelicia because of the earlier death of her twin daughters. She had the artist inscribe "Laura and Corinne" (her deceased twin children from her second marriage) on the back of the piece. "The Sleeping Children" now lies in repose in the entrance hall at Belmont, a tribute to a mother's love and to her artistic sensibilities. These four sculptures are important in Nashville's history as perhaps the most significant works of art in the city at the time, and they still hold a place of importance at Belmont and at the Acklen mausoleum. All four were sculpted by important American artists working in Rome. The sculptures as a group also indicate something of the artistic tastes and interests of Adelicia Acklen.[13]

In March, 1866 the family's journey through Italy included Naples, Pompeii, Herculaneum and Florence, where they visited the Duomo and the Boboli Gardens. On the way back to Paris they travelled through Basel, Geneva, Verney, Chillon and Strasbourg. In June, 1866 the Acklens arrived back in New York City where Adelicia went shopping for a new carriage, and on September 9 they finally left for Nashville after a journey which had lasted a sixteen months.[14]

Adelicia Cheatham – The Mistress of Belmont

Adelicia Acklen's return to Nashville in September of 1866 marks the beginning of the last phase of her life, which would secure for her a place as the standard bearer of artistic activities within the city. Her life was increasingly connected to events of educational and artistic interests. On December 18, 1866 Adelicia held a reception for her visiting friend, Madame Octavia LaVert. LaVert, of Mobile, was known both in America and Europe for her social charm. 1000 invitations were sent and Adelicia wore the dress and diamonds she had worn when presented to the French court. Special attention was given to the music played at the reception.[15]

On June 18, 1867 Adelicia Acklen married for a third time to Dr. William A. Cheatham. On June 27 a wedding reception was held at Belmont with 1500 invited guests. Adelicia wore a coronet, a gift from the Emperor and Empress of France. A band of musicians played in the gardens, which were illuminated by a full moon and Japanese lanterns.[16]

In the months and years ahead, there were numerous mentions of musical and educational events connected to Adelicia Cheatham. She purchased a 4013-pound bell to be placed in the tower of her church, First Presbyterian in downtown Nashville. A great deal of information about this gift is mentioned in sources from the time. Apparently it arrived at the railroad depot on July 6 and was brought to the church on July 9. The officers of the church then met on July 15 to prepare a letter of thanks to Mrs. Cheatham for the gift of the bell. On July 25 the bell was hoisted up to its place in the tower, an operation taking about one hour. When the bell was finally in its place in the tower, Adelicia paid a visit to the church to see it. This bell became an important presence in the life of Nashville. As a large, sonorous bell, it was used for many years as the fire alarm bell for the Nashville Fire Department. Today the bell still makes a commanding sound when it rings from the Downtown Presbyterian Church on Church Street.[17]

In the post-war years the Belmont gardens received particular attention and soon returned to their pre-war beauty. In addition to the gardens, the summer houses, and statuary, a conservatory housed tropical plants and other plants that could be grown out of season. Notice was given to the magnificence of the gardens and conservatory in the May, 1868 issue of *The Gardener's Monthly*.[18]

In this time period numerous references are made in letters to musical and educational activities at Belmont, including references to piano and voice lessons for the children. In a letter from 1871 Adelicia wrote that "William has learned several new pieces on the guitar." William's journal recorded that Adelicia attended a performance of Gounod's *Faust* in Nashville where she was invited backstage to meet the soprano Christina Nelssohn who sang the role of Gretchen. Pauline, the youngest daughter, became a proficient singer, studying with Mrs. Iglehart, a musician who is mentioned several times in Belmont documents. In 1880 Pauline sang the role of the gypsy in "The Frog Opera" with Mrs. Iglehart singing the role of the Queen Frog.[19]

19

Increasingly the Cheathams supported artistic ventures in Nashville. In May, 1871 a number of statues and paintings were moved from Belmont for display at the Southern Industrial Exhibition held in Nashville. Again in May of 1873, Adelicia Cheatham loaned her large painting of Queen Victoria for display at the 3rd Industrial Exhibition. And in September of 1874, 14 of Adelicia's paintings were displayed at the 4th Industrial Exhibition. In May of 1880 the Centennial Exposition began and the Cheathams loaned 11 paintings and the sculpture "Rebecca at the Well" for display in the Art Building.[20]

On April 14, 1874, Adelicia donated a portrait of President Andrew Jackson to the state of Tennessee. (This portrait hangs today in the office of the Governor of Tennessee). In the following January (1875) the Tennessee General Assembly adopted a resolution thanking Adelicia for the portrait. Then in August of 1877 the American Association for the Advancement of Science met in Nashville with Alexander Graham Bell as the keynote speaker. A reception for Bell was held at Belmont on August 30 with refreshments and music. For entertainment Mrs. Iglehart sang "The Echo Song."[21]

On September 19, 1877 President Rutherford B. Hayes, Adelicia's third cousin, came to Nashville to dedicate the new Customs House on Broadway. Since Adelicia's carriage was the finest in Nashville, it was used to convey the President through the city.[22]

As Adelicia's children matured, opportunities for their intellectual development were provided in abundance. The children were all provided with the best education possible. In addition to William's learning the guitar, Claude studied violin with a Mr. Hofferman. In 1877 Pauline, Adelicia's youngest daughter, journeyed to Paris to continue her studies. In 1878 William began a correspondence with Henry Wadsworth Longfellow which continued for some time. In fact, in August of 1879, Adelicia and William travelled to Boston where William had an appointment to meet with Longfellow. While in Boston Adelicia visited the newly-constructed Trinity Church and was very impressed by the grandeur and the art work of the Richardsonian Romanesque church. After returning to Nashville in September, William sent a letter (including pictures of Belmont) to Longfellow, thanking him for the visit.[23]

In its heyday Belmont was graced with the visits of numerous important people. In addition to the previously mentioned Alexander Graham Bell, in July of 1876 Thomas Huxley, eminent British biologist and colleague of Charles Darwin, visited Belmont. A few years later, on May 12, 1879 Henry Ward Beecher, well-known minister and brother to Harriet Beecher Stowe, was a guest at Belmont. And on May 21, 1880 Dr. and Mrs. Cheatham were listed as sponsors of an opera performance at the Masonic Theater for the benefit of the Orphan's Asylum.[24]

Adelicia – The Final Years

At the outset of the 1880s, Adelicia's activity as a society leader appeared to decline. At the same time, activities of her daughter, Pauline, increasingly became more prominent as she participated in balls, galas and travels. For some time there was talk about selling Belmont, and eventually Adelicia sold the Belmont property for $54,000. Ultimately, Adelicia separated from Dr. Cheatham and moved to Washington, D.C., where she immediately became a part of the social life of the community. Adelicia bought property on Massachusetts Avenue in Washington and planned to build a home there. She and Pauline travelled to New York to purchase furnishings for the new home then under construction. Shortly thereafter Adelicia became ill from pneumonia and died at the Fifth Avenue Hotel on May 4, 1887. A remarkable life was over.[25]

Adelicia Acklen – A Legacy

It is important to recount the life and interests of Adelicia Acklen in order to set the stage for what would happen on her estate for the next 130 years. Her Mansion would become a school. The beauty of the grounds, the significance of the architecture, the artistic interests and history that surrounded the historic estate would influence the development of the schools which found a home on the campus. The life and legend of Adelicia would live on, sometimes taking on larger proportions than it deserved, but her desire for culture and love of art and music definitely set the stage for the educational institutions that bore her beloved home's name. In a more practical way, the architecture of Belmont influenced the design and structure of the first buildings of Belmont School for Girls in 1890, 1905 and 1913. In the 1990s and into the new Millennium a compatible architectural style would be seen in a series of buildings constructed as a fast-growing Belmont University required massive new instructional spaces.

Most importantly, in the late 20th century the Belmont Mansion became an important venue for concerts for Belmont's burgeoning School of Music. The Belmont Camerata, Belmont's faculty chamber ensemble, began to perform chamber music concerts in the Grand Salon in 1988 to great acclaim from the Nashville music community. The Belmont Camerata often celebrated Adelicia's birthday with concerts of music from her time. Surely Adelicia would be pleased to know that guests in large numbers were listening to beautiful music in the room that she had conceived a century and a half earlier.

A tradition of beauty and excellence was established on a hill in Nashville that would live on in many ways through the institutions that occupied the space in the years to come. Music would continue to ring from the "beautiful mountain" and the Grand Salon of the Belmont Mansion inspired by Adelicia's legacy of artistic and natural beauty.

PART II
MUSIC AT BELMONT COLLEGE
AND WARD-BELMONT COLLEGE

Ward-Belmont Orchestra (1914), Fritz Schmitz, Conductor

CHAPTER FOUR

Beginnings: Music at Belmont College (1890–1913)

In 1889 the Belmont Mansion, along with 15 acres, was sold for $30,000 to Miss Ida Hood and Miss Susan L. Heron, who planned to open a school for girls. Both women had served on the faculty of Martin College in Pulaski, Tennessee, and they were looking for a location for their new venture; the Belmont property fit their needs perfectly. By September of 1890 they were ready to open the school with an enrollment of 80 students. At first they used the Acklen house for dorm space, common spaces, and classrooms, but immediately began a building program, resulting in a large building which connected to the north side of the Mansion and faced downtown Nashville in the distance.[1]

As a finishing school for girls, music was, from the beginning, an important part of the curriculum. The first catalog for the school in 1891 lists five instructors in music, teaching piano, violin, voice, guitar, and mandolin. Three of the teachers were in piano, one in voice, and one in the plucked string instruments. The inclusion of instruction in guitar, mandolin and banjo might seem unusual, but a survey of girls' schools of that period indicates that these instruments were quite common in those schools, often including guitar and mandolin ensembles. It appears that in the early years of the school, the curriculum focused almost entirely on private instruction in music.[2]

In 1896 The Clara Schumann Club was founded for students of piano. Clara Schumann (1819-1896), considered to be one of the most significant pianists of the nineteenth century, was an appropriate role model for young women in piano study. According to yearbooks from the school, this club was active for several decades, finally disappearing by the 1940s.

By the end of the first decade there were seven music instructors (four piano, one voice, one violin and one for the guitar, mandolin and banjo). There were a total of 105 students taking music lessons with by far the largest number in piano with 68 students, followed by voice with 26. "Harmony" was added to the curriculum as the first academic course.[3]

Evidence of growth occurred soon after the new century began. Fidelity Hall, a large four-story building to the west of the Belmont Mansion, was built in 1903 and became the location for music instruction. Pictures of the era show large studios for instruction, often equipped with a grand piano and an upright piano. In 1904 the first choir at Belmont, called the Choral Club, was established under the direction of Miss Julia Taliaferro.[4] The Choral Club performed, in what seems to have been one of the first cantatas or major choral works to be heard at Belmont: "The Culprit Fay" by J.L. Ensign. The score of "The Culprit Fay," composed on a poem by Joseph Rodman Drake, is a cantata of 78 pages for unison and two-part treble voices accompanied by keyboard. The text concerns the mischievous nighttime activities of fairies, a popular subject for poetry and music in the nineteenth century.[5] From this point on, choral music became an important part of the music program at the school. As a part of the May commencement activities of 1905, the School of Music presented a performance of Franz von Suppe's (1819-1895) operetta *Ten Maidens and No Man,* certainly an appropriate opera to be performed in a young ladies' finishing school. Though nothing is known about the scope of this performance, it appears to be the first opera performed on the campus. On May 19, 1906, the Music School followed the previous opera with another one, Gilbert and Sullivan's *Trial by Jury.* This performance used several men from Vanderbilt's Glee Club to sing the men's roles.[6]

A Great Leap Forward for Music

Music instruction at the fledgling institution was growing, but it was clear that the principals of the school, Misses Heron and Hood, had grander things in mind. With excellent facilities in Fidelity Hall, a growing number of students, and the beginnings of a music curriculum, a major decision was made which would set the stage for Belmont's Music School to flourish. In 1905 the administration appointed an outstanding pianist and teacher,

25

Edouard Hesselberg, to become Director of the Belmont School of Music. Hesselberg was a Russian pianist who had performed throughout Europe and the United States. He previously taught piano at Wesleyan College in Macon, Georgia. He had impeccable musical credentials, and his fame both as a composer and pianist immediately brought attention to Belmont's music school. He evidently was given a mandate to establish a music school of importance, one with an appropriate curriculum, new faculty and adequate instruments.

The accomplishments under Hesselberg's leadership from 1905 to 1912 are clearly seen in the literature from the school during that period. Within a year music enrollment had grown to 159 students.[7] At the same time, numerous musical organizations began to involve students in learning, programming and social events. In addition to the Clara Schumann Club, the Music School offered the Ensemble Club (for piano ensemble playing), the Etude Club, the Leschetizky Club, the Glee Club (formerly the Choral Club), and the Cremona Club. It seems that most, if not all, of the music students were involved in at least one of these organizations. In his first year Hesselberg honored his new school by composing a March Two-Step entitled "Belmont Belles," which was printed in the 1905 yearbook *Milady in Brown*.[8]

In 1906 Hesselberg established the position of "Rehearsal Superintendent," held by a staff member who was assigned to the practice facilities to monitor whether students were meeting their established practice hours and to otherwise ensure that students were working seriously. Research at the archives at Wesleyan College in Macon, Georgia revealed that Hesselberg had established the same position at that school and brought the concept with him to Belmont.[9] This position remained in place at Ward-Belmont into the 1940s, showing the high priority the school placed on diligent practice.

A 1906 brochure advertised an intense Music Summer Session for that summer, but the summer music program does not appear to have continued.[10] Edouard Hesselberg was a Kimball artist, representing the Kimball Piano Company in his concerts. In 1908, under Hesselberg's leadership, Belmont purchased 52 Kimball pianos, one of the largest single purchases from that company up to that time.[11] On February 28, 1908 famous pianist Myrtle Elvyn (1886-1975) played a concert at Belmont to great critical acclaim. Since she was a "Kimball artist" (like Hesselberg), this concert was apparently connected with the purchase of

Kimball pianos and was a promotional event for Kimball. This is the first record of a major guest artist to perform at Belmont.[12]

"Belmont Edition" of *The Musical Herald*

It did not take long for Hesselberg to put Belmont College on the map. He used his influence to get a major focus on the School of Music published in October, 1908 issue of *The Musical Herald*, one of the leading musical journals of the time. This issue, devoted almost entirely to Belmont College's School of Music, helped Hesselberg reach his goal to attract students to Belmont and to spread the Belmont name around the country. The front page of the issue was comprised entirely of a photograph of Hesselberg with a bold signature in white over the black background of his jacket. The inside cover was dedicated to the printing of Hesselberg's "Belmont Belles" (The Official Belmont March Two-Step). The four pages of the march are reduced and printed on one page of the journal. The third page contains two articles, the first of which is biographical information on Hesselberg, highlighting his musical career in Europe and America and extolling the attributes he brought to Belmont and the second of which is about Belmont College itself entitled "Belmont the Beautiful – A School Idyl (sic) of Beauty and Usefulness – The Evolution of a Baronial Estate; Or, How a Great Mansion Became a Great School." This lengthy article describes in glowing terms the beauty of the campus and its interesting history. Information is given about the founders of the school, Miss Hood and Miss Heron, along with the College Regent, Rev. Ira D. Landreth. A separate article on "The Belmont School of Music" provides details on the strong program offered and the excellent facilities found in Founders Hall, the new School of Music Building. The next article, titled "Myrtle Elvyn at Belmont" describes the performance at Belmont in February, 1908 of this well-known pianist of the day, highlights excerpts from reviews of the concert, and lists the repertoire for the concert. A final article "Press Excerpts of Director Hesselberg's Success" quotes from reviews of his concerts in cities around the United States: New York, Chicago, Philadelphia, New Orleans, Kansas City, Memphis, Galveston, Minneapolis, Pittsburg, Portland (Maine), Dallas, Fort Worth, Trenton, Auburn (New York), Ithaca, Grand Rapids, Baton Rouge, Mobile, Westchester, Burlington (New Jersey), Camden, Wilkes Barre, York, Laramie, Denver, Atlanta, Macon and Nashville. Hesselberg's endorsement of Kimball pianos is made clear in the information about him and Belmont. The final article extols the attributes of the Kimball piano and Kimball's modern factory. Evidently Kimball encouraged or paid fees for the focus on Belmont and the Kimball Company, since it was in this year that Belmont made a large purchase of Kimball pianos.[13]

In 1909 the Assembly Room in Faith Hall (now Freeman Hall) was greatly enlarged to provide a large auditorium adequate for chapel services and concerts. In addition to the major piano purchase, Belmont acquired a large Kimball pipe organ at a cost of $10,000 for the newly-enlarged auditorium in 1910. The 1911 music catalog for Belmont boasts that its three-manual Kimball pipe organ is "said to be the finest in any girl's school in the nation." It was noted for its grandeur of sound and its variety of tone. While the tonal specifications of this organ are not known today, indications are that the organ had approximately 1500 pipes, comprising 30 ranks. While that is not a large instrument by modern standards, it was a remarkable instrument for a school early in the 1900s.[14]

Growth of the School of Music under Hesselberg

Hesselberg's leadership paid off in increased enrollment in music at Belmont. By 1910 (five years into his tenure), 319 students were enrolled in music study, about triple the number before his tenure at Belmont. In addition to piano, voice and string instruction, organ instruction was added with the arrival of the young organist Arthur Henkel, who joined the faculty.[15] Henkel had recently become Organist-Choirmaster of Christ Church on Broadway. A highly respected performer, church musician and conductor, Arthur Henkel's association with Belmont would continue all the way into the 1950s with the new Belmont College. When Hesselberg took a new position in 1912 to become piano professor at the Toronto Conservatory of Music, he left Belmont with better music facilities and instruments, increased enrollment, a thorough music curriculum, a capable faculty, and a strong music tradition that continued throughout the life of the institution.

Edouard Gregory Hesselberg (1870-1935)

Edouard Hesselberg (sometimes called "D'Essenelli" by the press) was perhaps the most distinguished musician to teach at Belmont College in its earlier years, and the school's progress during his tenure indicates something of his musicianship, leadership skills and prestige. Born of Jewish parents in Riga (Latvia), Russia in 1870, he inherited musical talent from his mother's side of the family. His great uncle, Charles Davidoff, was the most famous cellist of his day. His first major performance was as a teenage pianist with the Philharmonique Symphony in Moscow. A few years later he graduated with honors from the Royal Philharmonique Conservatory of Music and Dramatic Art, the only graduate receiving a medal in his class. For his graduation performance he played Liszt's celebrated "Dies Irae" paraphrase *Danse Macabre* with full orchestra. After his conservatory study, he began his study with the famous Anton Rubinstein (1829-1894). He performed before the royal family of Russia and numerous houses of European royalty in his early years. He began a successful career as concert pianist, performing with such artists as Sembrich, Marconi, Nordica and De Reszke. He performed concerts in the major cities of Europe including St. Petersburg, Moscow, Berlin and Paris. A gifted composer, he often played his own works in concerts.[16]

In 1892 he immigrated to the United States where he continued his performing career, to enthusiastic acclaim, in cities such as New York, Chicago, Philadelphia, New Orleans, Minneapolis, Kansas City, Pittsburg, Dallas, Ft. Worth, San Antonio, Little Rock, Trenton, Ithaca, Grand Rapids and Mobile. Prior to his time at Belmont, he taught at the Ithaca Conservatory (1895-96), the Music Academy in Denver (1896-1900), and Wesleyan College (Macon, Georgia) (1900-1905). He married a Tennessean, Lena Priscilla Shackelford, and their first son Melvyn Edouard Hesselberg was born in Macon in 1901.[17]

In 1905 Hesselberg was invited to become the Director of the School of Music of Belmont College, then only 15 years in existence. The school already had an active music program of private study with seven faculty members offering lessons in piano, voice, violin, guitar, mandolin and banjo. Since the aims of the college's founders Miss Heron and Miss Hood were much grander, the highly reputable Hesselberg seemed to be the right person to expand the school's image. In fact, Hesselberg set a high standard that would be followed in music study at Belmont (and later Ward-Belmont) for years to come.

In the Belmont School of Music Catalog of 1906-1907, the following "Testimonial" is given by the management of Belmont in regard to Mr. Hesselberg:

29

In presenting to our patrons the Director of the Belmont
School of Music, we take pleasure in stating that the
endorsements of Mr. Hesselberg as both musician and man
are in our hands from those who know him best – well-
known citizens, college presidents, boards of trustees and
others in schools where he has taught and in the
communities where he has lived.[18]

Hesselberg expanded the scope of the School of Music by founding
Belmont's first orchestra in 1910 with 13 players. By 1913, under the
leadership of Harry Ross, violin teacher, the orchestra had grown to 20
players, beginning its move toward becoming Belmont's premiere ensemble
for decades to come.

Hesselberg was an active composer of piano music, concertos, songs and
violin pieces. His wife was a poet and provided texts for several of his love
songs. His best known works for orchestra were his *Russian Suite* and *Russian
Rhapsody*. He also transcribed a number of works by Bach, Chopin and
Schubert for two pianos. A few of his transcriptions remained in anthologies
into recent times, especially his arrangement of Tchaikovsky's *Nutcracker
Suite*.

Hesselberg was a Kimball artist, promoting the Kimball piano brand in
his concerts. When Hesselberg set out to improve and enlarge the equipment
of Belmont, he turned to the Kimball Company of Chicago and arranged for
Belmont to purchase 52 Kimball pianos at one time. This encounter is
documented in Van Allen Bradley's book on the Kimball Company entitled
Music for the Millions:

One of the most successful sales operations occurred in
1912 at Nashville, Tennessee, when he [N.C. Hadley] sold
52 pianos at one time to Belmont (now Ward-Belmont)
College, a noted finishing school, over which the Reverend
Ira D. Landrith presided as regent. The sale was engineered
with the help of Edouard Hesselberg, a distinguished
Russian concert pianist who was director at Belmont from
1905 to 1912. Hesselberg was under contract as a Kimball
artist and arranged to give a concert to demonstrate
Kimball's virtues. Hadley recalls that in order to lend dignity
to the concert he scurried around all over town looking for

rental tuxedos for the various members of the company's Nashville agency who attended. With the sale, the agency acquired all the old pianos at Belmont. And Hadley set out to sell them. A resourceful man, he located an abandoned hospital in the heart of town, took an option on it and moved in the traded-in stock. ...He brought in an expert refinisher and a repair man from the Chicago factory. Hadley chalked in the grains on the piano cases, some of which were of green oak, and the refinisher, an expert on stains and varnishes went to work. Soon they had a dazzling array of refurbished pianos ready for the wareroom and Hadley took out a full-page ad in the *Nashville Banner* to proclaim "Beautiful Pianos from Belmont." Such was the school's reputation, he says, that for three or four years afterward Nashvillians kept coming into the store to ask for "one of those pianos from Belmont."[19]

Hesselberg taught a large studio of all-women pianists. The school yearbooks from his time indicate that he organized his studio into a study club with officers and with Hesselberg's young sons Melvin and Lamar as mascots. The yearbooks also reveal that there appeared to be prestige in being in the Hesselberg studio because other teacher's studios were given less space. Printed piano programs of Hesselberg's studio show his students playing pieces of a wide range of difficulty and sophistication. Not surprisingly, composers such as Beethoven, Mendelssohn, Chopin and Liszt were prominent in these concerts along with long-forgotten composers of lighter fare.

Although Hesselberg was at Belmont for only seven years, his accomplishments were remarkable: The enrollment of students in the School of Music more than doubled. He enlarged the faculty, bringing in some important musicians who would remain with the school for decades. He arranged for the purchase of 52 new pianos at one time from the Kimball Company. Also during his tenure Kimball installed a large three-manual pipe organ in the Belmont Auditorium which was said to be "the finest pipe organ in any girl's school in the country." In 1910 Belmont established its orchestra under the leadership of violin instructor Harry Ross. Hesselberg's time at Belmont set a new standard in music for the college and helped establish Belmont as perhaps the finest artistic institution in the city of Nashville.

Hesselberg left Belmont in 1912 to teach at the Toronto Conservatory where he remained until 1918. After that tenure he taught for a time at the School of Music at the University of Nebraska. He died in 1935 in Los Angeles.[20]

Interestingly, Hesselberg was the father of one of the most famous film, Broadway and television actors of the 20th Century. Melvin Edouard Hesselberg (1901-1981) who studied music at Belmont as a child, was better known as Melvin Douglas, taking his maternal grandmother's last name as his stage name. Douglas acted in 77 Hollywood films, winning two Academy Awards as Best Supporting Actor in *Hud* (1963) and *Being There* (1979). He was nominated for Best Actor for *I Never Sang for My Father* (1970). He also won a Tony Award for his stage work on Broadway and an Emmy for television acting. He played leading roles with actresses such as Greta Garbo, Gloria Swanson and Joan Crawford.[21]

CHAPTER FIVE

Music at Ward-Belmont
(1913–1939)
"The Golden Age"

The merger of Belmont College with Ward Seminary was an important crossroads in the history of both institutions. Established in 1865, Ward Seminary was located on Eighth Avenue in downtown Nashville. It also had a strong academic and musical tradition, but the downtown location proved problematic as Nashville expanded. In 1913 the two schools agreed to merge to become Ward-Belmont School. Ward Seminary was the older and larger school, but Belmont had the larger campus located in a suburban area away from the city. The merger of the two schools served as the beginning of what might be considered "the golden age" of the institution. When school opened in September, 1913 there were close to 800 students, approximately 500 of which were from Ward Seminary and 300 from Belmont. The President of Ward Seminary, Dr. John Diell Blanton, became the President of the new institution. A major building program began on campus with the completion in 1914 of the large Blanton Academic Building (this building burned in 1972). On the east side of the quadrangle, three dormitories were built - Pembroke (1913), Heron (1916) and Hail (1923) - and a Club Village near the Tower provided cottages for club meetings.[22]

The merger strengthened the Music School because Ward Seminary brought several gifted faculty members and a large number of music students. Emil Winkler, Piano and Harmony Professor from Ward Seminary, became the Director of the School of Music, replacing the departing Hesselberg. Other music faculty members transferring from

Ward Seminary included Florence Boyer (voice), Eva Massey (piano), Estell Roy Schmitz (piano), Fritz Schmitz (violin) and Mary Falconer Winkler (piano). Joining the faculty as Head of the Voice Department was Charles Campbell Washburn, who brought greater status to this area of study. While the music programs were growing in general, instruction in guitar, mandolin and banjo was dropped soon after the merger. The union of the two schools resulted in a music faculty of 13 members with over 300 music students.[23] This critical mass brought a number of advantages, which were soon evident. The first was that Ward-Belmont was now positioned to become Nashville's most important musical institution; in fact, it soon became Nashville's favorite place for concerts given by students, faculty and guest artists. The pride that the community took in the musical achievements of Ward-Belmont helps to explain the pain caused by the demise of the institution decades later. There was simply no place in Nashville that provided musical instruction and performance at such a high level. The faculty members of the Ward-Belmont School of Music were indeed the leading and most highly regarded musicians of the community.

An important addition in 1913 was the arrival of Fritz Schmitz as Professor of Violin and Conductor of the Belmont Orchestra. The year before the merger with Ward Seminary, the Belmont orchestra had 20 players; in 1914, with the additional musicians from Ward Seminary, the orchestra grew to 35 players.[24] The Belmont Orchestra became the premiere ensemble of the School of Music and the most active orchestra in Nashville. Prior to the establishment of the Nashville Symphony Orchestra in 1945, the Belmont Orchestra's concerts attracted large audiences from the Nashville community on campus, at the War Memorial Auditorium and at the Ryman Auditorium. Professor Schmitz died in 1917, by which time the Belmont Orchestra and string program had made great strides.

One positive development was the beginning of regular performances by famous artists of the day. Over the next three decades the parade of musicians performing in the Ward-Belmont Auditorium reads like a "Who's Who" of great artists of the era. This new endeavor indicates something about the funding for the music area of the College. Representative performing artists of 1910-1930 include:

John Freund, Lecturer, Editor of *Musical America* (October, 1913)
Ernest Hutcheson, Pianist (December 7, 1914)

Rudolph Ganz, Pianist (October 12, 1917)
Alma Gluck, Soprano (November 16, 1917)
Ernestine Schumann-Heinck, Contralto (March 11, 1918)
Amelita Galli-Curci, Soprano (April 15, 1918)
Josef Lhevinne, Pianist (March 8, 1920)
Leopold Godowsky, Pianist (November, 1920)
Rosa Ponselle, Soprano (October 21, 1920)
Guiomar Novaes, Pianist (March 27, 1926)
Giuseppe de Luca, Baritone (October 20, 1927)
Percival Price, Carillon (April 12, 1929)[25]

On April 16, 1915 Ward-Belmont Choral Society and the Vanderbilt Glee Club joined together to present a concert version of Friedrich von Flowtow's opera *Martha* at the Ward-Belmont Auditorium under the direction of Browne Martin. Arthur Henkel accompanied the performance at the organ. A review in *The Nashville Tennessean* the next day stated that "the room was full and hundreds were turned away." The article further stated that it was probably the largest audience to ever hear a concert of this type in Nashville history.[26] In 1916 the Choral Society presented a similar concert of Balfe's *The Bohemian Girl* followed by the Ward-Belmont Choral Society's critically acclaimed performance of Cowen's *The Rose Maiden* on May 8, 1917. An article about the Cowen concert with a photograph appeared in the June 9, 1917 issue of *Musical America*. At this concert Browne Martin conducted a women's chorus of 85, a group of 25 young men from Vanderbilt, and four soloists accompanied by Arthur Henkel on the organ. The unnamed reviewer said the following about Professor Martin's leadership: "Mr. Martin has succeeded in moulding (sic) a body of young singers into an organization which can present choral works with notable distinction. In attack, precision, tone shading and all the beautiful effects one expects from a body of trained singers, the society rose to an unexpected degree of perfection. The fresh young voices of the girls, with the robust voices of the Vanderbilt Glee Club, thrilled the audience again and again."[27]

In 1917 Edouard Potjes, formerly at the Royal Conservatory of Ghent, Belgium, was hired to be the Director of the School of Music. It appears that his hiring was an attempt to recover the European prestige which had been lost with the departure of Edouard Hesselberg five years earlier. Potjes had impressive credentials with a degree from the Cologne Conservatory of Music and music study under Ferdinand Hiller and Franz Liszt, the greatest pianist of the 19th century. Not much is known about Potjes' work during the two years he was at Ward-Belmont as Director. While in Nashville, however, he composed a song for voice and piano entitled "American Battle Song," inspired by the entry of The United States into "the Great War," which he dedicated to President Woodrow Wilson.[28]

The year 1917 also brought the death of Fritz Schmitz, conductor of the Ward-Belmont Orchestra and teacher of violin. The 1918 yearbook, *Milestones*, gave this memorial: "Greatly beloved and most gifted, he was an inspiration to his pupils and friends."[29]

After the merger, Ward-Belmont began to advertize widely in major periodicals, extolling the strengths of Ward-Belmont as a place to educate young women. Many of the ads feature music study as one of the strengths of Ward-Belmont. Apparently these national ads began to attract students who were more serious in their music study;[30] student recital programs show that students who majored in music were performing works of more substance and difficulty. While Ward-Belmont still had the reputation as a finishing school for upper-class young women, the image of the serious musician was growing as the school became more widely known nationally, attracting more experienced and talented students. In 1918 Ward-Belmont added to the prestige of the School of Music by hiring the Italian tenor and teacher Gaetano Salvatore de Luca.

In 1919, after the short tenure of Edouard Potjes as Director of the School of Music, Lawrence Goodman from the piano faculty was appointed to the position. By this time some dissatisfaction with the numerous Kimball pianos purchased in 1912 during the Hesselberg era had surfaced. Under Goodman's leadership, the school upgraded by purchasing nine Steinway grand pianos and, in the future, Steinway became the piano of choice. In 1922 a new administrative structure was established under the guidance of Goodman. The administration of the School of Music was called the Board of Music Directors, allowing several area directors to assist in the administration of the growing music program. The Board consisted of Lawrence Goodman, director of the department of piano; Gaetano Salvatore de Luca, director of the department of voice; Kenneth D. Rose, director of the department of violin; Frederick Arthur Henkel, director of the organ department; Alfred Hoskins Strick, instructor in musical sciences. At this time there were a total of 17 music faculty members, with two listed as teachers in musical sciences (theory and music history) and one listed as a teacher in piano sight playing. The 1922 music catalog of

Ward-Belmont included extensive biographies of all music faculty with schools attended and teachers of each. The same catalog mentions the larger number of pianos, the pipe organ which is "second to none in the country," as well as some new items such as a two-manual practice organ, a Steinway duo-art piano and a Victrola with a large record collection.[31] (Many of these recordings remain in the Music Special Collections in the Bunch Library of the University).

In 1922 the Castner Dry Goods Co. presented to Belmont the Chickering grand piano supposedly used to accompany Jenny Lind when she sang in Nashville at the Adelphi Theater in 1851. The piano was placed in the Belmont Mansion where it became affectionately known as "The Jenny Lind Piano." While in more recent years this piano has been shown not to be the one that accompanied Lind, it remained an object of interest to visitors of the Belmont Mansion.

Events of 1924

In May, 1924 a momentous event occurred at Ward-Belmont when John D. DeWitt, Jr. presented the first radio broadcast in Nashville's history from the Faith Hall Auditorium (now Freeman Hall). Craig Havighurst gives this account of the first broadcast:

> Dr. Clayton E. Crosland, associate vice-president of one of the Southeast's finest finishing schools wasn't exactly sure what to say, but he did not wish to be misunderstood. "This is Ward-Belmont, Nashville," he said, a bit too loudly into his "microphone." The contraption wasn't entirely foreign – quite like a telephone without the ear-piece – but it was *most* modern. After a pause Crosland spelled out the name of the school, as if to make sure: "W-A-R-D – B-E-L-M-O-N-T." He continued, "We have today installed a radio sending station and will tonight broadcast the concert by Mr. Philip Gordon, the distinguished American pianist.[32]"

The concert took place in the presence of a large audience of young ladies with the broadcast ranging two hundred miles into the distance.

Soon thereafter, voice instructor Gaetano de Luca introduced and played recordings of Enrico Caruso over the new broadcasting station. The

37

recordings from de Luca's personal collection were simply played on a Victrola with the microphone placed nearby. Ward-Belmont used the station to broadcast promotional ads for the college and to broadcast important speakers from the auditorium. After a short period, administrators of Ward-Belmont decided that the venture was too costly and decided to close the station. John DeWitt soon thereafter became the manager of the new station WSM which opened within the next year.[33] In years to come Nashville would become a leader in broadcasting, and Belmont can claim that it began on its campus with concerts and recordings of operatic arias performed by Caruso. A historical marker in front of Freeman Hall marks this important event in Nashville history.

About the same time, at nearby Vanderbilt University, a group of poets emerged called the "Fugitives," who espoused a conservative style of poetry reflecting a southern attitude. The group was led by John Crowe Ransom, who wrote perhaps his most famous poem in 1924, presumably about the nearby campus of Ward-Belmont:

Twirling your blue skirts, traveling the sward
Under the towers of your seminary,
Go listen to your teachers old and contrary
Without believing a word.

Tie the white fillets then about your hair
And think no more of what will come to pass
Than bluebirds that go walking on the grass
And chattering on the air.

Practice your beauty, blue girls, before it fail;
And I will cry with my loud lips and publish
Beauty which all our power shall never establish,
It is so frail.

For I could tell you a story which is true;
I know a lady with a terrible tongue,
Blear eyes fallen from blue,
All her perfections tarnished—yet it is not long
Since she was lovelier than any of you.[34]

The poem is at once a tribute to Ward-Belmont and an observation about the transitory nature of beauty which the institution espoused.

Reaching Out to the Nashville Community

By the mid-20s the Ward-Belmont Orchestra was presenting concerts both on campus and at the War Memorial Auditorium. Building on the foundation started by Fritz Schmitz in 1913, Kenneth Rose brought the ensemble to a higher level in the 1920s. A printed concert program from 1923 of a concert in the Ward-Belmont Auditorium lists 50 players. 15 of the players are young men, mostly in the woodwind and brass section, and seven players are listed as "Mrs.," indicating that a number of the performers are community players.[35] The 1927 *Milestones* stated that "The orchestra is contributing in a most helpful way to the artistic development of the South."[36] And the 1928 *Milestones* added that "the Ward-Belmont Orchestra is one of the best known school orchestras in the country." The repertoire for the Ward-Belmont Orchestra Concert on May 10, 1928 was Schubert's Unfinished Symphony and Mendelssohn's Violin Concerto.[37]

On May 17, 1927 Ward-Belmont drama, dance, and music students presented the Greek play *Elektra* on the steps of the Parthenon in Centennial Park to a large audience present.

Gaetano Salvatore de Luca

At the beginning of the 1918 school year Ward-Belmont acquired the services of Signor Gaetano Salvatore de Luca as Director of the Voice Department. De Luca came to Belmont with impressive European credentials. He had studied with Chevalier Edouardo Carrado of Italy, Chevalier Alfredo Sermiento, Enrico Caruso's coach, Commendatore B. Carelli (Director of the Naples Conservatory), Lombardi of Florence, Buzzi Peccia and Carbone in New York and Signor Baraldi of London.[38] De Luca was an effective teacher, based on a number of pupils who had successful singing careers. And he was a man with big ideas. One of the grandest was his plan to produce and lead a fully-staged performance of Mascagni's *Cavalleria Rusticana*, mustering the forces of local talent in what was to be the largest operatic production to date in Nashville using local performers. The performance was held on May 12, 1927 at the Ryman Auditorium. The expenses were backed by Ward-Belmont, whose president, J.D. Blanton,

39

considered it as a gift to the Nashville "music-loving public." He was correct in that the college was highly praised for its support for the project. There was no charge, but rather free tickets were distributed through the Claude P. Street Piano Company. Elaborate sets decked the stage of the Ryman. Signor de Luca's students sang the main roles backed by a large cast of extras and chorus members. At the same time, Sarah Jeter of the Ward-Belmont Dance Department trained the dancers who presented a ballet between the two acts. Finally, Arthur Henkel conducted the 30-member orchestra. All accounts indicate that the performance, given to a packed house with several thousand people turned away, was successful beyond anyone's expectations. Because of the crowds, a second performance was hastily scheduled for the following evening. Nashville's response to this operatic venture was in some ways surprising, since travelling operatic troupes had often performed before in Nashville to cool response. The free tickets no doubt were a factor, but also a production presented by local singers, players and dancers caused interest. Another factor has to be considered as well – Gaetano Salvatore de Luca was the ultimate enthusiastic promoter. The production was his idea, he motivated the community to pool its resources, and his enthusiasm brought the performance together. Nashville music lovers must have been encouraged about the success of the performance, which may have suggested the possibility of a local opera company. No one could have known that the Great Depression was just two years away and that Nashville's own opera company was decades away.[39]

Signor de Luca may have seen the successful production of *Cavalleria Rusticana*, supported largely by Ward-Belmont, as a stepping stone to a larger vision for Nashville – the establishment of an independent conservatory of music. But he still had one year remaining on his five-year contract with Ward-Belmont. He requested release from his position, a request that was denied. It appears, however, that de Luca forged on with his plans for opening a conservatory while completing his final year of teaching at Ward-Belmont.[40]

He found financial support among several important Nashville businessmen who founded a corporation to fund the new Nashville Conservatory of Music which opened its doors in 1928. De Luca's personality and European experience persuaded well-connected business leaders in Nashville that supporting a conservatory would be good for Nashville, positioning the city as a cultural leader in the South. The Foreword to the Conservatory catalog states clearly the aims of the

40

Conservatory:

> The Nashville Conservatory of Music was founded by a group of distinguished business and professional men who were actuated by a desire to make Nashville the musical center of the South. The need for such an institution, equipped to develop talent in the South, has long been felt and has served as an inspiration for the founding of this great civic enterprise. In choosing Signor Gaetano S. de Luca to be president, the Board of Directors has selected one of America's most noted teachers, and he, in turn, has surrounded himself with a faculty of artists and teachers of outstanding merit.[41]

Signor de Luca served as President and General Director of the Conservatory with an impressive faculty and a large staff to administer the school. The Conservatory was located in a three-story building located at 2122 West End Avenue, next door to what was then the Governor's Mansion. The building was a combination of two palatial West End Avenue homes with the elaborate concert hall added at the back of the facility. The catalog touts its location near major schools (Vanderbilt, Scarritt College, and the YMCA Graduate School). Tellingly, de Luca omits nearby Ward-Belmont from whence he came, which in some ways was a competing institution. The verbal descriptions and photographs of the Conservatory building reveal it to be a well-appointed, opulent building reminiscent of great European spaces. Grand staircases, heavy draperies, great artwork, fine teaching studios and practice rooms are described in glowing terms, down to the plush carpets, gold leaf frames and tasteful paint colors (one can almost hear de Luca describing his new place of work). The Joel O. Cheek Auditorium seated 400 and was furnished with fine pianos and a new Moeller pipe organ of 54 stops. The Conservatory included 10 practice rooms, a library and dormitory near the Conservatory.[42]

The Conservatory developed a full curriculum for the Bachelor of Music degree majors in Piano, Organ, Voice, Violin, Theory and Composition and Public School Music. The Masters Degree in Performance was also provided. The Conservatory's programs were soon accredited by the National Association of Schools of Music, making it one of only five such schools in the South.[43]

41

In regard to the faculty of the Conservatory, it is noted that de Luca brought with him from Ward-Belmont Arthur Henkel, the revered teacher of organ, and Sarah Jeter from the Ward-Belmont Dance Department. In addition, de Luca brought Browne Martin from Ward-Belmont to be faculty dean and instructor in violin.[44] Henkel would return to Ward-Belmont after a two-year tenure at the Conservatory. One of the Conservatory's youngest teachers in the 1930s was Elizabeth Wall, who would later join the Ward-Belmont faculty in 1941. De Luca attracted noted teachers from outside of Nashville, most notably the famous pianist and composer Wiktor Labunski (1895-1974). Of Polish origins, Labunski studied at the St. Petersberg Conservatory before coming to the United States. He made his Carnegie Hall debut in 1928.[45]

The Conservatory very quickly established itself as a viable institution with wonderful facilities, a fine faculty, NASM accreditation and a good enrollment. It is to de Luca's credit that the foundations were established so thoroughly and quickly. However, de Luca's timing was unfortunate with the Great Depression beginning only one year after the Conservatory's establishment. Eventually, the Depression affected the Conservatory's level of financial support from local businessmen. The Conservatory carried on for a few years; however, Signor de Luca became ill with cancer and died in June of 1936. Without the financial support of its founders and the energetic leadership of its president, de Luca, the Conservatory closed in 1936, only eight years after its founding. Meanwhile, nearby on Belmont Boulevard, Ward-Belmont College moved forward, maintaining its musical programs with only slight indications of the effects of the Depression. The conservatory concept of musical education would never be attempted again in Nashville. A lesson had been learned: Musical instruction was more financially stable within the context of larger institutions of higher education. This lesson was to be borne out in decades to come with the music programs of institutions such as Ward-Belmont College, George Peabody College for Teachers, Belmont University and Vanderbilt University.

The Ward-Belmont Chimes

The idea of converting the old Belmont Tower into a bell tower as a World War I Memorial came from Miss Leila D. Mills, Dean of Ward-Belmont from 1915-1927. The class of 1921 started the memorial fund for what would be known as the "Alumnae Chimes."[46]

The 23-bell carillon was cast by the Gillett and Johnston Bellfounders of Croydon, England at a cost of $13,000 and was installed in November of 1928. The carillon was notable for several reasons: It was only the second carillon built in the South, the 25th to be built in the U.S., and the only carillon installed in a girl's school. The first carillonneur was Henry S. Wesson, organist for the college and Director of the Department of Musical Sciences. Wesson had replaced organ professor Arthur Henkel, who left Ward-Belmont in the same year to teach at the Nashville Conservatory of Music.

For the carillon dedication concert Ward-Belmont engaged Percival Price, probably the greatest carillonneur in North America at the time, specifying that he was to include the college song "The Bells of Ward-Belmont" in the concert. Price, the Carillonneur for the Peace Tower in Ottawa, Canada, played the dedicatory concert on April 12, 1929 to a large and enthusiastic crowd of students, alumni, faculty and Nashville residents. Several hundred alumnae attended out of the over 3,000 who had been invited. The event was broadcast over WSM radio, broadening the audience to numerous alumnae and friends of the college. Before the concert Miss Linda Rhea, representing the Alumnae Association, presented the bells to the college followed by a speech in response by Dr. John W. Barton, Vice-President of Ward-Belmont. A plaque (currently in the Tower) has the following dedication:

> The Ward Belmont Chimes
> Dedicated April 12, 1929
> A gift of the Alumnae Association
> The project was proposed by
> Miss Leila D. Mills,
> Dean of Women 1915-1927.
> This was made possible by donations
> of former students of Belmont
> College and Ward Seminary
> As well as students and faculty
> of Ward-Belmont.[47]

Henry S. Wesson took up the duties as carillonneur with seriousness. On the one year anniversary of the dedication, April 12, 1930, he played a concert which was broadcast over WSM radio. In June of 1930 he travelled to Mechelen, Belgium to study carillon at the Carillon School under the great Jef Denyn. As it happened, Wesson did not return to Ward-Belmont, but Arthur Henkel returned to Belmont after two years at the Conservatory of Nashville. Upon his return and throughout the 1930s, he played the carillon, including a series of Sunday evening concerts. Moreover, from 1935-1945 Henkel played a Christmas Eve concert which became known as "Arthur Henkel's Christmas Card." In the 1940s, however, Henkel turned the carillon duties over to Mrs. Florence Irwin, a member of the piano faculty of Ward-Belmont. The carillon became an important part of the traditions of Ward-Belmont and was significant in the prestige it brought to the college through concerts and the uniqueness of the instrument. While the 1929 Gillett and Johnston carillon would be removed from the Tower in 1952, the tradition of the Belmont carillon would be resurrected in a significant way in the 1980s.

Concert Artists of the 1930s

Even though the Depression caused financial hardships throughout the country, Ward-Belmont continued and even expanded its prestigious artist series with the following artists presented in concert:

> Ernest Hutcheson, Piano (March 10, 1930)
> Carlo Zecchi, Piano (February 17, 1931)
> Nathan Milstein, Violin (March 3, 1931 and March 7, 1935)
> Nelson Eddy, Baritone (March 18, 1931)
> Rudolph Ganz, Piano (April 17, 1931)
> London String Quartet (March 7, 1932)
> Jose' Iturbi, Piano (April 6, 1932)
> Robert Goldsand, Piano (December 8, 1932)
> Jascha Heifetz, Violin (October 31, 1933 and October 29, 1936)
> Kathryn Meisle, Metropolitan Opera Contralto (March 15, 1934 and October 12, 1937)
> Robert Casadesus, Piano (February 12, 1935)
> Frederick Jagel, Metropolitan Opera Tenor (April 16, 1936)
> Charles Kullman, Metropolitan Opera Tenor (February 16,1937)
> Eugene List, Piano (November 18, 1937)
> Mischa Elman, Violin (February 3, 1938)
> Robert Virovai, Violin (November 17, 1938)
> Saint Louis Sinfonietta (March 11, 1939)

Richard Bonelli, Baritone (March 28, 1939)
Hilda Burke, Metropolitan Opera Soprano (October 12, 1939)
Zino Francescatti, Violin (November 9, 1939)
Marcel Dupre, Organist (November 28, 1939)[48]

A Distinguished Visitor

A significant event occurred at Ward-Belmont on November 17, 1934 when President Franklin Delano Roosevelt, then in his first year as President, briefly visited the campus. Classes were cancelled so students could be ready to line the circle as his limousine approached the campus. Originally his appearance was scheduled for 9:30 am, but his entourage was delayed because of a breakfast for the President at the Hermitage. The tour through the campus eventually began at 11:00 am. The President's car drove slowly around the circle with all the students standing in order around the quadrangle. As the President's car entered the campus, Arthur Henkel in the Tower played "Hail to the Chief" on the Belmont Carillon.[49] One legend from the time says that Roosevelt was served lunch in the private dining room in Founders Hall, following the drive around the campus, but there is no proof of such a luncheon.

In the early 1930s the Ward-Belmont School of Music became "The Conservatory of Music," elevating the music program to higher status and highlighting music as a special area of study at the College. In the May 1931 issue of *Good Housekeeping*, an ad appeared promoting the Ward-Belmont Conservatory of music, picturing a young woman singing beside a grand piano.[50] In 1934 Lawrence Goodman, Dean of the Conservatory, left Ward-Belmont for another position, though he returned to Nashville in retirement.[51] For a period of three years there was no dean, and the Board of Musical Directors - consisting of Kenneth Rose, violin; Lawrence Riggs, musical sciences; Sydney Dalton, voice; and Roy Underwood, piano - was responsible for the administration of the Conservatory. All were long-term faculty members of the Conservatory. In 1937 Roy Underwood was appointed Dean of the Conservatory and the Board of Musical Directors was abolished, although the members of that group continued to be the Directors of their respective areas. Roy Underwood remained Dean until Alan Irwin replaced him in 1941.

New Student Attitudes

During the late 30s there were indications that Ward-Belmont was changing with the times. In 1935 a student-led jazz ensemble called "The Captivators" was formed and continued to exist until the closing of the school in 1951. The ensemble used saxophones, sometimes other woodwinds and strings, piano and drums. The group played for club dances, Halloween parties, and assembly programs. The Captivators were always prominently featured in the yearbook, *Milestones*, and was a source of pride for the student body.

A momentous concert by a guest artist occurred on November 18, 1937 when the 18-year-old Eugene List (1918-1982), just beginning his career, performed at Ward-Belmont. The review by Alvin S. Wiggers in the *Nashville Banner* the next morning was glowing, but of more interest to the reviewer was the reaction of the Ward-Belmont girls to the suave young pianist; he suggested that the girls responded to List as a crowd might to a matinee idol of the day. List was indeed called to play encore after encore, prompting the reviewer to make this comment: "Perhaps impressed as much by the youth's wavy blond hair as his superior skills, the large audience which included all the school girls, recalled him for three encores."[52] This event was quite a change from the more serious concerts of the past.

Ward-Belmont Conservatory Is Awarded Accreditation

Before 1924 when the National Association of Schools of Music (NASM) was established, there was a wide range of quality of instruction and curricula in music schools in the United States. NASM required rigorous standards for schools of music, and soon the more serious and prestigious schools sought NASM approval. The Ward-Belmont Conservatory achieved accreditation by NASM in 1938, the first junior college conservatory in the South to attain this status.[53] By taking this step, Ward-Belmont met the strict standards of NASM in the areas of curriculum, student performances, faculty credentials, funding and facilities. This status set Ward-Belmont apart from the traditional women's finishing schools of the time.

CHAPTER SIX

Ward-Belmont's Last Decade (1940–1951)

The Ward-Belmont Orchestra, High and Low Points

The Ward-Belmont Orchestra continued to be the flagship ensemble of the Conservatory, and through the 30s the ensemble's spring concerts were highlights of the Nashville musical season. The Spring 1939 Concert at War Memorial Auditorium included these formidable works: Bruch's Violin Concerto in G Minor, with Mathilda Weaver Duke as soloist; and Beethoven's Symphony No. 2 and Selections from Tchaikovsky's *Nutcracker*. The fortunes of the Ward-Belmont Orchestra suffered a setback, however, with the birth of the Nashville Symphony Orchestra in 1945. With the ending of World War II and its attendant economic growth in Nashville, the time was right for the development of a professional (or at least a semi-professional) orchestra. For the first concert of the Nashville Symphony Orchestra on December 8, 1946, Kenneth Rose, violin instructor and orchestra conductor of Ward-Belmont, was a member of the violin section. Moreover, Sydney Dalton, Ward-Belmont voice teacher, wrote a glowing first review in the *Nashville Tennessean* of the young orchestra with a headline which declared, "Strickland Direction of Group Lauded."[54] As active musicians in the community, Ward-Belmont faculty must have been enthused about having a new professional orchestra in Nashville, but the immediate effect at Ward-Belmont was the loss of a number of community players in its collegiate orchestra. As a result, in 1947 the orchestra with 21 players became known as "The Sinfonietta," made up mostly of string players from the college. Another group which received occasional mention was called "The Chamber Music Society," an ensemble of approximately 18 players, including some younger community players. As the Nashville Symphony became a viable orchestra, the Ward-Belmont Orchestra was never to be the large and important ensemble it had been since the leadership of Fritz Schmitz in 1914. In fact, by 1949 no orchestra existed at Ward-Belmont, but instead a modest group of 11 instrumentalists called "The Ensemble."[55]

Dean Alan Irwin and Changes in the 1940s

In the early forties the Conservatory moved from its long-time location in Fidelity Hall to a large house across Belmont Boulevard. (The Conservatory building stood where the Belmont University Bunch Library now stands). Meanwhile, the practice facilities remained in the practice building on the east side of campus. In the early 1900s Belmont had commandeered the old Acklen Bowling Alley building, which stood east of the Mansion, for practice rooms. This long narrow building, divided up into numerous practice rooms with a long corridor onto which all the practice rooms opened, was used for this purpose until the mid-1950s when it was demolished.

In 1940 Alan Irwin was appointed Dean of the Conservatory. Irwin received his music education at the Bush Conservatory of Chicago and Northwestern University. He continued his study at the Julliard School in New York City and received the M.A. degree from Columbia University. He was trained as an organist and served as the Minister of Music of the Belmont Methodist Church near the campus until his death in 1949. Alan Irwin and his wife Florence (also on the Conservatory faculty) were both active concert pianists.[56] As a leader in a new decade when society was changing drastically, he updated the Ward-Belmont Conservatory in ways that appear to respond to the new attitudes of the 1940s. While all of the directors of music at Ward-Belmont left their mark on the school in noticeable ways, the changes under Irwin are particularly visible. He seemed to sense that it was a new day, that music education was changing, and that Ward-Belmont had some catching up to do.

One of the first and most obvious changes involved redefining the job of "Practice Superintendent," established in 1905 under Edouard Hesselberg, to "Practice Supervisor and Secretary for the Conservatory," the first time a secretary is mentioned in the music area. Soon afterward the "Practice Supervisor" half of the title was dropped. The first person to hold this new job role was Lady Corinne Myers.

Early in Irwin's tenure publicity for music scholarships appeared in the 1943 college catalog. There were five $200 scholarships offered to outstanding performers, sizeable scholarships for the time. The most outstanding student was given the Grace Moore Scholarship, named for former Ward-Belmont student, Metropolitan Opera soprano and Hollywood movie actress, Grace Moore (1898-1947).[57] In 1941 Grace Moore visited Ward-Belmont where she was pictured in two photographs, one posed with several faculty members, including Dean Irwin. In another she is shown surrounded by a group of students enjoying tea.[58] The publicizing of music scholarships for the first time indicated that the school was interested in attracting talented students who might not have the financial means to attend Ward-Belmont. As the demand for girl's finishing schools declined in the 1940s, this appears to be an attempt to broaden the appeal of the college, making it available to a wider constituency. In addition to the listing of the new scholarships, "The Morley Cup," and "The Genet Cup," awards given annually to outstanding students in the Conservatory, are also referenced for the first time.

Two new music organizations appeared in the decade which replaced the older clubs such as the "Clara Schumann Club." For example, the Music Club was formed. Through the Music Club all music students could participate in sponsoring concerts and supporting musical events on campus. In the 1947-48 school year, the Music Club sponsored concerts by two guest artists, Joseph Knitzer, violin and Katherine Bacon, pianist. Dean Alan Irwin served as the faculty sponsor for the group. Furthermore, new honorary music sorority called Mu Sigma Phi was formed to honor students who had excelled both academically and musically.

Several new music ensembles were established in the 1940s, although they seemed to have existed only for a few years. A 1943 yearbook picture shows "The Southern Belles," a small string ensemble dressed for concert in ball gowns. Moreover, a creative new small vocal ensemble was called "The International Singers," dressed in folk costumes from different countries, presumably performed folk songs from these cultures. After two years, however, this group seems to have changed into a small select group called "The Singers," and then shortly thereafter was re-named "The Octet." Also, a new ensemble that seems to have met with good success was the

Harp Ensemble. Harp instruction had been offered at Ward-Belmont since the 1920s, and in the 1940s, under the leadership of harp instructor Frances Helen Jackson, the harp program flourished. An impressive photograph in the 1945 *Milestones* shows seven young harp players performing in evening dress.[59]

Also during this time, the Conservatory announced in its publicity materials that the school had acquired tape recording machines so students could hear their progress as performers. A photo from the 1940s shows a singer and a piano accompanist recording their practice session on one of the new tape recorders.[60]

Beethoven, Chopin and French Music Festivals, 1945-1947

The Beethoven Festival of February 28 – March 4, 1945 was among the most impressive music events at Ward-Belmont in the 1940s. The Beethoven Festival involved 22 students from all piano studios who performed a wide array of Beethoven works, including 13 complete sonatas, Variations, Bagatelles, Contradanses, and movements from concertos. While serving as Dean, Alan Irwin was also a part of the piano faculty, and this event seems to have been his brainchild. Ward-Belmont's impressive piano faculty were all represented by their students in the concerts. The piano faculty in 1945 included Verna Brackinreed, Alan Irwin, Florence Irwin, Hazel Coates Rose, Amalie Throne and Elizabeth Wall.[61] With this concert the Conservatory was making a statement that the Ward-Belmont Conservatory was no longer a finishing school for music dilettantes, but rather a place for serious music students. The breadth of works performed in the four concerts is impressive by any standard and indicated that Ward-Belmont could compete with well-known music schools.

With the success of the Beethoven Festival in 1945, the Conservatory embarked on an even more ambitious festival for 1946, featuring the music of Frederic Chopin. The number of concerts was expanded from four to six. One of the additional concerts was a faculty recital given by Alan Irwin, performing a formidable program of Chopin works including the Impromptu in A-flat, the Nocturne in B-flat minor, three Etudes, the Barcarolle in F-sharp, the Fantasy in F minor, the Ballade in F minor, and the A-flat Polonaise. A total of 60 piano students performed in the remaining five concerts. The repertoire included major works such as the Ballades and Scherzos along with shorter works such as the Nocturnes,

50

Waltzes, Marzurkas and Preludes.[62] The piano program of Ward-Belmont reinforced its reputation as a serious place to study.

The Piano Festival concept continued in May of 1947 with a focus on music by French composers. Five concerts were planned featuring the music of Debussy, Dubois, Lack, Philipp, Rameau, Ravel, Saint-Saens, and others. This festival was expanded beyond piano literature and included vocal, violin and organ selections.[63]

Concert Artists of the 1940s

The Conservatory kept its tradition of sponsoring a strong Artist Performance Series as it had since the early days of Ward-Belmont. Some of the outstanding artists in the 1940s included:

Muriel Dickson, Metropolitan Opera Soprano (October 24, 1940)
Marjorie Edwards, Violin (November 28, 1940)
Thomas Ingram, Piano (January 16, 1941)
Vitya Vronsky and Victor Babin, Duo-Pianists (February 20, 1941)
Lansing Hatfield, Baritone, Metropolitan Opera Audition Winner
    (May 1, 1941)
William Kapell, Piano (October 2, 1941)
Kathryn Meisle, Metropolitan Opera Contralto (May 7, 1941)
William Primrose, Viola (October 26, 1944)
Hart House String Quartet (January 11, 1945)
Ida Krehm, Piano (February 1, 1945)
Frank Asper, Organist, Mormon Tabernacle (April 12, 1945)
Ernst Wolff, Baritone (December 6, 1945 and February 5, 1948)
Eugene Istomin, Piano (January 10, 1946)
Leona Flood, Violin (February 14, 1946)
Roth String Quartet (March 28, 1946)
Yves Tinayre, Baritone (January 16, 1947)
Henry Cowell, Pianist and Lecturer (March 24, 1947)
Pasquiet Trio (April 3, 1947)
Joseph Knitzer, Violin (November 20, 1947 and February 26, 1951)
Samuel Dushkin, Violin (November 11, 1948 and March 29, 1949)
Maurice Eisenberg, Cello (November 18, 1948)
Paul Matthen, Baritone (February 11, 1949)
Robert Rounseville, Tenor (January 12, 1950)[64]

The artists are almost equally divided between piano, voice and string performers, indicating that administratively the funds for concerts were divided somewhat evenly among the three main performance areas of the college. The list also contains three chamber ensembles and one organist. While some extremely well-known names are on the list, the great superstar performers are less present than they were in the two previous decades. Granted, two of the most famous performers of the era - William Primrose (1904-1982), one of the greatest violists of all times, and William Kapell (1922-1953), considered to be one of the greatest pianists of his generation - but Kapell was only 20 years old at the time of his recital and was on the verge of a career breakthrough, so the Conservatory attained him at a time when he was still affordable on an academic concert budget. The others were all excellent performers of the era, but their names are not remembered widely today. The most interesting name on the list of performers is Henry Cowell (1897-1965), the famous American musical iconoclast, composer and pianist. Cowell was famous for his experimental pieces of the 1920s and 30s such as "The Tides of Maunanaun," "The Banshee," "Aeolian Harp" and "Tyger" which used huge tone clusters and unorthodox techniques of playing inside the piano by plucking and scraping strings. Prior to his 1947 Ward-Belmont appearance, he had served five years in San Quentin Prison on a morals charge. These factors made him an unlikely candidate for an invitation to perform at a sedate girl's school. Nevertheless, his appearance at Belmont included lectures on his use of American folk idioms in his music and how he was influenced by attitudes from the East through his study in the Orient. One of his lectures was entitled "Music in the Department of War Information." In addition, he presented an evening lecture-recital demonstrating music using his unorthodox piano techniques.[65] Again, the leadership of Alan Irwin was present, attempting to expose Ward-Belmont to the emerging styles of music.

The Significant Musical Career of Arthur Henkel

One of the most important local musical personalities in Nashville in the 20th century was Arthur Henkel. Known as a church musician, a teacher, a composer, an organ recitalist and a conductor, he began his musical studies at the age of five under the guidance of his father. One year later he began piano studies with Frederick Werner Steinbrecher, a pupil of Chopin, and Henkel's first organ teacher was Henri G. Andre of New York City. Later he studied both piano and organ at the Cincinnati College of Music, eventually devoting himself to organ, where his teachers at Cincinnati were Sydney Durst and W.S. Sterling. He not only played the great Music Hall organ in symphony concerts in Cincinnati, but he was also organist in leading churches in the city. Ultimately he was a graduate of the Metropolitan College of Music in Cincinnati, and in 1906 he became organist and choirmaster at Christ Church in Nashville, a position he held until his retirement in 1958, a total of 52 years![66] Upon his arrival in Nashville, and for a few years thereafter, he also taught music at the Tennessee School for the Blind. His strong leadership at Christ Church brought positive changes, evidenced by a church report in 1913 that spoke of "the splendid work of the choir. They not only sing harmoniously but what is rarer in choirs, they work harmoniously."[67] Always involved in the wider musical community, Henkel composed the music and conducted the chorus for the Greek Pageants at the Parthenon in 1913 and 1914.

Henkel began his teaching career at Ward-Belmont in 1910, a relationship which lasted until the end of the institution and two years into the formation of the new Belmont College – that is, until 1953. At Ward-Belmont he presided over the new three-manual Kimball organ in the Auditorium, said to be "the finest organ in a girl's school in the country." He regularly played for the chapel services at Ward-Belmont and developed a large studio of organ students. The first orchestra at Belmont College, depicted in the 1910 yearbook, shows Arthur Henkel in the group playing viola.[68]

He gave annual organ concerts each year at Ward-Belmont as well as Christ Church and other Nashville churches, including the dedication concert on the new 22-rank Wirsching Organ at the Immanuel Baptist Church on West End in 1913 when the church moved into its new Italianate sanctuary. Over the years he played a series of concerts at Christ Church under the auspices of the "Nashville Art Association," which presented him with an award of a silver pitcher at his 100th concert inscribed: "To Arthur Henkel – 100th recital - A token of appreciation for the work done in encouraging and elevating the taste for good music in the city of Nashville – by organ recitals given at Christ Church – from the Nashville Art Association."[69] When the Nashville Chapter of the American Guild of Organists was begun in 1933, he was the chief organizer for the Guild, often hosting meetings and concerts of the Guild of Organists at

Ward-Belmont. Henkel owned a three-manual organ in his home at 1600 Linden Avenue just a few blocks south of the Belmont campus. During the 1920s, the early days of WSM Radio, he played concerts which were broadcasted over the radio from his home. Concert programs of Henkel's recitals at Ward-Belmont show that he played only the best repertoire, including standard composers such as Buxtehude, Bach, Brahms, Franck, Rheinberger and Bossi. His strong performances continually brought critical acclaim in the Nashville press.

On May 12, 1927 Ward-Belmont presented a free performance of Mascagni's *Cavalleria Rusticana* for the Nashville public at the Ryman Auditorium. Students of Gaetano de Luca were the principal singers. Dancers were Ward-Belmont students trained on campus. Arthur Henkel directed a 30-piece orchestra. Five thousand people were turned away and a second performance for the next night was hastily arranged because of the demand.

In 1928 Gaetano de Luca founded the Nashville Conservatory of Music, and for two years Arthur Henkel joined him in this new musical venture. It seems likely that Henkel had a hand in the design and purchase of the new Moeller organ which was installed in the Conservatory Concert Hall. In 1936 the Conservatory closed due to the Great Depression, loss of funds from major donors, and the death of de Luca. Before the Conservatory closed, Arthur Henkel returned to his post of teaching at Ward-Belmont.

During the 1920s Arthur Henkel conducted an ensemble of professional and amateur musicians called the Nashville Symphony Orchestra. A number of Nashville businessmen supported the venture, among them Rogers Caldwell and Luke Lea. The orchestra, which performed in various venues and with varying success, folded in 1930 with the beginning of the Depression. There would be no community symphony orchestra again in Nashville until 1945, after World War II, when the present Nashville Symphony was born.[70] In addition to the Nashville Symphony Orchestra, Henkel conducted a small orchestra which performed regularly before movies at the Belmont Theater on 21st Avenue.

Upon the resignation of Henry Wesson from Ward-Belmont in 1932, Arthur Henkel became the carillonneur for Ward-Belmont's 23-bell carillon. On November 17, 1934 when President Roosevelt visited the Ward-Belmont campus, Henkel played "Hail to the Chief" as the President's limousine drove around the circle with the students lined along the drive. He continued to play the Ward-Belmont Carillon throughout the 1930s, including a traditional Christmas Eve Concert which came to be known as "Arthur Henkel's Christmas Card."[71]

In 1945, after 35 years of service at Ward-Belmont, the yearbook *Milestones* honored Arthur Henkel with the dedication for that year. The tribute to Henkel is titled "Special Delivery":

> To the man who displays an untiring energy, typifying the real Ward-Belmont spirit that we all strive to attain, we wish to pay tribute. His is the organ music which makes chapel services more impressive. It is he who plays the famous chimes in the old tower that bring a serious and misty expression to the eyes of each girl, making her realize more fully the beauty that is the heart of her Alma Mater. In appreciation for his many years of faithful and unceasing service we wish to dedicate our nineteen hundred forty-five *Milestones* to Mr. F. Arthur Henkel.[72]

Henkel taught during the first two years of the new co-ed Belmont College in 1951, but he did not return the third year as the young college forged its new direction. Apparently, the new President, R. Kelly White, wanted to build a new faculty not related to Ward-Belmont; therefore, most of the WB faculty left Belmont College at the end of the second academic year.

Henkel continued his duties as organist-choirmaster at Christ Church until 1958 when he retired. His career as a teacher, a conductor of a forerunner to the Nashville Symphony, a church musician, a concert organist and composer causes one to wonder how he managed it all. He died on July 7, 1958, with no real period of retirement in which to enjoy his accomplishments. Arthur Henkel made a major impact on all the important Nashville cultural institutions of his time; for that reason, he could be called one of the most important musicians in Nashville during the early 20th Century.

Operetta Productions of 1943-1949

Opera productions had not been a frequent part of Ward-Belmont's musical offerings. In fact, other than the performance of a Von Suppe' operetta *Ten Women with No Man* in May of 1905, the modest production of *Trial by Jury* in 1906, and the extravagant production of Mascagni's *Cavalleria Rusticana* under the leadership of Signor de Luca in 1927, there is little evidence of operatic activity other than individual arias sung on vocal recitals. However, this situation changed in 1943 when the Ward-Belmont Conservatory partnered with the Castle Heights Military Academy[73] Glee Club to present a production of Gilbert and Sullivan's *Patience*. Again, as with many musical events of the era, the driving force of this initiative was Dean of the Conservatory, Alan Irwin, who directed the production. The 1943 *Milestones* presented pictures of the performance with a large cast and professional quality costumes and sets. Apparently the opera was performed twice, once at Ward-Belmont and once on the following evening in Lebanon, Tennessee at Castle Height's McFadden Auditorium.[74] It seems that the restrictions of war time hindered further operatic production until three years later in 1946 when the two schools partnered a second time for a performance of Gilbert and Sullivan's *H.M.S. Pinafore*, again with elaborate sets and costumes. The tradition was thus established, and in 1947 Gilbert and Sullivan's *Mikado* was performed, by the two schools in a similar fashion.[75]

The operetta for 1948 was another Gilbert and Sullivan operetta – this time *The Gondoliers*. The printed program for this production indicates that there were 16 singers in the various roles with 40 chorus members drawn from the choirs of the two institutions. As in the past, this production used professional costumes and sets rented from a professional theatrical company. Pictures from the production show that it was elaborate in every respect, but one concession to cost was the use of piano to accompany the performances rather than orchestra. An interesting footnote about this performance is that Ward-Belmont student Sylvia Stahlman, in the leading role of Casilda, sang what was probably her first operatic role. Stahlman would become a leading operatic soprano in Europe and the U.S after her graduation from Ward-Belmont, only a few weeks after this production. In 1949 the two schools combined to perform another production of Gilbert and Sullivan's *Patience*, the operetta which began the Gilbert and Sullivan tradition back in 1943.[76] 1949 was the last year of an operetta performance, due, no doubt, to the death of Dean Alan Irwin, who had been the director of all of the productions, beginning in 1943.

56

The Ward-Belmont Choir Makes a Recording (1950)

In 1950 the Ward-Belmont Choir recorded what appears to be the only recording of a Ward-Belmont ensemble that was widely distributed. Under the direction of Sydney Dalton, the choir performed school songs such as "The Bells of Ward-Belmont," "College Senior Class Song," and "Preparatory Senior Class Song." Standard classical works performed were Bach's "Blessing, Honor and Wisdom," Scheutley's "Send Forth Thy Spirit," Kopylov's "Heavenly Light, and Guiney's "Out in the Fields." The album consists of two 78 RPM discs, attractively bound in a gold case with a modern representation of the Belmont Mansion. The recording fidelity of the time and the quality of singing in regard to blend, precision and intonation make the recording weak when compared to choral performance standards of the present day. Ironically, this recording, made in 1950 was distributed on two 78 RPM recordings, even though Long Play recordings began to be made in 1948 and by the early 1950s were the standard medium for recordings.[77] Ward-Belmont was using old technology while the new was becoming available, which could be seen as a metaphor for the College itself, doomed to close within a year, though no one seemed to anticipate its end.

Sylvia Stahlman, Ward-Belmont's Operatic Success (1929-1998)

Sylvia Stahlman, Nashville native and a 1946 graduate of Hillsboro High School, was perhaps Ward-Belmont's most distinguished music graduate in its later years. Graduating from Ward-Belmont in 1948, she is pictured in the 1948 *Milestones* in the Glee Club and the Mu Sigma Phi music honorary society. She performed what was probably her first operatic role at Ward-Belmont as Casilda in Gilbert and Sullivan's *The Gondoliers* in May of 1948. At Ward-Belmont she was a student of Sidney Dalton. Upon completing the two-year program at Ward-Belmont, she studied for a time at the Julliard School of Music in New York City. It was not long before she came to the attention of producers on Broadway; her first breakthrough was on the Broadway stage performing in Kurt Weill's *Love Life* alongside Nanette Fabray, directed by Elia Kazan.

She soon left for Europe where she made her debut at the Brussels Opera in 1951 as Elvira in *I Puritani*. She remained with the Brussels opera until 1954. She performed major roles in Amsterdam, Frankfurt, and

Vienna, singing under the stage name Giulia Bardi. In 1959 she sang at the Glyndebourne Festival as Ilia in Mozart's *Idomeneo*. She regularly appeared as a leading soprano at the Frankfurt Opera from 1958 until 1971.[78]

The liner notes of the recording of Verdi's *Un Ballo Maschera* states that "Europe made her its own before she was discovered by American audiences."[79] In the United States she sang regularly for the New York City Opera Company, including Offenbach's *Orphee' aux enfers* (Eurydice) conducted by Erich Leinsdorf and the role of Gilda in Verdi's *Rigoletto* under Julius Rudel. Later she sang with the San Francisco Opera Company and the Lyric Opera of Chicago. In San Francisco, she sang the role of Sophie in *Der Rosenkavalier* and the role of Sister Constance in the American premiere of Poulenc's *Dialogues des Carmelites*. She also sang the title role for Richard Strauss' *Daphne* in its United States premiere at the Santa Fe Opera in 1964.[80]

As her career progressed, she often recorded operatic and choral works on major labels. Some of her recording credits include:

Mahler, Symphony No. 4 with the Concertgebouw Orchestra of Amsterdam, George Solti, Conductor (London Records)

Haydn, *Mass in D Minor (Lord Nelson Mass)* with the King's College Choir, David Willcocks, Conductor (Argo Records, 1962)

Orff, *Carmina Burana* with the Hartford Symphony Orchestra (Vanguard Records)

Beethoven, *Fidelio* (role of Marzillene), Europaescher Phonoklub Verlag, Stuttgart

Works by Rossi, Stradella, Cesti, and A. Scarlatti (Chamber Music for Soprano and Continuo) (Pleiades Records, Decca)

Verdi, *Un Ballo in Maschera* (role of Oscar), L' Accademia di Santa Cecilia, Rome (London Records)   r

Bellini, *La Sonnambula* (role of Lisa), Maggio Musicale Fiorentino, Richard Bonynge, Conductor (Decca Records, 1963)

Handel, *Belshazzar*, Stuttgart Kirchenmusiktage, Helmut Rilling, Conductor (Vox Records)[81]

This partial, but representative list of recordings indicates that she was associated with many of the prominent conductors of the period. She was highly prized for her musicianship and for the suitability of her voice for a wide range of roles. As one listens to her recordings, her voice exudes admirable qualities which are still fresh. It is a lovely, flexible voice with a controlled vibrato and a voice that is always in tune.

Stahlman appeared several times as a soloist with the Nashville Symphony Orchestra during the 1950s and 60s and was appreciated by her hometown. Upon her retirement in the early 70s she moved to St. Petersburg, Florida. She died in 1998, leaving a legacy as the most gifted graduate of Ward-Belmont as a classical music performer. Her repertoire of operatic and oratorio roles was vast. She excelled in coloratura and soubrette roles and was always in demand by opera companies throughout Europe and the United States. She exemplified well the foundational education in music she received at the Ward-Belmont Conservatory.

Upon her death in 1998, her heirs presented a number of important items to Belmont University, including a life-sized portrait of Stahlman in operatic costume, which hangs today in the vocal area of the Wilson Music Building. Other items presented to the Belmont Music Library included a portfolio of operatic costumes designed for her and copies of most of the recordings in which she had performed.

Death of Dean Alan Irwin

Alan Irwin's sudden death on December 1, 1949 was a blow to the Ward-Belmont Conservatory. He had made many contributions and changes to the Conservatory that had modernized the school and had strengthened the academic and performance levels among the students. He seemed to be moving the Conservatory to a stronger position in order to compete with the growing music schools in universities of the post-war era, and to change the image of music as a pastime for young women. He modernized the Conservatory in numerous ways and brought attention to the school through festivals featuring large numbers of student performers. All photographs of Irwin show him to be an engaging, personable professor, different from the stern leaders of the past. He was the last leader to make an impact on the Conservatory because only one year remained in the life of Ward-Belmont at the time of his passing. In the 1950 issue of the yearbook *Milestones*, this tribute is found with his picture:

> Dean Alan Irwin – To those who knew him and to those who did not – his influences as a friend and musician will not be forgotten. Here was a man inspired in spirit and mind by music. Serving for many years as Dean of the Ward-Belmont Conservatory, his cheerfulness, ever-

winning smile, and understanding thoughts will not be forgotten. His pupils were continually inspired by this great man and his influence was a great part of every student's experience. His life was dedicated to inspiring music in every phase of his life activities. His thoughts were only of helping and leading those interested in music. His work was not in vain as his cheerful smile will live on in our memories as will that which he inspired – Music.[82]

With the death of Alan Irwin, Nashville pianist and teacher Werner Zepernick was appointed as Chairman of the Music Faculty. Zepernick was a graduate of the Staatliche Hochschule für Musik, Berlin with the MM degree from the Chicago College of Music. He served for only one year before the closing of Ward-Belmont. He went on to have a distinguished teaching career in piano, until his retirement in 1976, at nearby George Peabody College for Teachers, which was beginning its post-war growth to become Nashville's leading School of Music.

End of an Era

On February 28, 1951 the Nashville morning newspaper, *The Tennessean*, carried the stunning news of the impending closure of Ward-Belmont. Even before students and faculty could be assembled to hear the news, *The Tennessean* had discovered the news and publicized it throughout the community.[83] A shock wave ran through the campus and throughout Nashville. Nashville's beloved institution for over 60 years was suddenly closing. Accounts of students and faculty indicate that the final spring of Ward-Belmont's existence was similar to a long wake, as traditions were enacted one-by-one for the last time.[84]

Ward-Belmont's indebtedness had become unmanageable, and the college was sold to the Tennessee Baptist Convention, which planned to establish a Baptist-related co-educational college on the campus. The transaction sealing Ward-Belmont's fate was completed on March 3, 1951 when the Tennessee Baptist Convention Executive Committee voted to take over the $600,000 debt in exchange for the campus and all its assets.

One can only imagine from today's perspective how Ward-Belmont students, faculty and alumni must have felt, especially since no one seemed to have an inkling of the impending closing. Were there signs that the College was in trouble? Could the College have been saved if financial changes had been made earlier? In hindsight, several observable changes were taking place which could have sounded a warning. First, after World War II the demand for colleges for women declined sharply. Statistics indicate that Ward-Belmont's college-level enrollment dropped from 290 in 1939 to 144 in 1949.[85] The list is long of women's colleges that either closed or became co-ed in the decades after mid-century. Ward-Belmont was just one of the earlier casualties in this trend.[86] Secondly, after World War II women rapidly joined the work force as they had during the war, and the image of the stay-at-home mother and homemaker changed drastically. Thirdly, the type of environment maintained at Ward-Belmont was very expensive. Throughout its life and even into the forties, the students dined with fine china on tables covered with Irish linen table cloths and napkins. The school maintained a large staff to meet the needs of the often wealthy students who came to the school. Enrollment dropped in the late years of the school, evidenced by elaborate recruitment materials sent out in the forties. The Great Depression of the 1930s had taxed the school financially and set the stage for the decline in the 40s. Maintenance of buildings was neglected and the campus was in poor condition by the end of its life. A telling announcement was inserted into in the 1948-49 Ward-Belmont Catalog. After the catalog was printed, an addendum was stapled to the page concerning fees noting that the tuition for the 1948-49 academic year for the Music Conservatory was being raised to $1475 from the original $1360.[87] This decision, made too late to be printed in the catalog, perhaps indicates that the administration of the College was aware of financial problems.

How did students and faculty of the Conservatory react to the news of the sudden demise of their beloved school? It certainly would have been received as more bad news after the death of the beloved Dean Irwin just a year earlier. The efforts of Irwin during the 40s to make the school stronger have already been noted: the major opera productions, the Beethoven and Chopin festivals, the modern recording equipment, and the recording made by the choir all seemed outwardly to be the efforts of a thriving Conservatory. Ironically, about the same time that Ward-Belmont was moving toward extinction, her most illustrious music graduate from the 40s, Sylvia Stahlman, was making her European operatic debut at the Brussels, Belgium Opera Company.

PART III
MUSIC AT THE NEW COEDUCATIONAL BELMONT COLLEGE (1951–1968)

The Beltones (top photo) and Belmont Glee Club (1959),
Dee Wayne White, Director

CHAPTER SEVEN

A Difficult
First Decade

The new Belmont College was officially born on March 3, 1951 when the Executive Committee of the Tennessee Baptist Convention voted to acquire the Ward-Belmont property by taking over the $600,000 debt. It made sense that the Baptists needed to found a college in Middle Tennessee since there was already one in West Tennessee (Union University in Jackson, TN) and one in East Tennessee (Carson-Newman College in Jefferson City, TN). It seemed an easy enough move, though it was fraught with complications. First of all, there was great animosity from Ward-Belmont students, faculty, alumni and Nashville citizens, who loved, supported and admired Ward-Belmont for its accomplishments and felt that the school had been acquired underhandedly. An immediate movement was started by Ward-Belmont supporters to see if funds could be raised to save the school. That failing, they began to form a new school, Harpeth Hall, which was to replace the preparatory school of Ward-Belmont. Secondly, the Tennessee Baptists planned, as part of the process, to close Cumberland College in Lebanon, which was then under the control of the Baptists, though not officially owned by them. Lebanon citizens were adamant that their college should not close and immediately set about to keep Cumberland alive in Lebanon. Thirdly, the Tennessee Baptists had only five months from the time of the acquisition to prepare for the opening of the new school: to recruit students and faculty, to appoint an administration, and to decide what programs to offer.[1]

Some of the earliest publicity materials found in the Belmont University Archives advertise the opening of "Cumberland-Belmont College and Music Conservatory." The Cumberland name was quickly dropped and the term "Conservatory" disappeared sometime within the first year. In fact, the first year of the new Belmont College seems to have been somewhat improvised. Without a president, the Executive Board of the Tennessee Baptists appointed Dr. Warren Jones, Sr., President of Union University, as part-time President to launch the school, while still attending to his duties at Union. He served from April, 1951 through May 31, 1952. The student recruitment yielded 136 students for the first term, a small start indeed.[2] Some Ward-Belmont faculty were retained, and a few new faculty were hired. It became clear over time that the facilities of the college were in terrible condition. Maintenance had been deferred for years, and almost 30 years had passed since any new construction had taken place on campus. For an institution that would become a nationally recognized university within a few decades, it was truly an inauspicious beginning.

When Belmont College opened on September 13, 1951, the *Nashville Banner* noted that the first male in the history of the school had enrolled. The article qualified this claim by acknowledging "The famous actor Melvyn Douglas studied piano at Belmont in the early 1900s. His father Edouard Hesselberg was the head of the School of Music at Belmont from 1905-1912."[3] This claim can be further qualified by mentioning that young men had enrolled as part-time students at the Ward-Belmont Conservatory for private lessons since the 1920s.

Belmont Music Department in its First Year (1951-52)

The first catalog for the new college calls Belmont "A Coeducational Junior College and Conservatory of Music." The catalog basically includes the curriculum from Ward-Belmont with few changes; there had been little time and no leadership to do otherwise. The catalog also lists the musical assets of the college, which were essentially the space and equipment left from the previous school: two concert Steinway grand pianos, 10 Steinway pianos in teaching studios, a Duo-art Steinway with 200 rolls, a large three-manual organ, and two small practice organs. Also mentioned is a large library of books, recordings and scores, complete with listening rooms. Ensembles listed in the catalog included Sinfonietta, the small orchestra concept from Ward-Belmont, which was not to develop in the new school. Other ensembles listed were Choir and small instrumental ensembles.[4]

The music faculty for the first year were all holdovers from Ward-Belmont, including Sydney Dalton (Acting Chair), voice; Arthur Henkel, organ; Florence Irwin, piano; Kenneth Rose, violin; Marilyn Van Sickle, voice; and Elizabeth Wall, piano. All of these individuals were experienced and highly regarded teachers who had been a part of the success of Ward-Belmont. Sydney Dalton was a wise choice as Acting Chair because he had been at Ward-Belmont since 1933 and was widely esteemed in the Nashville community as a leading figure in the arts, as well as a regular concert reviewer for the *Nashville Banner*.[5] All of the faculty members had long associations with Belmont. (Arthur Henkel and Amelie Throne had both taught at Ward-Belmont for more than 35 years.) Whether all of these seven faculty members taught full time is not clear, but the music enrollment that first year would not have warranted that many full-time faculty. Some may have taught part-time, supplementing their teaching with their private studios, because they were highly regarded in the community as private teachers.

The first yearbook of Belmont, the 1952 *Tower*, shows that only two ensembles were active in the first year: a Boy's Octette, directed by Florence Irwin and a Women's Choir of 19 voices, directed by Sydney Dalton. One of the members of the Belmont Women's Choir that first year was Barbara Feldkircher (now Barbara Feldkircher Lutz).[6] When asked about her experience in the Women's Choir, she remembered that Sydney Dalton was business-like and demanding, getting good results from his choir. She made this interesting observation: She had graduated from Nashville's East High School, which in those days had an outstanding choral program with several large choirs. At first she felt that going to Belmont was a step down in that regard.[7]

She remembered well her piano lessons with Amelie Throne, one of Nashville's most highly regarded piano teachers. She taught in a manner that reflected her European musical training. She taught in a physical manner, often singing the melody with the student in a croaking voice, or playing along at the top of the piano range, urging the student to bring out the melody. She also walked around the studio, shouting instructions as the student played. Mrs. Lutz has great respect for Mrs. Throne's teaching, and she still plays the piano 60 years after her time at Belmont for her own enjoyment as well as the enjoyment of others.[8]

Mrs. Lutz did not take any classes with Arthur Henkel. She originally thought of him as being a rather severe person, but once she encountered him, she found him to have a sharp wit and a keen sense of humor. She was aware that Elizabeth Wall from the piano faculty was a quiet presence and was respected for her cooperative spirit and her thorough approach to teaching.[9]

What did the music faculty of that first year think about their new situation? Certainly they would have mourned the passing of their previous school and its students, and probably they worried about the stability of their positions in the new college. Still, Barbara Lutz observed that she did not see any regrets on the part of the faculty. Although much had been lost from that tradition, they seemed to understand that the old tradition of finishing schools for young women was a thing of the past. Moreover, they seemed to genuinely like their new co-ed environment and the lively spirit of the new students, moving naturally into their roles of teaching males as well as females, many of whom had different backgrounds from the Ward-Belmont students.[10] From a practical standpoint, the faculty were pleased to have teaching positions after the demise of their former school and took to the task with seriousness and enthusiasm.

The 1951-1952 academic year for the Music Department (or Conservatory) began with a scaled-down version of the Ward-Belmont music curriculum, faculty and ensemble offerings. This trial year represented a tenuous step into what would become a decade of change, challenge and struggle as the tiny new college made its way into the future.

The Second Year (1952-53)

On August 8, 1952, the Belmont Board of Trustees appointed Dr. Ransom Kelly White as the first president of Belmont College. Dr. White came from the First Baptist Church of West Palm Beach, Florida to take the presidency. He was a former pastor of nearby Belmont Heights Baptist Church and knew the community well. It would be difficult to imagine a new college president with more challenges ahead than Dr. White had. The fledgling Music Department had a major role in Dr. White's Inauguration in the Belmont Auditorium on May 18, 1953. There were two ceremonies, one in the afternoon and one in the evening. In the first program Arthur Henkel played the organ and Sydney Dalton led a mixed choir called the Belmont College Choir in Handel's "Hallelujah, Amen." The evening ceremony began with organ music played by Henkel. Schubert's "The Almighty" was sung by new voice teacher Genter Stephens. The Belmont College Choir sang "Onward, Ye People" by Sibelius. The accompanist for the choir was music student Betty Skelton, whose parents would later endow a church music scholarship in her honor in the 1970s, called the Betty Skelton Brewer Church Music Scholarship.[11]

Sydney Dalton, Acting Chair, continued in his role in 1952, while basically the music faculty also remained essentially the same. On August 11, 1952 Dalton began a series of music programs on WSM radio on Sundays at 10:30 p.m. entitled "Exploring Music." On this weekly program he discussed musical topics and played recorded examples. With its focus on classical music, this programming met an important need before the days of public broadcasting.[12]

On September 11, 1952 *The Tennessean* reported that Belmont was offering its first music scholarship. The scholarship was funded by Belmont music faculty member Florence Irwin in memory of her husband, Alan Irwin. This award was to be given to a pianist. On October 31, 1952 an article in *The Tennessean* announced that the Alan Irwin Scholarship was awarded to pianist Sandra Pullen, who planned to enroll at Belmont for music study in the fall of 1953.[13]

In the second year students were asked to submit words and music for an Alma Mater for the new College. The chosen song written by student Kenneth Anderson Floyd, was used for three years until Dr. William Mathis wrote a new Alma Mater in 1955.

At the end of the 1952-1953 academic year, some dramatic changes occurred among faculty members of the Music Department of Belmont. Louis Nicholas reported on June 7 in *The Tennessean* that Sydney Dalton had resigned as Acting Chair of the Music Department to begin a private teaching studio in Nashville. The article further stated that Arthur Henkel and Amelie Throne were retiring from Belmont.[14] Arthur Henkel was still Organist and Choir Director at Christ Church, and Amelie Throne was a respected piano teacher, continuing to teach privately for several years. In addition, none of the original Ward-Belmont music faculty (with the exception of Elizabeth Wall) were retained after the second year. Clearly the new president, Dr. White, was seeking to reinvent the faculty. Barbara Lutz, who was finishing her two-year program in music at the time of these changes, surmises that Dr. White wanted to bring in newer faculty members and move away from the Ward-Belmont culture.[15] Whatever the reasons for the changes, the ties with Ward-Belmont were broken and a new direction was being forged. The one music faculty member retained from Ward-Belmont, Elizabeth Wall, had excellent credentials and had taught at Ward-Belmont for ten years before the new college was formed.

The fact that she was a Baptist, and also organist at Eastland Baptist Church may have kept her on the faculty as Belmont forged its Baptist identity.

Loss of the Belmont Carillon

A sad episode in the early history of Belmont College was the loss of its carillon in the Tower, one of only a few such instruments in the south. Not long after the founding of Belmont College, Schulmerich Electronics, Inc. contacted the college about the possibility of exchanging the Gillette and Johnston carillon bells for a Schulmerich Carillonic electronic bell system. The carillon, now in poor condition, was not being used, and the Schulmerich Company convinced the administration and trustees that an electronic system would be easier to play, would sound better, and would require little maintenance. The negotiations went on for six months, with Schulmerich waging an aggressive campaign to convince the college that the exchange was in the college's best interest. On March 29, 1952 Belmont sent to Schulmerich a contract that agreed to the acceptance of a carillonic bell system in exchange for the 23 cast bronze bells. When the new system was installed, neighbors complained about the amplified sound and Ward-Belmont alumnae bemoaned the loss of yet another part of their heritage. The Nashville newspapers reported widely the concerns of Belmont neighbors and Ward-Belmont supporters, bringing bad publicity to the college. The new electronic system was not used after its first few months and by 1958 was inoperable. In 1968 the Schulmerich Company offered to sell Belmont a new system, offering a discount because of a trade for the old inoperable system. After the summer of 1952 Belmont's historic tower was silent. The Ward-Belmont carillon was historic in that it was only the second carillon built in the South and the 25th carillon in the entire United States. The Gillette and Johnston Bellfounders who made the bells were highly regarded masters of their craft. The loss of this asset was a short-sighted decision and sad occurrence in the early days of the college.[16] Three decades later, however, another chapter in the story of the Belmont carillon would unfold.

1953-54 – A New Faculty

In 1953 Dr. William S. Mathis was named the Chair of the Division of Fine Arts. With the arrival of a new Chair and new faculty members, the

Music Department was combined with Drama and Art to become the Department of Fine Arts. Dr. Mathis was the first music faculty member of either Ward-Belmont or Belmont College to have the doctorate degree and appeared to be an excellent choice to move the Music Department forward. He had the BM degree from Stetson University, the MM from the University of Michigan and the PhD from Florida State University. Josephine Cook Harper, Ward-Belmont and Cincinnati Conservatory graduate, taught piano for one year. Other new faculty members were Peggy Jo Tapp Turman, piano; Nyra Turbeville, piano; and Genter Stephens, voice and choral ensembles. Elizabeth Wall, piano and music history, completed the faculty for that year.[17]

The use of the word "Conservatory" was dropped from the catalog as the Division of Fine Arts came into being, and the Bachelor of Music degree was listed in the catalog with majors in Applied Music, Church Music and Music Education. With the beginning of this school year, Belmont added a third year with the intention of graduating students with four-year degrees by the spring of 1955. Whether the accreditation by the National Association of Schools of Music still was in force in the new college is unclear. In fact, the coveted accreditation had probably been rescinded with the closing of Ward-Belmont. The catalog states, however, that the Applied Music study "conforms" to standards set by NASM.[18] Although the goal of NASM accreditation would not be attained for another two decades, that goal remained ever-present in the minds of the music faculty.

In the mid-1950s the Music Department moved to facilities in Hail Hall. Formerly a dormitory at Ward-Belmont, the building was refitted to serve as classrooms and teaching studios. The Music Department used the first floor of Hail, which provided three classrooms, two listening rooms, the Division of Fine Arts Office, the music library, and seven teaching studios. The lower level of Hail Hall provided a space (later known as the Little Theatre) that was used for small recitals and drama productions. This arrangement remained until the completion of a permanent home for the Music Department in the Massey Fine Arts Building in 1967. Until the mid-1950s, music students practiced in a building that had once housed the old Acklen bowling alley. The long, narrow building, located near the current Massey School of Business, was made into extended hallway of practice rooms during Ward-Belmont era. These practice rooms had little sound isolation, so students from the early 50s called the building the "Monkey House" because when all the rooms were filled with practicing students, the cacophony sounded like chattering monkeys. This historic building from Adelicia Acklen's estate was torn down in the mid-1950s.

Dr. Mathis immediately formed a mixed-voice choral group called "The Choraleers." This choir made a good impression and was invited to sing for the Southern Music Educators Convention in New Orleans in the spring of 1954, making the choir Belmont's first touring ensemble. Dr. Mathis also chaired a new Artist Series Committee which appears in a list of faculty committees. No doubt he was aware of the illustrious artist series presented in the past by Ward-Belmont and wanted to use performances by well-known artists to draw attention to Belmont, particularly from the Nashville community. There is no record, however, of any guest artists actually performing during these early years, and after a few years the committee no longer existed.[19] Very likely the reason was lack of funds. As a young college, Belmont had not yet developed financial resources to afford such programming; its departmental budgets were lean.

Belmont's First Music Graduate, 1955

Belmont College's first music graduate was Barbara Redden (Burnett) (BM '55). She was a vocal major, studying voice with Sydney Dalton and Dr. William Mathis and studying piano and music history with Elizabeth Wall. She was the only graduate in music in the spring 1955 commencement and therefore the first music student to finish the four-year Bachelor of Music degree. Upon graduation, she became Minister of Music of the First Baptist Church of Crossville, TN. She left her active church music work for a time after her marriage, devoting her time to raising her children. In 1967 she began to teach first grade at the Gene Brown Elementary School since there were no full-time music teachers in schools at that time. In 1990 the school opened a music position for kindergarten through fifth grade, which she took in order to use her musical skills. As of 2014 she remained at Gene Brown School as the elementary music teacher. Her teaching career at this time spanned 46 years. While teaching, she continued to be active in the music programs of the churches where she was a member. The first music graduate of Belmont indeed had a long and productive career of service to churches and schools through the use of her music education.[20]

Degree Changes in Music

In the 1955-56 school year, the Board of Trustees decided to remove the Bachelor of Music degree and to substitute the Bachelor of Arts in Music instead. The Bachelor of Arts curriculum was considered to be a much less rigorous degree from a music standpoint. In response, the music faculty prepared a self-evaluation proposal to reinstate the BM degree, which they hoped to present to the National Association of Schools of Music at their November, 1955 meeting in St. Louis. This 17-page document stated Belmont's approach to meeting the NASM criteria. Elizabeth Wall appeared before the Belmont Board of Trustees on behalf of the music faculty to request approval to present the application for NASM membership. The Board of Trustees rejected the faculty request voting to retain the Bachelor of Arts degree as it appeared in the catalog for that year.[21] In an interview with Professor Elizabeth Wall, she stated that the Board of Trustees' rejection of the proposal to seek NASM accreditation was the most disappointing event in her long career at Belmont.[22]

Changing Leadership 1956-1964

Dr. William Mathis remained at Belmont as Chair of Fine Arts only until the spring of 1956. He had been the author of the Self-Evaluation Document written for NASM. The Board of Trustee's rejection of that document must have been a severe blow to Dr. Mathis, whose vision for the Music Department included a strong, accredited music curriculum. No doubt his resignation within a few months of this incident was prompted by this disappointment. He had come to Belmont with the expectation of being able to build a stronger music program. Limited budgets and small enrollments thwarted his vision. While at Belmont he composed a new "Alma Mater" for Belmont, replacing the student-composed song which had been in use for three years. A number of faculty changes occurred in the 1955-56 school year. Robert Sawyer, Betty Lawson and Dee Wayne White were added, while Genter Stephens, Josephine Harper and Peggy Jo Turman were no longer present.[23]

By 1956 the music faculty had again changed dramatically. Upon the resignation of William Mathis, Dee Wayne White, who had joined the faculty a year earlier, was appointed Chair of the Department of Fine Arts. Other faculty were Cyrus Daniel, theory; Fred B. Pearson, voice and choral;

and Elizabeth Wall.[24] The ensemble offerings continued to evolve. There were two choral ensembles: The Belmont Choir with 26 mixed voices dressed in robes, directed by Fred Pearson; and the Belmont Glee Club, a choir of 24 voices, dressed in tuxedos and dresses, directed by Dee Wayne White. In addition to these choirs, a male quartet called the Bellaires and a Girl's quartet called the Bellettes were established. By 1956-57 school year Belmont College had become a four-year institution and the Music Department graduated five students with BM degrees in 1957. One of those five graduates was Robert Mulloy, who would join the Belmont music faculty a few years later, the first Belmont graduate to do so. Ironically, the Bachelor of Music degree had been dropped the previous year, and future music majors would graduate under the new BA degree program.

In 1957-58 Dee Wayne White further changed the choral ensemble arrangement. He had received his undergraduate degree at Oklahoma Baptist University where Warren Angell had developed a unique choral group call the Bison Glee Club, influenced by Angell's work with the Fred Waring Chorale. White developed a Men's Glee Club along the lines of the OBU Bison Glee Club, which involved a TTBB choir with a small group of women for added vocal color. At the same time, a women's choir called the Beltones was organized. Due to this new ensemble arrangement, the mixed group called the Belmont Choir dropped in numbers and was eliminated the following year. This arrangement of separate groups for men and women remained in place until 1969.[25] In 1957 the Men's Glee Club was invited to sing at the Southern Baptist Convention meeting in Chicago, with concerts presented along the way to the event. Chairman White also made an attempt in 1957 to reinstate the Bachelor of Music degree. He updated the NASM document prepared by Dr. Mathis in 1955 in order to make a request to the Belmont Board of Trustees for the reinstatement of the BM degree, but nothing indicates that he made any progress with the appeal.

In 1958 Helen Trotter Midkiff, who was in the process of completing her master's degree at George Peabody College, joined the faculty to teach organ and theory. Mrs. Midkiff became a long-time faculty member, retiring in 1988. Midkiff reports that when she came to Belmont in 1958, the old Kimball organ in the auditorium was inoperable; the pipes were dismantled and stored in rooms behind the organ case. The College acquired a Hammond organ which was placed in the auditorium to be used for chapel services and teaching.[26] The Ward-Belmont Kimball organ was in use at least into the 1955-56 school year because it is listed as an asset in the 1955 NASM Self-Evaluation Document.[27] The organ was built in 1910, and if maintenance had been neglected in the late Ward-Belmont era and into the early years of Belmont College, the Kimball organ probably needed a drastic restoration by the mid-1950s. The fate of the organ echoes that of the carillon: The young College had few resources and the cost of a major overhaul was most likely prohibitive. The old instrument was removed and replaced for a time with an electronic substitute. Fortunately, the organ situation would improve dramatically in years to come.

In the fall of 1959, the Department of Music formed a new Oratorio Chorus whose purpose was to perform large works from the choral repertoire. The first concert of the Oratorio Chorus occurred on December 4, 1959 with a performance of Handel's *Messiah*, directed by Dee Wayne White with J. William Thompson, tenor; Robert Mulloy, baritone; Fay Jennings Thompson, soprano; and Linda Miller, contralto as soloists. The Chorus presented its second concert in the spring of 1960 with a performance of a new work, *The Resurrection Story* by Claude Almand. For the first five years of its existence, the Oratorio Chorus performed portions of Handel's *Messiah* every December. The tradition of the Oratorio Chorus eventually took hold at Belmont and flourished. The philosophy that all music students should participate in the singing of great choral masterpieces with orchestral accompaniment eventually became ensconced in the music curriculum, enduring for the future.[28]

Dr. Herbert Gabhart Becomes New Belmont President - 1959

The 1950s at Belmont College concluded with some dramatic and positive events. In the Fall of 1959, Dr. Herbert Gabhart became President of Belmont, beginning a new era of increasing in size, facilities and academic reputation. Gabhart would serve as president of Belmont for 23 years and afterward as Chancellor of the University until his death in 2009, a period of 50 years of service. His predecessor, Dr. Kelley White, had laid the groundwork for accreditation of the young school, and Gabhart received the news in December, 1959 that Belmont had been fully accredited by the Southern Association of Colleges and Schools (SACS). This important step gave Belmont College full standing in the academic community, allowing its credits to be accepted by other colleges and students to move freely into graduate study.[29]

The Music Department, however, received a serious blow on August 21, 1960 when Hail Hall, the location of music instructional facilities, was engulfed in a fire, causing serious damage to music classrooms, studios, equipment, and faculty-owned books and music. The upper two floors of the building were gutted, but the lower two, housing music and drama, were only damaged. Dr. Herbert Gabhart gives this account of the Hail Hall fire: "Lightning struck Hail Hall on August 21, 1960. About midway through my Sunday evening sermon (along with my presidential duties, I was serving as interim pastor at Dalewood Baptist Church), the telephone in the outer office started ringing. The call brought distressing news that Hail Hall was on fire. 'Congregation dismissed!' I sped to the campus.... Upon arrival we found that the Nashville Fire Department had the fire nearly under control. We were extremely grateful that only a few students were in the building that evening."[30] The Music Department was displaced for a time as the building was rebuilt and cleaned.[31]

The fire in Hail Hall capped off a decade of trial and error, numerous faculty changes, and a curriculum constantly in flux. In a period of only nine years, there had been three heads of the Music Department, over 20 different faculty members, and a constantly evolving ensemble arrangement, as well as the loss of the BM degree, the Kimball pipe organ, and the college carillon. Enrollment in music was still small, and money for new equipment and programming was non-existent. At the end of the decade only four music faculty members were serving, the lowest number in the history of the school. In the first decade of the college a mere 12 student had graduated from the Music Department and the music program needed visionary leadership and a college strong enough to support that vision. With Herbert Gabhart in the presidency, Belmont was poised for growth – including the possibility for growth in music. In the next decade some critical foundations were to be established.

CHAPTER EIGHT

Belmont Music in the 1960s: A New Home

In 1961 Robert Mulloy, a 1957 graduate of Belmont, joined the Belmont music faculty after completing his Master of Music degree at George Peabody College. His position included voice teaching and choral ensembles. When Dee Wayne White left Belmont in 1963, Mulloy took over the Men's Glee Club. Over the years of his career, he figured prominently as a mentor for students and a faculty member who was often active in campus activities. He was helpful in the establishment of Belmont's Phi Mu Alpha Sinfonia fraternity in 1966 and served as its faculty sponsor in its formative years. When the new Music Business major was established in 1974, he gradually devoted more time to the development of that program, eventually relinquishing his teaching role in the Music Department.

In 1963 Mulloy wrote the music for a new Belmont Alma Mater with words by highly respected English Professor, Janet Wilson. This Alma Mater replaced the one written by Dr. William Mathis in 1955 and became an important part of Belmont tradition. The Board of Trustees voted to adopt the new Alma Mater with its poetic text and singable melody on June 13, 1963. The Belmont Alma Mater has been sung at every commencement ceremony and opening convocation since its creation in 1963. Professor Robert Mulloy died from cancer on January 22, 1998 after a long and significant career of service to his Alma Mater.

An historic groundbreaking for the new Williams Library took place on June 30, 1963. The library was the first new construction on campus in 40 years, the last being Hail Hall in 1923. At last Belmont was moving beyond the old Ward-Belmont buildings to develop a modern campus. The new building was planned to provide ample library space for the growing college, replacing the cramped Ward-Belmont library in Blanton Hall. The three-story building would eventually be rebuilt in 1995 to serve as the Wilson Music Building.

In the early 60s the number of music majors remained small as did the number of graduates in music: 2 in 1962, 5 in 1963, and 3 in 1964.[32] In 1963 Chair of the Fine Arts Department, Dee Wayne White, resigned as Chair to join the faculty of Campellsville College in Kentucky. John C. Burgin came to Belmont and taught in his place for one year. During the year without a Chair of Fine Arts, Miss Elizabeth Wall, the longest tenured music professor, served in the position.

The Kenneth Hartley Era, 1964-1969

With the coming of Dr. Kenneth R. Hartley, the Belmont Music Department had a capable, academically strong music leader. Hartley earned the BS degree from the University of Missouri, the MSM from the New Orleans Baptist Theological Seminary, and the Ed.D from Florida State University. Prior to coming to Belmont, he served on the faculty of the Music Department of the New Orleans Baptist Theological Seminary, where he taught church music and served as Acting Dean for one year. At Belmont Hartley directed the Beltones and the Oratorio Chorus, although he changed the name of the Oratorio Chorus to "Belmont Chorale" for a time (not be confused with the later use of the title).

In December 1965 Belmont received delivery of a new Wicks pipe organ for use in the old auditorium, replacing the Hammond instrument that Professor Helen Midkiff had played and used for teaching since 1958. The organ was placed on the stage of the old Ward-Belmont Auditorium (called by Belmont simply "the Auditorium") in front of the case of the old Kimball organ which had been removed. This organ (Wicks, Opus 4248) was a modest instrument of four ranks (sets) of pipes unified for a fuller sound and flexibility.[33] Though small, it had the capability to fill the room with sound, and was used for performances, chapel services, and teaching for about three years until it was moved to the new Harton Concert Hall, in the Massey Fine Arts Building. This organ remained in Harton Concert Hall until 1996 when it was moved once again, this time to an organ teaching/practice studio in the Wilson Music Building.

One of Dr. Hartley's goals for the Music Department was to begin a

BELMONT MUSIC IN THE 1960S: A NEW HOME

viable instrumental program. Since 1951 instrumental music had been only incidental in the music program and there had never been a regular instrumental ensemble. With this aim in mind, in 1967 Dr. Hartley was able to hire E.D. Thompson as Band Director and teacher in the instrumental area. Thompson held the BA, MA and EdS degrees from George Peabody College and had been a veteran band director in Metro Nashville Public Schools. Belmont's first band, pictured in the 1968 *Tower*, was quite modest with only 19 players.[34] This ensemble served as a pep band for the basketball games and made appearances in concerts. It was a small start, but it was the seed from which a vital, new area of the Music Department would sprout and eventually flourish.

The New Massey Auditorium and Fine Arts Building

The most significant event of Hartley's tenure was the completion of the Massey Auditorium and Fine Arts Building, providing for the first time adequate, new, dedicated space for music instruction on the campus. The groundbreaking was held September 26, 1966, the cornerstone was laid September 17, 1967, and the dedication of the building was held on April 21, 1968. Faculty members from the time of construction indicate that the music faculty had little input into the design of the building, but they were nevertheless pleased with the wonderful new facilities the space provided. It included three large classrooms, which could double as choral or instrumental rehearsal rooms; 12 practice rooms; eight offices/teaching studios; and an office for the Fine Arts Department, in addition to which Harton Concert Hall, on the lower level, provided an excellent recital space for small audiences. The small Wicks organ that had temporarily been located in the old auditorium was moved to Harton Hall. Harton Concert Hall became the prime venue for student and senior recitals, as well as for guest artist concerts. Massey Auditorium was a vast improvement over the old auditorium in North Front. It seated 1200 and provided a large stage and orchestra pit. It was well-suited for chapel services and large-scale concerts, such as instrumental ensembles and musicals. The new organ in Massey Auditorium was a three-manual, 39-rank Wicks instrument - an excellent instrument for teaching and performance. The number of organ majors was growing, and the instrument would receive much use in the years ahead.

One of the striking things about Massey was that it was *modern*. Its sleek, trim lines broke tradition with the historic architecture of the campus and made a statement about Belmont's "look" for the future. Massey Fine Arts Building was connected to the recently completed Williams Library by a pleasant open courtyard, which became an outdoor gathering place for music students. The placement of a new library and a modern music facility together near the center of campus made a clear statement about the key roles of the library and the arts in the growing young college. Along with the recently completed Stripling Gymnasium, built along Belmont Boulevard, the Belmont campus was dramatically changing under the leadership of Herbert Gabhart with his considerable fundraising capabilities.

The dedication of the Massey Fine Arts Building on April 21, 1968 honored Jack C. and Elizabeth Massey for their support of the college, with former Belmont president R. Kelley White serving as speaker for the occasion. The ceremony started as typical celebration of a new facility, but it became a much more significant event when Mr. Massey announced that he was making a contribution of $1,200,000 in order to build and fund a strong School of Business at Belmont College. The unanticipated announcement riveted the Nashville media, which covered the event in great detail. Henceforth, doubts about Belmont's financial viability disappeared, and the Nashville community began to follow Massey's lead in supporting the developing college.[35]

The celebration of the opening of the new music facility continued on May 2, 1968 with the debut performance in Massey Auditorium by the Nashville Little Symphony, conducted by Thor Johnson, the Conductor of the Nashville Symphony Orchestra. The Little Symphony was a smaller ensemble of 19 players that played outreach concerts in the community. Over the following summer, the group continued to rehearse in Massey Auditorium in preparation for its New York debut at Town Hall on September 30, 1968.[36]

When Massey Auditorium was dedicated in April of 1968, there was not yet an organ in the room. Herbert Gabhart gives this account of the completion of the organ in his book *Work: the Soul of Good Fortune*:

> The college… needed a "respectable" organ for the new auditorium under construction. Helen Trotter Midkiff (now Mrs. Robert Capra) asked for permission to solicit a donor for $50,000 for the chapel organ. Since I had planned to ask the same donor for a much larger sum, I denied her request, explaining that if we succeeded in

securing the gift, $50,000 would be made available for the organ. It wasn't long before Massey Auditorium was equipped with a beautiful new Wicks pipe organ.[37]

Helen Midkiff played the dedicatory recital on January 28, 1969. This organ continues to accompany religious and academic services today and was the instrument on which a host of organ majors learned their craft.

The music students and faculty who moved into the Massey Building in the fall of 1968 must have felt a measure of pride in their new space. Music enrollment was steadily growing, and the building adequately met the Music Department's space needs (for a short time, at least). Still, the new space had its shortcomings. There had not been sufficient funds for new furnishings and equipment, so audio equipment for classrooms and a new concert grand piano were still needed. Moreover, the acoustics in Massey Auditorium were not ideal for singers or small ensembles, and the lack of fly space above the stage hampered the staging of dramatic productions. But these issues could be worked around, and the facility brought the Music Department a sense of importance within the College and the Nashville Community.

The Importance of Jack Massey (1904-1990)

Jack Carroll Massey was Nashville's most important entrepreneur of the 20th century. He was noted as the only businessman ever to take three different companies to the New York Stock Exchange. His business venture in wholesale medical supplies was just beginning as the fledgling Belmont College neared its 10th anniversary. As a Baptist layman, he was attracted to the struggling college and began making substantial, but nevertheless modest gifts. As Herbert Gabhart forged a stronger relationship with Massey, he decided that it was time to ask Massey for a major gift to support the construction of a new facility for music instruction and performance. Massey's gift to support the building of the Massey Auditorium and Fine Arts Building furthered this remarkable relationship between a donor and an educational institution. Massey was responsible for the outright funding of three buildings on campus: The Massey Auditorium and Fine Arts Building (1968), The Center for Business Administration (Later the Bunch Library) (1972), and The Jack C. Massey Business Center (1990). He also supported other construction on campus on a smaller scale and gave substantial amounts to build and endow the Massey School of Business. By the time of his death in 1990, his contributions to the University amounted to more than $18,000,000. It was appropriate that Belmont University honored Jack Massey four days after his death with a memorial service in Massey Auditorium. The service, entitled "A Celebration of Talents Multiplied," involved music faculty musicians, the Belmont Chorale and numerous faculty and friends in a joyful tribute to Belmont's most revered benefactor.[38] How appropriate that the service was held in the building named for Massey which was enabled by his first major gift to Belmont.

Music Graduates in the Early Years

The number of music graduates was small during the 1950s and early 1960s; however, growth began by the late 1960s, setting the stage for even larger growth in the 1970s. Graduates from the early period were outstanding church musicians and music educators, and include the following representative alumni: Barbara Redden Burnett (1955), elementary music educator; Robert Mulloy (1956), Professor, Belmont University; Parker Holder (1960), music educator; Linda Miller Towe (1960), music educator; Larry Flanagan (1965), minister of music; Bert H. Coble (1969), Head, music department, Cumberland College; Charles Crocker (1969), minister of music; Morgan Lowrey (1969), church music, Baptist Sunday School Board (LifeWay).

The Legacy of Kenneth Hartley

During Dr. Hartley's tenure at Belmont, both Phi Mu Alpha Sinfonia fraternity for men and Sigma Alpha Iota for women were formed within the Music Department. The Omicron Rho Chapter of Phi Mu Alpha was chartered on May 7, 1966 with 25 members under the guidance of Robert Mulloy as faculty advisor. Enrollment in its early years was large, involving a high percentage of the male music majors plus students from other majors who were interested in music. The Epsilon Lambda Chapter of Sigma Alpha Iota was chartered on April 26, 1969 with 22 charter members and Elizabeth Wall serving as faculty sponsor. 13 SAI Patronesses (women of the Belmont community) signed the charter as supporters of the organization. Both fraternities provided a social and service outlet for music students on campus, and the role of these two organizations have continued to be vital elements in the life of the Music Department.[39]

Dr. Kenneth Hartley resigned his position at Belmont at the end of the 1968-69 academic year, moving to Union University in Jackson, TN where he became the Chair of the Music Department of Union University, an older and much more established institution. During his four years at Belmont, the Music Department achieved a permanent home in the Massey Fine Arts Building, a modest instrumental program was started, and the music faculty had grown to seven full-time instructors (Hartley, Kliewer, Lyall, Midkiff, Mulloy, Thompson and Wall). Dr. Hartley expanded the horizons for choral music during his time. As he directed the Belmont Chorale (later called the Oratorio Chorus), he chose to perform more cutting-edge works whereas in the past Handel and Mendelssohn had been the most common repertoire for this ensemble. Under his guidance, the choir performed Honegger's *King David*, Kodaly's *Psalmus Hungaricus* and Stravinsky's *Symphony of Psalms*. With the Beltones he introduced Britten's *Ceremony of Carols*. Clearly he wanted to stretch the repertory for choirs at Belmont and in doing so, he paved the way for others who would lead the choral program.

PART IV
BELMONT MUSIC UNDER JERRY WARREN (1961–1991): A FIRM FOUNDATION

Dr. Jerry L. Warren, Head, Department of Fine Arts (1969-1983); Dean, School of Music (1983-1991); University Provost (1991-1999); Interim University President (1999-2000); University Professor (2000-2007)

CHAPTER NINE

Challenges and Achievements (1969–1979)

At the end of the 1960s Belmont had weathered significant challenges in developing enrollment and improving facilities. After a decade of leadership by Herbert Gabhart, enrollment had grown dramatically and three new buildings now graced the campus: Williams Library, 1964; Stripling Gymnasium, 1965; and Massey Auditorium, 1968. With major funding by Jack Massey and others, Belmont was gaining a reputation for academic excellence, which provided a firm foundation on which in which a strong music program could be built. At this opportune time a new leader for the music program arrived.

Dr. Jerry L. Warren came to Belmont as Head of the Department of Fine Arts in the Fall of 1969, where he would lead the Department of Music (later the School of Music) until 1991, when he was appointed Vice-President for Academic Affairs and shortly thereafter Provost of the University. He was uniquely suited for the task ahead. Dr. Warren completed his BM degree from Howard College (now Samford University) and the MCM and DMA from The Southern Baptist Theological Seminary. He had served as Minister of Music at the First Baptist Church of Auburn, Alabama, and spent three years on the music faculty of Shorter College before coming to Belmont.[1] He was an experienced church musician, voice teacher, choral conductor and administrator, yet most of his career lay before him. He recognized immediately Belmont's potential and challenges. In an interview Warren said, "I felt that Belmont had unlimited potential with its location in Middle Tennessee and the heart of Nashville. We had a small faculty who was willing to work hard to achieve goals. We had a very good relationship with Middle Tennessee churches which was a major plus in recruiting." When asked about challenges the Music Department faced in 1969, he recalled the lack of financial resources, which resulted in inadequate equipment, as well as limited programming and scholarships. Because of meager music scholarship funds, building a large group of music majors and attracting the most talented students was difficult.[2]

There were 45 music majors at Belmont when he arrived, and the curriculum needed to be overhauled. Dr. Warren was willing to work hard, often on a shoestring budget, to build a program that would attract students. As a result, when he left the School of Music in 1991, 257 undergraduate music majors and 25 graduate students were enrolled. He had also quadrupled the size of the faculty and guided the music program to accreditation by the National Association of Schools of Music. Moreover, by this time the strength and quality of the School of Music attracted students from all across the country. This section of the book deals with the dramatic changes that took place over the 22 years of Jerry Warren's leadership of the Belmont University music program.

Reorganization of the Choral Program

One of Dr. Warren's immediate goals was to reorganize the choral program. For 15 years the choral groups had been divided into the Men's Glee Club and the Beltones for women. Philosophically he believed that students going into church music and music teaching positions would be better served by participating in a mixed-voice choral experience. He decided to abolish the single-sex choirs and form The Belmont Chorale in their place. The term Oratorio Chorus (then named the Belmont Chorale) was reclaimed for the large choir performing major works. This transition was not easy because both previous choirs had developed a camaraderie and tradition. Especially, the Men's Glee Club had developed an identity something like a "fraternity." The new choral configuration moved forward with some dissatisfaction at first. In a short time, however, the Belmont Chorale developed its own traditions and became not only the flagship choral ensemble of the college, but also a leading choir among small colleges. Within three years of its founding, the Belmont Chorale was invited to participate in the 1973 St. Moritz Choral Festival in St. Moritz, Switzerland. On that journey the Chorale performed in Switzerland, Austria and Italy, becoming the first Belmont ensemble to concertize overseas and to receive international recognition.[3]

Development of the Faculty

Within a year of Warren's arrival, in 1970, he was informed that funding had been cut for the new instrumental position begun under Dr. Hartley in 1967 and that the position of E.D. Thompson would not be continued. Thompson had already enlarged the band to a sizable ensemble by the time the new Massey Auditorium opened. This setback was critical for a new Department Chair with growth on his mind. Warren himself took over the leadership of the band for a year, and then Patrick McGuffey, an adjunct teacher of trumpet, continued the role until the time when a new faculty member could be hired for the job. Since the number of music majors steadily grew over the next few years and thus the need for faculty did as well, Warren was able to expand the faculty while gradually increasing percentage with doctorates. (Warren was the only music faculty with the terminal degree at the time of his hire.) In rapid succession the following faculty were hired: Dr. Richard Lamar, an experienced piano teacher and concert artist (1972); Dr. Paul Godwin, professor of music theory and leader of the Concert Band (1973); Dr. Richard Shadinger, professor of music history, piano and church music (1974); Sherry Kelly, teacher of voice and choral conducting (1975); Linda Ford, teacher of piano and later founding director of the Piano Pedagogy Major (1976) and Dr. Albert Wood, Belmont's first full-time faculty member in Music Education (1976). Two years later, in 1978, John Pell joined the faculty as instructor of guitar. His wide range of skills in both classical and popular styles gave him an important role in the development of the guitar program. In 1979 four new faculty members were added: Randall Ford, clarinet and Concert Band; Marjorie Halbert, voice and director of Company; Rachel Lebon, commercial voice; and Robert Marler, piano. While steadily adding full-time faculty, Warren called on capable local Nashville music talent to teach part-time in areas not covered by full-time faculty. In the early years these appointments included Linda Ford, piano (later hired full-time); Ken Krause, percussion and theory; Patrick McGuffey, trumpet; Fran Powell, music education; Jerry Roberts, guitar; Norma Rogers, flute; Robert Taylor, oboe; and Samuel Terranova, violin.[4] These teachers were experienced performers, teachers and players with the Nashville Symphony Orchestra. These faculty additions brought strength and status to the Music Department, and the use of part-time (adjunct) faculty became a regular way of meeting the need for music faculty in an environment of growth.

85

Curriculum Development – Gaining NASM Accreditation

While Warren was enlarging the faculty, he also attended to the development of the music curriculum. He was concerned that Belmont offered only a Bachelor of Arts degree, although he was aware of the reasoning behind the Bachelor of Music degree's elimination in the 1950s. The Bachelor of Music degree, with its higher concentration of music content was considered to be the best avenue for training professional musicians. With support from the college administration, the music faculty - under Warren's leadership - began to build a Bachelor of Music degree plan that would meet the standards of the National Association of Schools of Music. While it was fairly easy to design the curriculum on paper, securing approval from the College Curriculum Committee and the College faculty was not as easy. In those days the small faculty of the College served as a "committee of the whole" to approve or reject curriculum changes, and they discussed at length and often disagreed about what type of college Belmont should be. Some regarded Belmont as a liberal arts college and preferred little emphasis on professional programs. Since more faculty members were from the humanities and sciences departments, the liberal arts proponents had a strong voice. Professional programs were few, but growing, and the debates sometimes became quite heated. Eventually, in 1971 the Bachelor of Music degree - with majors in Performance, Church Music and Music Education - was added to the catalog.

While the type of institution Belmont should be was often contested in the early years, Belmont consistently pursued the pathway to professional programs. When the Music Department joined Business, Nursing and Education as a new professional program on campus, the die was cast. In fact, out of this debate evolved Belmont's Vision of the 1980s and 90s: "to be a premier teaching University bringing together the best of liberal arts and professional education in a consistently caring Christian environment." Dr. Warren indicated in an interview that convincing the entire campus community of the value to the College of having a strong music program was not an easy task. But in 1973 Belmont was granted "Institutional membership" in NASM, meaning that the school had taken the first critical step toward accreditation.[5]

By 1977 the Department of Music was ready to submit its application to become a full member of the National Association of Schools of Music.

Created with input from all music faculty, the NASM Self-Study Document showed great progress in meeting the standards of the Association. In the fall of 1977 a visiting NASM committee came to Belmont for an on-site visit to examine the programs, procedures, faculty and facilities of the Music Department. The Self-Study Document included a proposal for a major in Music Therapy. This program, however, was not begun due to the lack of appropriate resources; it was ultimately dropped from the curriculum.[6] The progress of the Department was evident to the visiting committee, which recommended that Belmont be made a full member of the National Association of Schools of Music. That status was voted on by the Association and became official in 1978, placing Belmont among the better schools of music in the country.[7] Dr. Warren's steady leadership had brought the Music Department far in the eight years since his arrival. The attainment of accreditation was a major achievement, bringing numerous advantages in terms of curricular strength, status and recruitment.

Founding of the Music Business Program

In 1972 Dr. Warren invited leaders in the music industry to campus to discuss ways Belmont might educate students to work in the growing music industry of Nashville. The connection between Belmont and the music industry seemed like a natural fit. Geographically, Music Row - with its plethora of recording studios, performing rights agencies, and publishing companies - rolled right up the hill and ended at Belmont's doorstep. And like the music industry itself, Belmont was young and entrepreneurial. The meetings concluded that the music industry needed leaders who were musically literate, but who also had a good knowledge of business. Given this direction, Warren involved faculty members from the growing Massey School of Business and asked them to design a Bachelor of Business Administration degree that focused on the music industry. The degree included standard business courses, new courses related to the music industry and a small cohort of music courses. Launched in the fall of 1973, the degree was to be directed by the School of Business.[8] With its focus on recording technology, the Music Business program attracted much attention to Belmont because it was one of the first degrees of its type in the country. Fortunately, on February 21, 1974, the young program dedicated a fully functioning state-of-the-art recording studio, located in the lower level of the Massey Center for Business, through the generosity of Mr. and Mrs. Edmund W. Turnley, Sr., who made a grant through the Turnley Family Foundation for this studio. This acquisition immediately gave the program credibility, which helped it get off to a strong start.[9] As the program got underway, music professor Robert Mulloy began to teach music industry courses, dividing his time between his music teaching and the new Music Business Program. But as the program grew, Mulloy relinquished his music teaching and moved to the Music Business program full time, eventually becoming the head of the program until his untimely death in January of 1998.

Community Involvement

While curriculum development demanded a great deal of Warren's time, he did not neglect opportunities to reach out to the community. Publicity for Belmont and its music offerings had been almost non-existent; In the 1970s, however, several opportunities emerged for media coverage. In 1972 the Belmont Chorale sang on a half-hour television program on WSIX entitled "This Is Belmont." In addition, Belmont revived an old Ward-Belmont tradition held in the Belmont Mansion called "Hanging of the Green." In 1974 and 1975 this event was taped for television and broadcasted over WSM. The expenses for the telecast were provided by a gift from Belmont Trustee Albert B. Maloney.[10]

At the same time, on March 10-13, 1975 The Church Music Department of the Baptist Sunday School Board hosted a church music conference called "PraiSing" to celebrate the inauguration of the new *Baptist Hymnal 1975*; Belmont's Music Department had a major role in the four-day event. Belmont hosted two days of concerts by guest artists and choirs from Baptist colleges in Massey Auditorium. Under Dr. Warren's direction, the Belmont Chorale performed a concert at Belmont Heights Baptist Church on March 12 and participated in a program at the Municipal Auditorium as part of "The Great Choir," singing hymns from the new hymnal. On March 13 at 3:00 a.m., as part of the "Singing Through the Hymnal" event, the Belmont Chorale sang an hour-long segment, including a series of hymns from the new *Baptist Hymnal*.[11]

Halloween Departmental Recital

A popular music event in the 1970s and 80s was the Halloween

Departmental Recital held on the Thursday afternoon nearest to Halloween. The program usually included performances of "spooky" music, musical spoofs and skits. Students and faculty alike participated, often in elaborate costumes. Phi Mu Alpha and Sigma Alpha Iota often took the lead in planning and promoting the event. Memorable acts included a student portrayal of a music faculty meeting, with students acting the parts of each faculty member; Dr. Pursell playing a "wrong-note" version of a popular piano sonata; students presenting spoofs on music history and theory classes; a group of non-singers performing the quartet from *Rigoletto;* and a faculty performance of "The Grasshopper Opera." The highly anticipated program, held in Harton Concert Hall, varied widely from year to year, but became a casualty of a growing concert schedule and the activity of an increasingly busy music department.

A New Concert Grand for Harton

A major problem Warren faced was the inadequacy of pianos and equipment and practically no capital budget with which to meet the needs. In the summer of 1973, a major gift met two important needs – a new concert grand piano for Harton Concert Hall and a new 12-unit piano laboratory for use in teaching secondary piano. Tree International Music Company and its employees honored one of their employees, Mrs. Joyce Bush, who was suffering from cancer, by donating these items to Belmont; this tribute to her made the presentation of the gift a meaningful and emotion-filled event. On August 7, 1973 the new Steinway Concert Grand piano and the new Wurlitzer Piano Lab were dedicated in a concert which honored Mrs. Bush and celebrated the gift to Belmont. In the dedicatory program Dr. Richard LaMar played a selection of Chopin Etudes which showcased the new Steinway. Professor Max Lyall performed a Chopin Ballade and Prokofiev's Toccata. A consummate improviser, Lyall concluded the program by improvising on a selection of songs composed by Tree International song writers.[12]

The Wurlitzer piano lab was a godsend to the Music Department. All music majors were required to study piano and to pass a piano proficiency exam. As enrollment grew, a piano lab was needed so a class of students could be taught proficiency requirements at the same time. This new lab, which was state-of-the-art at the time, allowed the Music

Department to teach these students efficiently and in a financially productive way.[13]

Building a Music Library

In the early 1970s, the music collection in the Belmont Williams Library greatly needed to be strengthened. Little budget money had been allocated for purchasing library materials, and that deficit was obvious now that the Music Department wished to seek accreditation. When the Music Department was located in Hail Hall, recordings and scores were kept there, where there were two listening rooms. Materials were checked out through the Fine Arts Department secretary. Many of the recordings and scores, from the Ward-Belmont needed to be replaced. The new Williams Library, built in 1964, provided a dedicated space for music materials; having all music materials housed in one facility was obviously advantageous. In 1974, after 10 years at Ward-Belmont and 23 years at Belmont College, Professor Elizabeth Wall retired from teaching. She had been responsible for library materials during part of her career, thus making it natural for her to become the part-time music librarian during retirement. Under her guidance Belmont's music library began a systematic updating of books, scores and recordings. Following NASM guidelines for an effective music library, she used a limited music library budget to fill in the library's gaps. Miss Wall worked as Music Librarian for 5 years until her "second retirement," amassing a total of 38 years of service to Belmont. When she retired fully from the music library in 1979, the facility had acquired an adequate listening room with several thousand long-play records, a large score collection, collected editions of major composers, all the standard research reference works, and a fine collection of books representing all the curriculum areas of the Music Department. Elizabeth Wall must be credited for building the foundation of the Belmont Music Library, a resource which would grow into a massive collection in years ahead.

Growth and Space Needs

Music enrollment was gradually growing: from 45 music majors in 1969, Dr. Warren's first year, to 85 music majors (almost double from 1969) in 1977. In 1973 seven music majors graduated, compared to 12 in 1977.[14]

Belmont's music program was beginning to develop a critical mass of majors, which allowed for a wider variety of ensembles and programming.

In the 1970s Belmont lacked a unified program of overseas study for its students, but Dr. Warren recognized the importance of these student experiences. In May, 1977 Dr. Warren, along with Richard and Marilyn Shadinger, led a group of music majors on a musical tour of Europe. The three-week journey focused on concerts and sites of musical importance in London, Brussels, Bruges, Ghent, Cologne, Bonn, Munich, Innsbruck, Interlaken and Paris. Highlights of this journey included operatic performances at Covent Garden in London and the Brussels Opera, concerts at venues such as Notre Dame Cathedral in Paris and a visit to Beethoven's birthplace and museum in Bonn. This was a modest beginning, but later in the 1990s Dr. Warren's leadership would bring a full complement of Study Abroad experiences for Belmont students.

By 1976, finding adequate space for a growing Music Department presented a problem. When the Music Department had moved into the new Massey Fine Arts Building eight years earlier, in 1968, the facility was ample for the 40 music majors at the time, with room for growth. The rehearsal rooms in Massey, however, were not big enough for a traditional-size concert band. Consequently, the band rehearsed in the old Ward-Belmont Auditorium, which was no longer in regular use. Eventually, the old North Front Building, where the Auditorium was located, deteriorated and was closed, though, and some discussion ensued about demolishing it. In 1976 the old Physics Building, which housed science labs for Ward-Belmont, was reconfigured to make a band rehearsal space. At the same time, more teaching studio and classroom space was needed. Ironically, the first floor of Hail Hall, which had previously been the Music Department location in the 1960s before Massey Fine Arts Building was built, served as the overflow teaching space for music classrooms and studios, the first of several makeshift music teaching spaces in the years to come.

Development of the Piano Pedagogy Major

In 1977 the Music Department initiated a new major in Piano Pedagogy, a degree designed to educate teachers of piano. This move, the first addition of a new major to the Bachelor of Music curriculum, aimed to meet the need for competent, educated teachers of piano. It was the vision of Mrs. Linda Ford, the coordinator of the major, to establish a program at Belmont that emphasized teaching of pre-college students. This vision led to the founding of the Piano Preparatory Department, which opened in the fall of 1981. The purpose of the Belmont College Piano Preparatory Department was threefold: to offer solid piano study for young students in the academic setting of Belmont; to provide laboratory teaching settings for Belmont students majoring in Piano Pedagogy; and to recruit students for the Music Department. Belmont Alumna Karen McCarty (BM '81), graduate of the Piano Pedagogy program, was the first administrator of the program. By 1996 the Piano Preparatory Department grew into Belmont Academy, offering pre-college study in piano and a variety of other instruments.

Development of the Commercial Music Major

One of the most significant decisions made by the Music Department in the 1970s was the establishment of a Major in Commercial Music under the Bachelor of Music degree. This possibility had been discussed for several years, first arising when Belmont was planning the new Music Business degree to be housed in the School of Business. Now that students could opt to study music business as business majors, should students not also study popular and jazz styles as music majors? Nashville certainly seemed to be the right place for a commercial music major, and Belmont with its intense creative energy seemed to be the college to pull it off. Belmont's recent growth and stature reinforced the idea.

Thus, in 1977 planning began for the Bachelor of Music Degree in Commercial Music. A number of important issues had to be dealt with. First, no models existed for such programs. A few universities offered Jazz Studies programs, but Belmont's aim was broader – to offer study in a wide variety of popular styles, including everything from country music to jazz. The National Association of Schools of Music simply had no guidelines for such a curriculum. Secondly, the problem of space and adequate budgets for equipment were chronic. A Commercial Music program would require sound equipment and space for more students, ensembles and faculty. Thirdly, what type of faculty would be needed for such a program, and where could they be found? The music program would need to find faculty members whose musical and academic backgrounds prepared them to teach popular music within an organized academic curriculum. Perhaps most serious of all was the problem of the music faculty's comfort with the decision to begin such an innovative program. The current faculty, who might feel that their areas of interest would be threatened, were likely to object to bringing forward the serious study of popular music. In an interview with Jerry Warren, he expressed that this was his major concern as the Music Department moved into this new direction.[15]

In fact, none of these issues were solved quickly or easily. When devising the curriculum, the planning committee wisely decided to retain a certain level of classical performance and academic coursework in the Commercial Music Major. Using NASM guidelines for ratios of music content and general education, and the hours of credit for areas of performance, music history and music theory, the committee forged ahead to plan a curriculum. The original curriculum was revised several times in the early years as better ideas for the program were discovered through experience.

The Commercial Music Major provided three Emphasis Areas from which students could choose to focus their degree: Performance, Music Business, and Composition and Arranging. The Performance Emphasis Area was analogous to the Performance Major in classical study, requiring both a Junior and Senior Recital. Only outstanding performers in popular styles were allowed into this emphasis area. The Music Business Emphasis Area allowed students to take a strong cohort of courses in the Music Business program. The Composition and Arranging Emphasis Area was designed for students with interests and abilities in composition and arranging in popular styles.

The problem of space and budget was ever-present. (In fact, there was no time after 1975 when space for music instruction and performance was not a problem.) The Commercial Music program began in 1978, starting slowly at first with small enrollments, to avoid overtaxing space and monetary resources. As enrollment in the Commercial Music Major grew, so did budgets for needed equipment and options for space expansion.

The problem of faculty resources for such a program was solved over time as well. There were, in fact, faculty in academia with the necessary skills, and Belmont intentionally searched them out. In addition to full-time faculty, it became clear that much of the teaching expertise was available in the Belmont neighborhood. Numerous local musicians had exactly the skills that Belmont needed. These were artists who were not available full-time, but who could teach on a part-time basis. Because of this, the Music Department's adjunct teaching roster began to swell in the

1980s. Early full-time faculty members in Commercial Music were Dr. Jay Collins, percussion and theory; Rachel Lebon, voice; John Pell, guitar; William Pursell, composition; John Arnn, piano; James Ferguson, voice; Roy Vogt, bass; Dr. Michael Harrington, theory and music history, and Jeannine Walker, voice.[16] These excellent faculty members served as perfect foundational faculty for a growing program. The last problem - that of faculty support for the Commercial Music Major had to be worked on for years because faculty attitudes tend to change slowly. The faculty had agreed wholeheartedly to begin the Commercial Music major, but living this decision out into the future was not easy. It was an ongoing challenge. But history reveals that, with time, the faculty did grow to be mutually supportive across the various disciplines.

The first graduate of the Major in Commercial Music was Carlisle Jewel (Charlie) Miller, Commercial Piano Major, who completed the program in December of 1979. In many respects he represented the best of what Belmont hoped graduates in this program would be. He was a gifted pianist in both classical and jazz styles and an academically strong student. He completed the MM degree at Western Kentucky University in 1981. Miller developed an impressive career as a church musician, accompanist, solo pianist, recording artist and composer. Settling into his career in Greenville, SC he often played keyboards for Broadway touring companies in both Greenville and Charlotte, NC. His numerous piano arrangements were published over the years by Lillenas, Inc., and he has recorded several albums of piano performances. In an interview, he expressed appreciation for the close attention he received from faculty in the emerging Commercial Music Major. Decades after his graduation as Belmont's first Commercial Music graduate he continued to make his mark as a highly regarded director, composer and pianist.[17]

By 1982, just four years after the founding of the Commercial Music Major, the program received national notice when it was featured in an article in the January, 1982 issue of *Keyboard* magazine. The article, entitled "Music Education for a Changing Job Market," by Diane Rappaport, stated that although many programs of this type are in the fledgling stage, the two basic approaches are "most easily exemplified by the two majors offered at Nashville's Belmont College." The article focused on both Belmont's Commercial Music Major and Music Business Major as two ideal ways to meet the needs of students and the music industry in a changing job market.[18] As more colleges and universities began to consider developing programs of study in commercial music, Belmont College became a model for such programs; eventually, the National Association of Schools of Music began to use Belmont's curriculum as a model for accreditation purposes.

As part of the Commercial Music program, a number of new ensembles were started to meet the performance needs of majors. Belmont had established a jazz ensemble and a show choir before the major was launched, but the importance and ability of these groups increased quickly with the influx of majors in Commercial Music. In addition to the Jazz Ensemble and Company (the show choir), commercial performing groups founded in the early eighties were Jazzmin, the Bluegrass Ensemble and Small Jazz ensembles. In the May, 1982, the show choir "Company," under the direction of Marjorie Halbert, competed in the Johnny Mann Great American Choral Festival, placing third in the competition. Company brought home an award of $10,000, which was used to purchase sound equipment and a new synthesizer for the Music Department.[19]

Events of 1978

In the summer of 1978 Belmont produced the outdoor drama "Miracles," based on the English miracle plays of the Middle Ages. Dr. Anderson Clark of the Belmont English Department was the producer, while Lynn Eastes from the Department of Drama directed and Dr. Richard Shadinger served as music consultant. In addition to local actors, several British actors came to Nashville to participate in the production. A large multi-level stage was constructed in the space between the Humanities and Science Buildings with the Blanton Annex as the backdrop. The outdoor drama received strong press coverage and ran for four weeks during the summer of 1978.

The outdoor Miracle Play production was just one indication of events that were bringing attention to Belmont from the Nashville community. In 1977 George Peabody College for Teachers closed its revered School of Music. While Vanderbilt took over the Peabody School of Education, and retained Peabody's pre-college Blair Academy of Music, it did not preserve the School of Music. The closing of the Peabody College School of Music was a severe loss to the Nashville music community. For decades Peabody had educated performers, teachers, composers, conductors, and church musicians in degrees ranging from the BM to the PhD. The school was nationally known for its production of music teachers and music

95

administrators as well as important scholars. Since Vanderbilt's foray into collegiate music education was still almost a decade away, Belmont emerged as the leading collegiate music program in Nashville, receiving publicity and visibility with more and more frequency. With the demise of the Peabody College Music School, Belmont was asked to host the 1979 summer International Trombone Workshop of the International Trombone Association, which had previously met at Peabody. The Trombone Workshop continued to meet annually at Belmont throughout the early 1980s, bringing the finest trombone players from all over the world for workshops and performances on campus.

The tradition of an annual Christmas Music Festival was begun in 1978, gradually becoming an anticipated kick-off event of the holiday season for many Nashvillians, as well as the Belmont community. An article from *The Tennessean* on November 30, 1978 announced the concert to be held on Friday and Saturday evenings, December 1 and 2. The cost was $2.00 per person. All ensembles of the Music Department were involved, including all choirs as well as the Concert Band and Collegium Musicum. The combined choirs and band performed Robert Shaw's "The Many Moods of Christmas." The second half of the concert presented secular Christmas music in the setting of a holiday party, complete with falling snowflakes.[21] The Christmas Festival became a tradition, though it experimented with different days such as Sunday afternoons and other week nights, and with different themes. For example, the 1980 Festival featured faculty member William Pursell's Christmas Suite "An American Christmas." Originally composed for the American Bicentennial and published as a record album by National Geographic, it was performed live for the first time by the choirs of Belmont. The 1982 Festival was done in the style of a Moravian Lovefeast, while the 1984 Festival used the order of Lessons and Carols. The ninth Festival in 1988 was performed in memory of beloved English Professor Janet Wilson, who died in the fall of that year.[22] The Christmas Festivals eventually grew into "Christmas at Belmont," which gained national recognition through broadcasts on PBS after 2000.

Amidst all the successes, there was also loss. A sudden death of an important person in any institution is a tragic blow. And so Dr. Richard LaMar's death on October 22, 1978 truly shocked the close-knit Music Department family. On the morning after Dr. LaMar's death, Dr. Warren called music majors in from all their 8:00 classes to gather in Harton Hall for the sad news. Having come to Belmont in 1972, Dr. LaMar had proven himself to be a passionate, demanding and caring teacher for his piano students. LaMar was also a frequent performer of piano concerts and possessed a piano repertory that was both broad and impressive. He could play at a moment's notice any Bach Prelude and Fugue or Chopin Etude, as well as many other major segments of the standard repertory. The closeness of the Music Department helped students to deal with the loss. All of LaMar's piano students were absorbed temporarily into the piano studios of Linda Ford and Richard Shadinger, teachers with whom they were already familiar. The Music Department held a memorial service for Dr. LaMar in Massey Auditorium on October 26, with Dr. Herbert Gabhart, President of Belmont, presiding and student Elaine Bailey-Fryd (BM '79), one of Dr. LaMar's piano students, giving a tribute to LaMar as a teacher. Max Lyall, a former Belmont colleague, returned to campus and played a Skriabin Prelude as a musical elegy for a fine musician.[20]

Representative Alumni from the 1970s

The music graduates from the 1970s reflect the largest majors at the time: Church Music and Music Education. Representative music alumni from the decade show a significant impact in churches and schools through their music careers: Wayne Randolph (1970), minister of music; Tommy Johnson (1972), high school choral director; Susan Smith Cauley (1973), minister of music/organist/music educator; Carol Rhodes Poston (1974), middle school music teacher/accompanist; Billye Browne Youmans (1974), voice teacher/recitalist; John Link (1976), minister of music; Pam Burrus Lovvorn (1976), music educator/pianist; Dr. Timothy Sharp (1976), Executive Director of the American Choral Director's Association/scholar/conductor; Jeffries Binford (1977), church musician/concert organist; Douglas Jones (1977), guitarist/performer/teacher at University of Louisville; Gary Lowry (1977), Guitar teacher/performer/recording artist; Dr. Larry McFatter (1977), Music Professor at California State University, San Bernadina; Beth Brown Shugart (1977), church musician/conductor; Anne Sanderson Cronic (1978), church musician/university teacher; Carlene Bradley Eastridge (1978), organist/church musician; Terry Taylor (1978), minister of music/ children's choir curriculum writer; Elaine Bailey-Fryd (1979), elementary music educator; Julie Thomas (1979), Alumni Office, Belmont University; Tony Cook (1979), music educator; Reece Holland (1979), performer on stage and television; Dr. Sharon

Leding Lawhon (1979), Professor of Music, Samford University: Carlisle (Charlie) Miller (1979), church musician/composer/recording artist.

Blanton Annex Used for Music Instruction

The beginning of the new decade at Belmont promised to be a time of growth for the Belmont Music Department. In the fall of 1980 155 music majors constituted 20% growth from the previous year. Teaching space, a continuing problem, was found in the old Blanton Annex, which had been part of the Blanton Hall Academic complex that was saved when Blanton Hall burned on the night of December 30, 1972. The Blanton Annex was not well-designed for music instruction, but it did provide large spaces for studios. The building also housed the old Ward-Belmont swimming pool, locker rooms and a gymnasium around which the offices were located. The old gym often accommodated such disparate activities as opera rehearsals, indoor baseball pitching practice during inclement weather, and evening student social events, making the Blanton Annex an interesting, noisy and quirky environment for music instruction.

Founding of the Nashville Area Music Teachers Association

On May 17, 1980, a group of music teachers from Nashville met at Belmont College for the organizational meeting of the Nashville Area Music Teachers Association to be affiliated with the Tennessee Music Teachers Association and the Music Teachers National Association. For many years Nashville music teachers had participated in the Middle Tennessee Music Teachers Association, which was headquartered at Middle Tennessee State University in Murfreesboro. Nashville teachers felt that it was time to start an organization to meet the needs of music teachers in the city of Nashville. An earlier meeting of interested teachers had occurred at Belmont on March 17, 1980 to discuss the prospect and process for starting the new organization. At that meeting two committees were elected to write up a charter and bylaws and to nominate officers. The organizational meeting on May 17 was hosted at Belmont by Richard Shadinger and Robert Marler, both of whom were listed among the 27 charter members. Dr. Shadinger was elected the first president of the organization, which became one of Nashville's most active professional music organizations.[23] This began a long association between Belmont and

98

NAMTA. In addition to Shadinger, Belmont professors who would serve as president of the organization in the future were Dr. Daniel Landes, Dr. Anthony Belfiglio and Dr. Kristian Klefstad.

Public Relations and Fund Raising

In a move to stay in touch with music alumni and friends, the Music Department began a newsletter called *Music News* which was published at various intervals from 1980-1992. Richard Shadinger was the first editor of the newsletter, which originally was a simple news sheet without pictures. Later, with the addition of a Music Public Relations staff person, the newsletter became more professional in content and appearance. The newsletter helped to publicize concerts and events to alumni and friends, and helped to inform supporters of needs for the department, particularly the need for music scholarships.

As part of an initiative to raise funds, Dr. Warren organized the Belmont Music Foundation to support the work of the Music Department. At its organizational meeting on December 6, 1980, the following officers were elected: Elizabeth Wall (Nashville Area Chair), Norma Benz (Alumni Chair), Nancy Lesch (Current Student Chair), Mr. and Mrs. Richard Lutz (Parents Chairmen), Tommy Johnson (High School Chair), Chris Krause (Church Relations Chair), Susan West Richardson (Communications Chair), Gordon Stoker (Music Industry Relations Chair), Steve Smith (Annual Fund Chair), and Jerry Warren (Executive Secretary-Treasurer). The Foundation planned an annual fund drive for March 26-28, 1981 with a goal of raising $10,000.[24] While the goals of the Foundation were modest, it served as the beginning for larger fundraising efforts of the future. As these fundraising initiatives were beginning, a matching grant of $3,000 from the Presser Foundation was added to funds given to the department in memory of Dr. Richard LaMar. The funds provided for the purchase of six new upright practice pianos. Within a year, in 1981, the Joseph Cates Company of New York established the Roy and Mildred Acuff Scholarship fund. Roy Acuff himself contributed $25,000 to the scholarship, adding greatly to the endowment and making it the largest endowed music scholarship to date. Students receiving scholarships from this endowment were known as "Acuff Scholars." This endowed scholarship continues to honor the artistry and musicianship of one of Nashville's most revered country music artists.

Alumni and Student Achievements of the Early 1980s

In 1980 the significance of Belmont's major in Church Music was underscored when statistics indicated that Belmont supplied a large number of graduate students to the Baptist Seminaries for the study of Church Music. In 1980 13 Belmont alumni were working toward the MCM degree at The Southern Baptist Theological Seminary in Louisville, KY. Five students were working on the same degree at Southwestern Baptist Theological Seminary in Ft. Worth, TX, while two were pursuing the degree at the New Orleans Baptist Theological Seminary. It was a time of growth for music within churches, and Belmont was supplying a large number of musicians to meet this need, mostly in Baptist churches.

At the same time many Belmont students from the 1980s and 90s took the opportunity to gain professional performance experience at the Opryland USA theme park in Nashville. In the summer of 1980, at least 10 Belmont students were singing in major roles in the shows performed daily at the park. Over the lifetime of Opryland USA (1972-1997), scores of Commercial Music majors benefitted from the professional-level performance experience as they worked on their degrees at Belmont. Many of these students would pursue professional performance careers in the music industry. Representative students who performed at Opryland were Carolyn Binkley ('83), Bill Derifield ('82), Gaye Hudson ('83) , Keith McGregor ('81), Ginger Nickerson, Cindy Nixon, Chris Rodriguez ('83), Mike Satterwhite and Garris Wimmer.[25]

With an increasing number of talented music majors, Belmont students were beginning to make excellent showings in auditions in their performance areas. In the Spring of 1980, at the Regional Auditions of the National Association of Teachers of Singing, two students won their respective divisions: Soprano Ruth Anne Crabb (Volpe) (BM '83) won first place in the Sophomore Women's Division, while senior Baritone Charles Cooper won first place in the Intermediate Adult Division. Two years later piano major Dawn Dickinson Sharp (BM '82) was a winner in the Jackson (TN) Symphony Concerto Competition, which resulted in her performance with the Jackson Symphony Orchestra. In the future Belmont students would often bring similar awards to Belmont, showing the growing strength of the Music Department's student body.

Founding of Belmont Pi Kappa Lambda

In 1982 the Belmont Department of Music was honored to be invited to charter a chapter of the music honorary society, Pi Kappa Lambda, one of the oldest and most prestigious honor societies in the U.S. Belmont's chapter was chartered on April 22, 1982 with a ceremony in Harton Concert Hall. Dr. Wilbur Rowand, the Executive Director of Pi Kappa Lambda, was present to install the chapter. The first faculty members to be installed were Kris Elsberry, Paul M. Godwin, Sherry Kelly, Robert Marler, Jerry L. Warren, Rachel Lebon, Richard C. Shadinger, Helen Trotter Midkiff, Linda Ford, Marjorie Halbert, Randall Ford and William Pursell. Alumni members inducted were Peggy Byars Wiggs ('60), Carolle Tracy ('68), Steve Hall ('71), Gayle Breedlove Tankersly ('71), Susan Smith Cauley ('73), Altricia Pruitt ('74), Wilma Lamm ('77), Gary Lowrey ('77), Anne Sanderson Cronic ('78), Dennis McDuffie ('80), Michael Raley ('80), Nancy Lesch ('81), Karen McCarty ('81), and Linda Lucas Harmon ('82). Officers elected for the first time were Robert Marler, President; Richard Shadinger, Vice-president; and Kris Elsberry, Secretary-Treasurer.[26]

First Steps of Music Technology

In the fall of 1982, the Music Department began its first computer-assisted instruction under the leadership of Dr. Paul Godwin, Professor of Theory, who had undergone training in the new music technology. The addition of several TAP machines and several Apple computers brought Belmont students into contact with computer technology for the first time. At first, computers were used to aid theory and ear training instruction. With rapid change, technology became increasingly important, especially with students in Commercial Music. In addition to Dr. Godwin, adjunct instructor Martin O'Conner, made use of Belmont's Moog synthesizer, presenting electronic compositions in concerts at Belmont and guiding students in composing through the use of synthesizers. As music technology advanced, the use of the technology grew, leading to the establishment of a fourth Music Technology Emphasis Area option in the Major in Commercial Music.

101

CHAPTER TEN

A Comprehensive School of Music Emerges (1980–1991)

William E. Troutt – A New President for Belmont, 1982

Dr. William E. Troutt ushered in a new era for Belmont when he became the third President of the College on October 29, 1982. At the time he became President he was 33 years of age, the youngest president of a college or university in the United States. Troutt was uniquely qualified for the tasks ahead. A native of Bolivar, TN, he received the BA degree in religion from Union University, the MA in higher education from The University of Louisville and the Ph.D. in higher education from George Peabody College for Teachers. He completed additional graduate studies at The Southern Baptist Theological Seminary, the University of Michigan, Vanderbilt University and Harvard University. He had served as Assistant Director of the Tennessee Higher Education Commission and as a Senior Consultant with McManus Associates, an education consulting firm of Washington, D.C. Prior to becoming President of the college, he served a year as Executive Vice-President of Belmont during Herbert Gabhart's last year as President.

When Dr. Troutt came to the presidency, Belmont was a very different institution from the one begun in the early 50s. Belmont had grown from an initial enrollment of 136 students to 1,927 in 1982. The faculty had grown from 29 to over 150. The foundations laid during the Presidency of Dr. Herbert Gabhart had brought about growth, financial stability, accreditation, academic respectability and new facilities. The promise presented by a young new President gave a sense of optimism to the Belmont community.

Inauguration Events for President Troutt

The Music Department was strongly involved in the ceremonies planned for the Inauguration week. On Wednesday, October 27, 1982, a Belmont Family Worship Service was held in Massey Auditorium. Belmont faculty and student musicians involved were Ann Richards, flute; John Pell, guitar; Richard Shadinger, organ and harpsichord; Kathy Elmer Ganus, flute; and Marjorie Halbert, soprano. On the evening before the Inauguration, Thursday, October 28, 1982, the Music Department presented an Inaugural Concert, involving a large number of music faculty and students. Performers for this concert were Helen Trotter Midkiff, organ; John Reid, Trumpet; the Belmont Student Brass Quintet; the Belmont College Consort Singers with Sherry Kelly, director; Rachel Lebon, soprano; Marjorie Halbert, soprano; John Baker Thomas, tenor; Keith B. Moore, baritone; Richard Shadinger and Kris Elsberry, piano duet; Robert Marler, pianist; and the Belmont Chorale, with Irwin Ray, who was directing Chorale during the sabbatical leave of Jerry Warren.[27]

The Inauguration Ceremony on October 29 had a special mood of pageantry because of the music planned for the event. The Belmont College Band, directed by Randall Ford, provided a prelude and postlude along with the processional and recessional music. A new College Hymn entitled "Jesus Is the Christ" was commissioned for the event. F. Janet Wilson, Professor of English, wrote the text, and John Arnn, Associate Professor of Music, composed the tune. The collaboration of two professors provided a fortunate combination of words and music which resulted in the College Hymn's immediately becoming an important part of all academic ceremonies. Arnn named the tune "TROUTT" for the new President. In addition to the hymn, Arnn and Wilson were commissioned to compose a festival anthem for the ceremony. The work was entitled "Christ, the Hope of Glory" and drew from the text and tune of the new College Hymn, expanding upon its music and textual ideas. Performed by the combined Belmont choirs and Concert Band under the direction of Dr. Jerry Warren, the work was a festive addition to the event.[28]

Setting Goals for the Future

The beginning of the Troutt administration was an exciting time for the Music Department. The Department was benefitting from the

103

accomplishments of the last decade: enrollment growth, enlarged faculty, adequate facilities, NASM accreditation, and new majors which were attracting more students. The time was right for setting goals for the future and planning strategies for meeting those goals. Jerry Warren began the tradition of having an annual Faculty Retreat for sharing ideas, planning for the future, and enjoying the company of faculty outside the daily routine. The faculty retreat held on January 18-19, 1983 at Henry Horton State Park was especially memorable as important ideas for the future were discussed. The programming for this retreat allowed time when faculty members could express any idea or dream for the future. When every possibility had been expressed, the group gradually categorized and prioritized the ideas presented, coming to a consensus about some directions for the future. There was a unanimous feeling about two items in particular. The first was that the faculty wanted the Department of Music to grow to become a comprehensive department of 250 music majors. (The enrollment in music at the time was about 180 students.) The possibility was suggested that the Music Department could become a School of Music, though the faculty was aware that this structure would have to come through a larger reorganization of the College. When the word "comprehensive" was brought up, to many it suggested the enlarging of the instrumental program to match the already strong vocal and choral areas. Most felt that the establishment of an orchestra and string program to go along with the fledgling band program was the ideal direction. Of course, this required a full-time faculty member with the expertise to direct and build a program from the beginning. The primary idea from the Faculty Retreat of 1983 was thus to seek a new position for an orchestra director with the goal of building an orchestra and string program.[29]

Armed with the enthusiastic backing of the music faculty, Dr. Warren approached the Belmont administration with a request for a new faculty position for an orchestra conductor. It was understood that this faculty member could teach courses in conducting, music education, and other areas as well as develop the orchestra. The position was approved in the fall of 1983, and a committee was formed to search for the right person, recommending Dr. Robert Gregg for the position; he had recently completed his DMA degree at the University of North Texas and had served as Assistant Conductor for the North Texas Symphony Orchestra. Upon his acceptance he arrived at Belmont to begin the position in August of 1984. The task ahead of him was a daunting one, but he immediately began recruitment for the fledgling orchestra.

104

Events of 1983

The spring of 1983 was a time of good news for the Music Department. The Roy Acuff Endowed Scholarship was made even larger by a significant contribution from Roy Acuff himself. Another substantial scholarship was established in memory of Bill Justice, a well-known composer and arranger in the music industry. The Justice Scholarship provided financial assistance for a student who was a talented composer/arranger, the first scholarship of this type.[30]

Moreover, the strength of Belmont's voice students was validated in the Spring Metropolitan Opera Auditions held in Nashville. Soprano Ruth Anne Crabb (Volpe) (BM '83) and Tenor Cliff Forbis (BM '85) won the Middle Tennessee Metropolitan Opera Auditions. Belmont soprano Carolyn Binkley (BM '83) was a runner-up in the auditions, which meant that Belmont made a sweep of the Met Auditions that year. Crabb and Forbis went on to the Southern Regional Met Auditions in Memphis, where they both were finalists.[31] Both of these singers went on to have successful careers in opera. Ruth Anne Crabb (Volpe) became a regular singer with the Florence (Italy) Opera Company and Cliff Forbis continues to sing at many of the great opera houses in the world, including the Metropolitan Opera, the Munich Opera, and La Scala in Milan. Carolyn Binkley became a voice faculty member at Belmont and a regular performer in the Nashville area.

Expansion of Music Facilities

In 1983 the Music Department was forced yet again to find new space for music instruction. The old Blanton Annex, which had served for several years as a temporary space for teaching studios, was to be demolished in order to open up the campus quadrangle from the Belmont Mansion south to the Tower. The old Physics Building on the east side of the campus was chosen as the alternate place for the Music Department. In its original state, it did not seem like good teaching space for music. However, the College planned to gut the building and rebuild the interior to provide adequate space with appropriate soundproofing. When the renovation was completed, the building provided 14 teaching studios and one classroom. For lack of a better name, it became known as the "Music Annex" and served as teaching space for about a decade until the Wilson Music Building was provided in 1994. As is often the case with temporary space,

105

there were interesting experiences. Since the Annex backed up to the tennis courts, it was not unusual to have a voice lesson interrupted by a tennis ball slamming into the window screen, occasionally causing broken window panes. Since the Annex was the closest building to the baseball diamond and tennis courts, the lobby of the Annex also became the gathering place for baseball and tennis players looking for restrooms or a drink of water.

Founding of the School of Music

On June 3, 1983 Belmont College, under the leadership of President Troutt, announced that the College was to be divided into Schools instead of Departments. At that point the Music Department became the School of Music with Dr. Jerry Warren as Dean of the School. This change was in line with the music faculty's goals set at the retreat in January of that year; it provided a platform for a new organizational structure and slightly more autonomy within the College structure.[32]

Within the School of Music there was also a new structure; the School was divided into two departments, Academic Studies and Performance Studies, which allowed for wider leadership opportunities for faculty members, who served as Coordinators of various areas of study. While the original structure given below changed over the years, it basically became the organization of the School of Music over the next thirty years. Within this administrative structure, Paul Godwin and Richard Shadinger became "Department Chairs," later called "Associate Deans." These roles developed more fully over time and became important support for the Dean as the School of Music expanded.

The Department of Academic Studies, Paul Godwin, Chair
    Historical and Theoretical Studies, Paul Godwin, Director
    Theory, Paul Godwin, Coordinator
    Music History, Richard Shadinger, Coordinator
    Professional Studies, Cynthia Ann Curtis, Director
    Church Music, Richard Shadinger, Coordinator
    Music Education, Cynthia Ann Curtis, Coordinator
    Commercial Music, John Arnn, Coordinator
    Piano Pedagogy, Linda Ford, Coordinator

The Department of Performance Studies, Richard Shadinger, Chair

Traditional Performance Studies, Richard Shadinger, Director
    Voice, Sherry Kelly, Coordinator
    Keyboard, Richard Shadinger, Coordinator
    Instruments, Randall Ford, Coordinator
Commercial Performance Studies, John Arnn, Director
    Voice, James Ferguson, Coordinator
    Keyboard, John Arnn, Coordinator
    Instruments, Randall Ford, Coordinator[33]

In the fall of 1983, enrollment in the School of Music grew to 200 students for the first time, moving closer to the faculty goal of 250. This new enrollment level placed Belmont music program in a new category as one of the largest music schools in a private college in the South. New full-time faculty were added in that semester to meet the rising enrollment: James Ferguson, Commercial Voice, and Dr. Daniel Landes, Piano and Coordinator of Secondary Piano. In commenting about the move to "School" status, Dr. Warren said that one of the best experiences from his standpoint was the interaction with other deans at Belmont on common needs and goals. He particularly remembers the collegiality with Robert Simmons, Dean of Humanities and Donald Ramage, Dean of Sciences as they worked together to develop Study Abroad possibilities for Belmont students.[34]

Founding of Faculty Chamber Ensembles

The goal to build a strong instrumental program had to be approached from numerous angles, one of which was to find strong teachers in all instrumental areas. Many of these were adjuncts. To highlight the instructors in the instrumental area, Dean Warren established several faculty chamber ensembles that were charged to give regular concerts on campus and occasional concerts in the community and local schools in order to spread the name of Belmont. The first ensemble formed in 1982 was the Belmont Piano Trio, which was a great first step because it took advantage of the prodigious piano talents of a relative newcomer to the faculty, piano professor Robert Marler, who coordinated the ensemble. Other players were Dennis Molcahn, violin, and David Boyle, cello. This ensemble had considerable change in personnel over the years, and by 1985 it had become the Belmont Piano Quartet with Marler, piano; Pamela Sixfin, violin; Virginia Christensen, viola; and Roy Christensen, cello. The second ensemble formed was the

107

Belmont Chamber Winds composed of Ann Richards, flute; DeWayne Pigg, oboe; Randall Ford, clarinet; Robert Heuer, horn; and Pat Gunther, bassoon. The Chamber Winds became a permanent faculty ensemble, providing a performance outlet for faculty and giving students an opportunity to hear the chamber wind literature. The third ensemble was the Belmont Chamber Brass which involved Debra Martin and John Reid, trumpet; Tom Miller, horn; Doug Rogers, trombone; and Marcus Arnold, tuba.[35] Strategically, the formation of these faculty ensembles was significant because it raised the prominence of instrumental music on campus just as the School of Music was beginning an orchestra under the direction of Dr. Robert Gregg.

New Faculty of the 1980s

The steady growth of Belmont in the 1980s caused growth in the School of Music as well. The addition of new majors in music and Belmont's heightened profile in academia added to growth of the number of students enrolling in the School of Music. In response to the growth, there was unprecedented growth in the full-time music faculty during the 1980s with many of these new faculty making significant impact on the school and the students they taught. Important faculty added during this decade were:

1980 – Dr. Cynthia Curtis, music education and music history; Dr. Keith Moore, voice; William Pursell, composition and music history
1981 – John Arnn, commercial piano; Dr. Kristie Elsberry, music theory and piano
1983 – John Pell, guitar; Roy Vogt, bass
1984 – Dr. Robert Gregg, orchestra and music history; Dr. Shirley Zielinski, voice
1985 – Dr. Michael Harrington, music theory, composition and music history; Dr. Ted Wylie, voice
1986 – Dr. Keith Ellis, trumpet and Concert Band; Dr. Karren Ford, organ and music theory
1988 – Dr. Deen Entsminger, music education and music theory
1989 – Dr. David Bridges, music theory and music history[36]

Many of the faculty who joined the faculty during this decade would devote their entire careers to Belmont University and become leaders in their respective areas in the School of Music as well as in their professional areas outside of the University.

Early Stages of the Belmont Orchestra

When Dr. Robert Gregg began his duties as Conductor of Orchestra at Belmont, not only was there no orchestra, but there were also few students in the string area. He immediately set out to find string players on campus. He found them among music students who majored in other instruments, students who were not music majors, guest community players, and faculty. For example, the Concert Mistress of the first orchestra was Amy Macy (BM '86), a vocal music education major. One member of the cello section was Professor Sherry Kelly, Coordinator of the Voice Program, who had studied cello with Janos Starker while she was a voice major in college. For its first performance on November 6, 1984, Gregg called the first orchestra the Belmont Chamber Orchestra, an appropriate title for an ensemble of 34 players. Sharing its first program with the Belmont Concert Band, the orchestra played literature of only modest difficulty, but played it well. The first works performed were movements from Handel's *Royal Fireworks Music* and Stravinsky's Suite No. 2, and there was a sense of excitement that this new facet of the School of Music would add wonderful new dimensions to the concert life of Belmont. The second year of the orchestra began with greater possibilities. Since several colleges in the Nashville area were without orchestras, Dr. Gregg decided to involve players from those institutions by calling the ensemble the Belmont Intercollegiate Orchestra. This approach not only brought a few new players from Tennessee State University, Scarritt College and Trevecca Nazarene College, but it also provided the possibility of concerts at Scarritt and Trevecca during the 1985-86 school year. At the year's end the orchestra presented its first Concerto-Aria Concert with student soloists chosen by audition. This tradition continued through the years, becoming an important highlight of each spring by featuring outstanding student performers. The intercollegiate approach to the orchestra lasted for only one year, however, because the orchestra was primarily Belmont based, although students from other colleges continued to play with the orchestra from time to time. The term "chamber" was also dropped from the name of the ensemble as it began to perform the standard orchestral repertoire. By 1986 the orchestra was an established ensemble and an important part of the fabric of the School of Music. Within five years the orchestra grew to 50 players and continued to grow to symphonic size in the 1990s.[37] Occasionally the orchestra served as an accompanying orchestra for choral

109

performances, but philosophically Robert Gregg held that the orchestra must primarily be an ensemble that stood on its own, performing increasingly sophisticated repertoire as more string majors began to choose Belmont as a place to study.

The growth of the Belmont Orchestra coincided with the arrival at Belmont of Elisabeth Small as instructor in violin. Small was a Julliard graduate and a pupil of Dorothy DeLay, who had played as Assistant Concertmaster for the Atlanta Symphony Orchestra. She was a passionate teacher of violin and an accomplished chamber music player, performing with the Belmont Piano Trio beginning in 1985. She began to attract string players to Belmont, which in turn strengthened the orchestra. In 1988, Elisabeth Small became the Artistic Director of the Belmont Camerata Musicale, Belmont's unique faculty chamber ensemble.

The Beginnings of Graduate Study

Belmont's Massey School of Business planned to become the first area on campus to have a graduate program by offering the MBA degree. However, the charter of the Tennessee Baptist Convention specified that the Tennessee Baptist colleges were to provide only undergraduate programs. Belmont made one attempt to get a vote through the Tennessee Baptist Convention to allow graduate study, but the vote failed. Because of rivalries between the colleges, the other two colleges did not seem to want Belmont to overtake them in offering graduate programs. Thus, President Troutt approached Union University and Carson-Newman College about seeking this change together so that all three schools could offer graduate programs at the same time. This cooperative approach worked, and on November 20, 1985 the Tennessee Baptist Convention voted to allow graduate programs in education and business in the three colleges. Very soon Belmont was offering the MBA through The Massey School of Business. The possibility of master's level degrees in education opened the door for the School of Music to pursue a Master's degree in Music Education. As a planning step for the masters degree, the School of Music invited two consultants to visit in the summer of 1986 to help Belmont develop a curriculum. Dr. Charles Leonhard of the University of Illinois and Dr. Catherine Hadon-Gabrion from the University of Michigan visited for workshops in which the faculty committee looked at the feasibility of graduate study and the possible curriculum needs. At the time few options for graduate study in music education were available in the Nashville area, and with the growing school systems in Middle Tennessee, the need for the degree definitely existed. After planning the curriculum and getting approval from the College, Belmont offered its first graduate program in music beginning in the summer of 1987. Dr. Cynthia Curtis, Coordinator of the program, led in the beginning of other music education initiatives, including the summer Orff and Kodaly certification programs. Other graduate programs under the MM degree were added gradually to complement Music Education. After 1987 there was steady enrollment in the Masters degree in Music Education and Belmont quickly became a leader in Music Education in Middle Tennessee.[38]

The Tennessee Arts Academy

In 1985 the Tennessee Department of Education, under the leadership of Joe Giles, Director of Arts Education, began to offer high-level educational programs for art, drama and music teachers across the state. In 1987 the Tennessee Arts Academy was established at Belmont College because of its aesthetic beauty and its central location in the state. From the beginning, it was planned to be a top-flight program of learning and inspiration for arts teachers from across the state. Well-known teachers and clinicians were invited every year to work with the attendees. Nationally famous artists and musicians were brought to Belmont for performances, lectures, and workshops for the summer academy. The first dean of the Arts Academy was Dr. Cynthia Curtis, music education professor at Belmont (later to become Dean of the School of Music). After several years, the Academy began to offer a track for school administrators and in the early 1990s the Arts Academy began to invite "musers," high-level thinkers, writers and speakers about the arts, to speak to the Academy participants, providing a new level of challenge and inspiration. In the late 1990s the Tennessee Arts Academy Foundation was established to provide financial support and to insure the stability of the program. In 1998 Dr. Madeline Bridges came to Belmont to join the Music Education faculty and she was named Project Director and Campus Coordinator for the Tennessee Arts Academy. The Arts Academy America was established in 2002, giving the opportunity for teachers from outside Tennessee to participate. Highlights of the Academy each year are the TAA Chorale, the TAA Art Exhibit, and the presentation of the Academy Awards, recognizing outstanding artists,

111

musicians, dramatists, administrators, and teachers for their contributions to the arts. Representative performers and speakers of national stature who have appeared at the Academy are Lorin Hollander, concert pianist (1997), Mary Costa, opera singer (2000), Sheldon Harnick, Broadway composer (2001), Bob McGrath, singer and host of Sesame Street (2003) and Marvin Hamlisch, composer and conductor (2011). After 25 years in operation, the Tennessee Arts Academy continues to be longest running premier summer program in America for teacher training in music, visual arts and theatre. Since its inception the Tennessee Arts Academy has trained more than 5,000 teachers and administrators. The work of these teachers has impacted over two million students over the years.[39]

New Belmont Chorale Leadership

In 1984 due to pressing administrative duties, Dean Jerry Warren decided to relinquish the leadership of the Belmont Chorale which he had founded in 1970. The Chorale's tradition of excellence had grown over those 14 years. Sherry Kelly, who had directed the Belmont Consort Singers for a number of years, took over the leadership from Dr. Warren. In the summer of 1985, Mrs. Kelly's second year of leadership, she led the Chorale to their second performance at the St. Moritz (Switzerland) Choral Festival as part of a larger European concert tour.[40] In 1986 under her leadership the Chorale recorded the first available recording of the choral works of Jean Berger (1909-2002). Berger was one of the most significant choral composers of the time, and his works were often performed by college, high school and church choirs throughout the U.S. Belmont had a long association with Berger because he had visited Belmont twice in the past as a leader of choral workshops. He was an engaging composer and leader who had appealed greatly to the students at Belmont. For the recording, which was released on the Gasparo label, Berger was asked to supervise the recording sessions, which gave added authority to the performances. The January/February 1986 issue of *Fanfare* magazine gave positive reviews of the recording, making the point that it is one of the only recordings of this important composer's works and that it was supervised by the composer.[41] The recording sold well, bringing recognition to the Belmont Chorale. This project began a series of composer-related recordings that the Chorale released over a decade under the Gasparo label: *Jester Hairston Spirituals* (1989), *Exsultate Jubilate, The Choral Works of Daniel Pinkham* (1993), and

Earth Shall Be Fair, The Choral Works of Robert Ward (1996). In 1986, because of growth in the vocal area, a new ensemble, Women's Chorus, was begun to meet the demand, becoming the primary required ensemble for most freshman women vocal majors. Sherry Kelly was appointed director of this choir for women. In 1989 Sherry Kelly led the Chorale on a tour to Eastern Europe, performing in Austria, Czechoslovakia, Romania, and Yugoslavia. The Chorale performed 15 concerts in churches behind the Iron Curtain, often staying in homes of hosts because of the lack of hotels. Because the tour was mostly in Communist countries, the trip was an adventure into unknown territory for the group. For much of the tour John Robinson, Belmont's Fulbright Scholar studying in Romania, served as a guide for the Chorale.[42]

National Association of Schools of Music Accreditation Renewal

In October, 1986 the School of Music underwent a ten-year site visit by an evaluation committee from National Association of Schools of Music for renewal of accreditation. The large and thorough document prepared by the faculty was reviewed by the committee as were the curriculum, faculty and facilities of the School of Music. Because of the fast growth and change in the School of Music, several concerns emerged in the evaluation process. In December the School of Music received a letter from NASM deferring renewal of accreditation based on six issues: Shortage of practice rooms, lack of adequate listening space in the library, the combining of Theory and Composition under one major, concerns over budget for the School of Music, lack of exposure to non-western music, and the high number of hours in the BM degrees. While these issues were improving, budgetary and space concerns were still apparent. Consequently, new practice rooms were built in Founders Hall, and the administration promised budget increases for the music program. At the same time, plans were made for a new library space that would eventually meet the music library concerns, and curriculum changes corrected the concerns about the Theory and Composition Major, splitting the two areas , and thus coming into compliance with NASM guidelines. A heightened focus on non-western music was also added to the music history courses required of all music majors. A response to the Commission on Undergraduate Programs of NASM was sent on September 20, 1987, explaining the changes made in response to the issues cited by the visiting committee. After reviewing

113

Belmont's commitment to change in these areas of concern, Belmont's NASM accreditation was renewed for another ten years.[43]

Bells Return to the Tower

Since 1952 when the Ward-Belmont carillon was removed, Belmont's historic Tower had been silent, but the hope that a carillon could again resound on campus persisted. By the 1980s serious consideration was given to the possibility of purchasing the Gillette and Johnston bells that had earlier been in the Tower. The Belmont bells had been placed in a makeshift tower at the factory of the Schulmerich Bell Company in Sellersville, PA to form a carillon. Belmont inquired about the purchase and re-installation of the bells and received a contract proposal with a cost Belmont regarded as prohibitive. Perhaps the Schulmerich Company assumed that Belmont wanted the bells returned for sentimental reasons and that the college would pay the high price. Instead, Richard Shadinger guided the college to the I.T. Verdin Company in Cincinnati for a new proposal. Rick Watson of Verdin designed a 23-bell instrument of new Dutch bells that duplicated the earlier carillon, the price of which was considerably less than that of the Schulmerich proposal. Belmont was searching for a campus project to celebrate Tennessee Homecoming '86, a statewide celebration of Tennessee culture and history. About the same time an alumnus of Belmont College, Drew Maddox (Class of '55), became interested in the project and donated a major gift to purchase the bells. He also encouraged others to give in order to meet the full cost of $115,464. The carillon consisted of 23 bells cast by the firm Petit and Fritsen of Aarle-Rixtal, The Netherlands. The bronze bells ranged in weight from 1,188 pounds to 57 pounds. The bells were connected to a keyboard with the capacity for 20 additional bells that could be added in the future. The carillon was installed by Verdin in August of 1986, with a dedication concert planned for September 5. Rick Watson, the designer and installer of the carillon, played the concert for a crowd of over 500 invited guests. The carillon was dedicated to Dr. and Mrs. Herbert Gabhart for their many years of service to the college. The dedication plaque in the Tower honors the Gabharts with these words:

> The Belmont Carillon is dedicated in honor of Chancellor and Mrs. Herbert C. Gabhart in grateful

appreciation for devoted service to Belmont College and the Kingdom of God. The College is grateful to Drew R. Maddox, Sr. whose vision, leadership and personal support secured the Belmont Carillon.

Dr. Richard Shadinger agreed to play the bells and began instruction to learn the craft while on a sabbatical leave. Belmont was fortunate that a very experienced carillonneur, Beverly Buchanan, was moving to the Nashville area because her husband was working at the new Saturn automobile plant in Spring Hill, Tennessee. Upon her arrival in 1988, she began to play the carillon regularly and worked to develop the Tower and the use of the carillon. Buchanan was a highly trained carillon player, a student of Percival Price, the performer of the dedication of the Ward-Belmont Carillon in 1929. She previously served as carillonneur for Christ Church Cranbrook in Detroit and brought a wealth of experience and knowledge to Belmont. She first saw the need to improve the interior of the Tower and wrote up a five-year plan for those improvements, including interior painting, carpeting, dropped ceilings, storage cabinets, and heating and air-conditioning. The second crucial need was to acquire a practice keyboard so the carillonneur, as well as students, could learn music without playing on the actual bells. A fundraising campaign was begun among Ward-Belmont alumnae for Tower improvements and the practice keyboard. Buchanan was able to acquire a used practice keyboard from the Shrine of the Immaculate Conception in Washington, which was rebuilt by I.T. Verdin for Belmont's use. The new practice instrument was installed in April, 1992 on the third floor of the Tower, completing the major improvements begun several years earlier. With the installation of the practice keyboard, the School of Music began to offer carillon study to Belmont students. Over the years a number of students learned to assist in the playing of the carillon, first with Beverly Buchanan and later with Richard Shadinger. Belmont's carillon became an important part of the sound and fabric of campus communal and ceremonial life. The carillon was always played before and after commencement ceremonies, major concerts, special events, and Christmas events. The tradition of Christmas carillon concerts, begun in the 1930s by Arthur Henkel, was resumed in 1988 by Beverly Buchanan and continues to the present.[44]

115

Belmont's First Fulbright Scholar Is from the School of Music

In 1987 Belmont College produced its first Fulbright Scholar, John Robinson (BM '87), a Church Music Major from Waynesboro, TN. John distinguished himself as a scholar and musician in every way. He was a gifted singer with an impressive deep bass voice. He performed with choral groups and sang major roles in Belmont opera productions. In addition, he was an outstanding tuba player, performing regularly with the Belmont Orchestra. Most amazingly, he was a superb linguist, learning Russian, Romanian (his strongest language), Serbo-Croatian, Polish, Hungarian, and Czech. He developed reading ability in eleven languages and was mostly self-taught. His approach to learning eastern European languages involved finding eastern European names in the Nashville phone book and calling those individuals until he found one interested and able to teach him the language. His interest in language developed through his concern for Christians who were being restricted and persecuted in communist countries behind the iron curtain. He developed pen pals in these countries, which both helped his writing skills and gave him the opportunity to encourage Christians in these countries. In the summer of 1985 he worked in Austria and Yugoslavia with Romanian Christians in exile and did the same in 1986. He applied for a Fulbright Scholarship for the study of voice and opera at the Conservatory in Kluge, Romania. Because of his music skills and unusual language gifts, he was chosen for this coveted award, travelling to Romania in the fall of 1987 to begin his studies at the Conservatory in Kluge. This opportunity gave him an entrée into the country in which he was most interested. While there for the year, he was able to work with Baptist congregations through singing and preaching, providing encouragement to Christians who were suffering under communist rule. Letters from Robinson during his time in Romania told of the cold winter, often without heat and sufficient food. Because he was an American, he received extra rations, while the general population was in dire need. When he returned after his year abroad, he was considerably thinner than when he left, but also much richer in experience. In a short two years later when communism fell in Eastern Europe, Robinson went back to Romania as a pioneer missionary, working in churches throughout that area of Europe. In 1989 he served as a guide for the Belmont Chorale on their concert tour through Eastern Europe.[45]

Belmont Camerata Musicale Is Established

The instrumental program was growing steadily in the 1980s with the establishment of the Belmont Orchestra and the growth of the Belmont Concert Band. The faculty chamber ensembles gave visibility to faculty members and enriched the concert life of Belmont and the community. In 1988 Dean Warren had the idea to begin a new faculty ensemble that used faculty performers from all areas and offered educational value for students; he also wanted it to be creative and flexible. Working with the staff of the Belmont Mansion, permission was granted to present an annual series of chamber music concerts in the setting of the Grand Salon, the center of Belmont Mansion's grandeur. The space has been called the grandest domestic space in a home in the South built prior to the Civil War; a more appropriate place for chamber music concerts could not be imagined. The space was large, yet intimate. Depending on the seating arrangement the space could accommodate 100-150 audience members. Since performers were not on a stage, the space gave the audience the sense that they were actually in an informal home setting as they listened, giving an authentic experience of chamber music. Elisabeth Small, instructor in violin, was appointed to be Artistic Director of the ensemble. Her charge was to plan and prepare a creative, appealing, and varied annual series of chamber concerts involving a wide range of performances from the School of Music Faculty. The first performance of the Camerata was February 18, 1988 which established the path Camerata would take in its programming. The first half included a Handel Trio Sonata for violin and oboe, which was followed by two Handel sacred arias sung by Dr. Shirley Zielinsky and accompanied by the Baroque ensemble. The second half of the concert consisted of Stravinsky's *'l Histoire du Soldat*. In all a total of 14 players were involved in the concert, mostly School of Music faculty.[46]

The standard repertoire of Bach, Mozart, Haydn, Beethoven, Brahms, etc. comprised a part of the programming, but crucial also was the more adventurous repertoire, exploring works from off the beaten path. Over years of programming, the infinite variety of chamber music for all combinations of instrumentation was explored with a balance of standard and cutting-edge works. Some programs were topical, such as "Courtly Music of the Baroque," "Music by Twentieth-Century American Composers," "Celebration of Women Composers," "Music from the Time

117

of Adelicia Acklen," or the three-night "Les Six Festival." Other concerts were devoted to one composer such as Mozart, Schubert, David Amram, John Harbison, or Charles Ives. In some cases living composers were present to participate in the program or to present lectures for students, including John Harbison (1993), George Crumb (1993), and Joan Tower (2008).[47] The Camerata concerts, which met community approval and critical review in the press, quickly became a perennial favorite of Belmont and Nashville concertgoers.

Events of 1987-88

In the fall of 1987 Elizabeth Wall, Professor Emerita of the School of Music, was honored by Sigma Alpha Iota with the "Ring of Excellence" for her long service to the Belmont Chapter of SAI. She served as the founding faculty sponsor for SAI in 1967 and continued that role after retirement in 1979. Having joined the Ward-Belmont faculty in 1941, she served on the Belmont campus for 38 years.[48]

During the 1987-88 academic year, faculty members from the Belmont Camerata presented a series of five noonday chamber music concerts at Cheekwood Museum in the Upper Stallworth Gallery. Concerts were performed by John Pell, guitar; Shirley Zielinski, soprano; and two chamber concerts performed by Ann Richards, flute; Dewayne Pigg, oboe; Keith Ellis, trumpet; Richard Shadinger, harpsichord; Randall Ford, clarinet; Robert Heuer, horn, and Pat Gunter, bassoon. A student ensemble made up of Susan Gauger, flute; Tammy Rogers, violin; and Jeff Slaughter, harpsichord, presented a concert of Baroque chamber music as a part of the series.[49]

In the spring 1988 auditions of the Tennessee Music Teachers Association, two Belmont students won first place in their respective divisions of the TMTA collegiate auditions: Greg Hill (BM ' 87), a student of Linda Ford, won first place in the piano division; and Tammy Rogers (King) (BM '87), a student of Elisabeth Small, won first place in the string division.

On February 18, 1988 the Belmont Chorale, under the direction of Sherry Kelly, was chosen to perform a concert in Winston-Salem, NC for the Southern Regional Convention of the American Choral Directors Association. On March 25 the Belmont Jazz Ensemble, under the direction of Dr. Keith Ellis, performed a concert in Knoxville for the convention of the Tennessee Music Educators Association.[50]

On March 1, 1988 the School of Music presented its Plan Approval Document to the National Association of Schools of Music for approval of its first graduate program, the MME degree in Music Education. The degree was quickly approved by the association.[51]

On April 18, 1988 a new ensemble, the Belmont Chamber Singers, under the direction of Dean Jerry Warren, presented its debut concert. The choir was designed to accommodate graduate students and to sing repertoire appropriate for smaller choirs.[52]

On April 20, 1988 long-time faculty member Helen Midkiff retired after teaching organ, theory, and music appreciation for 31 years. At her retirement celebration she admitted that she would miss her students: "I'm so proud of them and all they have accomplished. They're the joy of my teaching and the reason I'm here." In paying tribute to Mrs. Midkiff, Jeff Binford (BM '77) said "She not only taught how to make music, but she was a wonderful Christian example. She never ceased to tell us that when we played, it needed to be for the glory of God alone." The School of Music honored her with the title of Associate Professor of Music Emerita, announced at a banquet attended by former students, faculty, and friends. Soon after her retirement, she married Rev. Bob Capra, a retired minister.[53]

In the summer of 1988 the School of Music initiated its first summer Kodaly Certification Workshop, which became a summer tradition for the future. The first instructors in the program were John Feierabend of the Hartt School of Music and Pam Bradford from the University of Oklahoma.[54] The Kodaly program became a regular summer offering for Belmont graduate students and Nashville area music teachers. Teachers in subsequent years included Philip Tacka and Micheal Houlahan from Millersville University (PA).

The young Nashville Opera Company was making tentative steps to become an established opera company with a regular series of productions each year. Belmont provided the Opera Company with free office space for several years while the company was gaining support from the community. In appreciation for Belmont's support for the Nashville Opera, Mary Ragland, the major supporter for the company, presented the Belmont School of Music an endowed voice scholarship in the amount of $50,000, which came to be known as the Mary Ragland Vocal Scholarship.

In the summer of 1989, the Belmont College music library was the recipient of a major gift of music materials. The Albert Uttinger estate left to Belmont over 5000 long-play recordings and over 1200 books on various subjects. Music Librarian Timothy Gmeiner worked for months to sort and catalog the collection, which more than doubled the library's holdings in recordings. In assessing the collection Gmeiner said, "You never expect to receive a quality collection this big... This gift has truly enhanced the quality of our music library."[55]

Belmont Professor of Composition, William Pursell, was commissioned by Nashville's Aladdin Industries to compose a symphony. Called *The Heritage Symphony*, the work was performed by the Nashville Symphony Orchestra on September 15-16, 1989 to critical acclaim. A highly regarded composer and recording artist, Purcell has works recorded with the Eastman Rochester Symphony Orchestra on the Mercury Label, has received two Grammy nominations, and was named Tennessee Composer of the Year in 1985 by the Tennessee Music Teachers Association.[56]

The Commercial Music Showcase

Ten years old in 1988, the Commercial Music Program was showing a new level of maturity and musical strength. The curriculum had been adjusted to better meet students' needs, and a strong professional faculty of performers and scholars were in place. At the same time the talent level of students in the program was increasingly strong. In 1988 the Commercial Music faculty decided to develop The Commercial Music Showcase as a way of presenting to the public the talent of student performers in popular styles. The faculty also wanted this event to involve musicians from the music industry. Students who wished to audition for the Showcase could sign up for an audition time to perform in front of experienced music industry professionals (managers, producers, performers), who were invited to be a part of a panel of judges for the auditions. Call-back auditions were scheduled for the second evening of auditions, and eventually the students chosen for the showcase were narrowed down to four or five performers. The chosen performers, usually vocalists, were assisted in choosing appropriate songs for their portion of the Showcase. Once the songs were chosen, student arrangers went into action to arrange charts for the concert. Outstanding student vocalists were chosen to be the background vocals for the concert, and the best instrumentalists from the Commercial Music Program were selected to serve as the Showcase Band. The featured vocalists were often given wardrobe, make-up, and hairstyle assistance from music industry professionals to add to the professional quality of the Showcase. Now a continuing tradition, extensive rehearsals bring the show together for an enthusiastic audience each year. The Showcase is promoted widely so that music industry managers and producers have an opportunity to hear Belmont talent. The Commercial Music Showcase, an annual event, serves as a springboard for the careers of young performers. Since 1988 over 100 students have been given the opportunity to present their talents to an audience of professionals and peers; most of these students have developed successful careers as performers in the world of popular music.[57]

Quality Improvement Comes to the School of Music

President William Troutt brought to Belmont College a style of administrative management called Quality Improvement, based on the teachings of industrial designer Edwards Deming. Deming developed a set of techniques through which the administrator involves workers on all levels of the organization to help improve work processes. While these techniques had often been applied to industry, they had rarely been tried in an educational institution. Troutt felt that Deming's ideas, which required listening to everyone's ideas and processing them until best practices emerged, held good possibilities for Belmont.[58]

President Troutt wanted the techniques to filter down into the academic departments, and in 1989 Dr. Jerry Warren became a disciple of the concept, bringing it to the administration of the School of Music. The faculty formed a group known as the TAG (Training Advisory Group), who would oversee problem-solving processes in the Music School. If a problem was identified by anyone, and if several other people were interested in the issue, it could become a topic of study by a Focus Group. Surveys could be taken, input gathered, solutions proposed, and decisions made. Areas being studied by Focus Groups were filtered through the TAG team for further input and approval. Town Hall meetings of the music faculty were held to get input from faculty about topics being considered. Improvement ideas were then sent on to the administrative leaders of the School of Music for input and approval. Areas considered for improvement could be either mundane or significant.

Some of the processes studied and improved through the TAG Team were: the acquisition of answering machines for faculty offices, practice

121

room space, studying the possibility of a Musical Theater Major, office policies and an office procedure manual, accompanist policies/guidelines, room scheduling problems, alumni development, sound reinforcement needs, public relations, a benefit concert, School of Music Vision and Mission Statement, student retention, recording of student ensembles, a faculty mentoring system, and fundraising. Over a period of several years, a large number of processes were improved due to this technique. All of the improvements came from the grassroots, based on concerns identified by faculty and staff. The improved processes were ones that the instigators cared about and therefore followed through on. In the setting of a School of Music that often experienced problems caused by growth, the Quality Improvement process gave ownership of problems and their solutions to workers on all levels. The results were positive and visible over the years that the TAG Team was active in the 1990s.[59]

The First President's Concert

Dr. Warren wanted to begin the tradition of an annual concert to honor the college's President, to showcase School of Music Ensembles, and to raise financial support for Belmont's School of Music. The first annual President's Concert was held on April 29, 1989, quickly becoming an anticipated tradition each spring. President Troutt hosted the event, which featured a wide variety of ensembles from the School of Music. The fundraising potential for the concert became apparent after the first year, and a dinner was added to precede the concert for invited supporters of Belmont. One of the most important aspects of the concert was how it portrayed in one evening's event the full breadth of music studied and performed at Belmont. Most Nashville citizens were familiar with only a small facet of the School of Music. In this setting the audience could hear everything – the orchestra playing a symphonic work to a commercial vocal group singing some of the latest hits of popular music. The concert offered an eclectic mix that was interesting, entertaining and impressive. President Troutt took his hosting of the event seriously and became engaged fully in the event. Having played saxophone as a youngster, he agreed in the 1990 concert to prepare and perform a solo with the Jazz Ensemble. Continuing with this tradition, the next year he took on the task of conducting the orchestra and chorus in a short composition. For one concert he even agreed to learn a soft shoe dance routine to perform with Company, the

College show choir. The audience and students loved his good humor and willingness to be an integral part of the celebrations. It was decided in 1992 to use the President's Concert as a platform for recognizing supporters of music at Belmont and in the Nashville community through an honor called the Applause Award. In 1992, the first recipient of the Award was Donna Hilley, CEO of Broadcast Music International.[60] As a part of the President's Concert that year, Hilley underwrote the recording and production of a cassette featuring numerous ensembles of the School of Music. This recording, entitled "Kaleidoscope," was a first for the School of Music – a recording featuring the wide range of achievement within the School of Music that could be used for public relations and student recruitment purposes. Over the years the President's Concert would raise hundreds of thousands of dollars for scholarships for music majors.[61]

Founding of the Nashville Children's Choir

In 1989 two Nashville music educators, Marilyn Shadinger and Frederica Braidfoot, saw the need for a community-wide children's choir. No institution in Nashville supported a choir giving young singers a high-quality choral experience. Nashville Metropolitan Schools did not have full-time music teachers in the elementary schools at the time, making a community choir even more crucial. Shadinger and Braidfoot, music teachers at Ensworth School, approached Dean Jerry Warren about the possibility of establishing such a group in cooperation with Belmont College. With his approval, the two directors went to work recruiting young singers through public schools and churches. They decided to call the group The Nashville Children's Choir, since it represented students from a cross-section of Nashville and Middle Tennessee. In the Fall of 1989 the choir had 30 singers. Rehearsing on Monday afternoons at Belmont, they soon became an important part of the life of the School of Music. Dr. Warren saw the founding of the choir as an important move toward the music education of pre-college students. As the School of Music was expanding into graduate studies, it also was expanding its pre-college options through the Piano Preparatory Program and the Nashville Children's Choir.

The choir's first concert was a Christmas program performed in Harton Concert Hall. It soon became clear that a small venue like Harton was inadequate for the large audience of families, friends and community people who wanted to hear the well-trained voices. Larger spaces such as

123

Massey Auditorium, Belmont Heights Baptist Church, and other Nashville churches were sought as performance venues. In the second year the choir was expanded to include two training groups which prepared children to sing in the advanced choir. The youngest group, for grades 3 and 4, was called the Preparatory Choir. The middle group, for grades 4 through 6, was called the Concert Choir. The advanced choir for children from grades 5 through 8 was called the Touring Choir. In its second year Frederica Braidfoot relinquished her leadership when her family moved away from Nashville. In her place Dr. Madeline Bridges from the music education faculty of Middle Tennessee State University became co-director with Shadinger, a partnership which lasted until Marilyn Shadinger retired from the choir leadership in 2007. During Christmas 1991, the Children's Choir performed a concert which was taped for Channel 2 WKRN for broadcast during the Christmas season. The Touring Choir began a tradition of spring tours which would take them to Atlanta, San Francisco, Chicago, Detroit, Orlando, Toronto, Boston, Dallas, St. Louis, New York, Williamsburg and Washington, DC. Twice the Touring Choir was invited to sing at Carnegie Hall in New York City. Special performances included a concert at the Governor's Mansion; Christmas television appearance with Reba McIntyre on the Nashville Network; performances with the Nashville Symphony Orchestra, the Nashville Ballet in *The Nutcracker* and *Carmina Burana*, and *La Boheme* with the Nashville Opera; regular appearances at Belmont's President's Concerts and Christmas at Belmont. The Choir was often asked to sing for national meetings of music educators, such as The Convention of the American Orff Society in Memphis and the Tennessee Music Educators Association. Recordings by the Nashville Children's Choir included back-up sessions for major country artists and for educational CDs for the Silver-Burdett textbooks for music teachers. A Christmas CD with the London Symphony Orchestra was sold internationally, and later they recorded with the professional men's choir, The Centurymen. In addition, the Touring Choir recorded its own CDs periodically. The Nashville Children's Choir became a Nashville treasure, providing excellent singing experiences for thousands of children through the years and enjoyable performances for audiences in Nashville and beyond.[62]

The Nashville Children's Choir program was expanded in the 1990s to include The Nashville Youth Choir, which provided a good singing outlet for alumni of the Children's Choir and other high school singers from throughout Nashville. In 2003, Robert King, Choral Director of Lipscomb

Academy, became the permanent Director of the Nashville Youth Choir.

Belmont's First Broadway Performer

Melissa Davis was a talented Commercial Music Major who became Miss Belmont in 1989. As a member of Company, Belmont's Show Choir, she honed her skills in dance and singing on stage. In February of 1990, the touring company of the musical *Les Miserables* performed at the Tennessee Performing Arts Center, and was also holding auditions for possible replacements in the company. On February 14 Melissa Davis auditioned with the *Les Miserables* Touring Company, and within a month she was called to join the cast in the role of Cosette. With only four days to say goodbye to family and Belmont friends, she flew to Boston to join the company. At the next stop in Washington, DC, she received the call to go to New York City where she joined the Broadway cast of the show in the role of Cosette. Regarding her fortune of gaining a Broadway role in a major show, she modestly said, "I haven't made it.... I am not a star... I was given a chance. Many people I know would be successful if given the chance." President William and Mrs. Troutt attended a performance of *Les Miserables* in New York and visited with Melissa after the show. In 1992 Melissa Davis came back to Belmont to perform in the President's Concert for that year, singing one of Cosette's songs from *Les Miserables* along with Belmont's choruses and orchestra, which also joined her for the rousing final chorus from the show.[63]

Representative Alumni from the 1980s

The careers of music alumni from the 1980s show the wider reach of Belmont into a large number of schools, churches, universities and major performance venues. Representative music alumni from the decade are: Elaine Cook Haley (1980), minister of music; Philip Mitchell (1980), minister of music; Rich Gable (1981), music educator; Pamela Howard (1981), university voice teacher; Karen McCarty (1981), piano teacher/church musician; Keith McGregor (1981), musical theater performer; Dr. Michael Raley (1981), Professor of History at Hanover College; Linda Harmon (1982), piano instructor, Belmont University; Dawn Dickinson Sharp (1982), music educator/pianist; Chris Rodriguez (1983), guitarist/performing and recording artist; Ruth Anne Crabb Volpe

125

(1983), opera singer, Florence, Italy; Dr. Daniel Lawhon (1983), organist/performer/teacher; Jana Wolfe (1984), minister of music; Mario DaSilva (1985), guitar instructor, Belmont University; Clifton Forbis (1985), internationally-recognized operatic tenor; Richard Suggs (1985), minister of music; Sabra Wright Buchheit (1986), pianist/performer/church musician; James Green (1987), musical theater director/composer; Greg Hill (1987), pianist/recording artist; Tammy Rogers King (1987), violinist/teacher/performing artist/fiddler/recording artist; Jonathan Nelms (1987), music minister; Jeff Parker (1987), minister of music; John Robinson (1987), minister/missionary/linguist; Gregory Walter (1988), musical theater performer/teacher at North Carolina School of the Arts; David Baker (1988), guitarist/performer in New York; Teresa Cheung (1988), Conductor, Alltoona (PA) Symphony Orchestra; Michael Mellet (1988), background vocals/recording artist; Carlos Colon (1989), composer/teacher; Todd London (1989), percussionist/performer/percussion instructor, Belmont University; Daniel Weeks (1989), Voice Professor at the Cincinnati College-Conservatory of Music/operatic tenor.

1990 – A Year of Significant Events

In January, 1990 the Belmont Camerata Musicale embarked on one of its most ambitious series of concerts with a "Les Six Festival," focusing on the works of Honegger, Poulenc, Durey, Talliaferre, Milhaud, and Auric from early twentieth century France. Three concerts in one week covered a wide range of styles and genres from all six composers. The concerts involved a large number of the music faculty from both instrumental and vocal areas. The concluding work of the Festival was Milhaud's *l' Creation du Mond*, a ground-breaking work of the 1920s known for its early use of jazz idioms. Jerome Reed gave an extensive account of the festival in his article in the February 1, 1990 edition of *The Tennessean*. He summed up his thoughts about the three concerts with these words: "Kudos to Elisabeth Small and the Belmont faculty and students for undertaking an enormous task and using the energy to present these infrequently played works from a fascinating period in music history."[64]

The growing string program of the School of Music prompted the establishment of student string quartets and other chamber ensembles. Depending on the number of students and instrumentation, several groups were formed each semester and coached by faculty. The first official concert by the Belmont Student String Quartet was on February 27, 1990. The quartet concert became a regular part of the annual concert schedule with a wide range of quartet literature played by the students.[65]

By the 1990s, the School of Music had produced a large alumni group to which it needed to connect. In 1980 an alumni newsletter called *Belmont Music News* had been started to provide information about events in the School of Music and to publicize the accomplishments of alumni. Throughout the decade this bi-annual newsletter helped to keep alumni informed. Expanding on that outreach, on April 21, 1990 the School of Music hosted a 20th Anniversary Reunion for the Belmont Chorale. A significant number of Chorale alumni returned for a weekend of singing, social events, and a concluding concert. This reunion weekend served as a model for future events designed to bring music alumni back to campus and help to forge a closer bond with them.[66]

New endowed scholarship funds were also given to the School of Music in 1990. In December of that year the Johnnie Wiley Endowed Scholarship was established by his family, who hailed from Gainesville, GA. Mr. Wiley was the father of Darrell Wiley, class of 1979. Soon thereafter, in 1991, the Florence Esther Mathis Music Scholarship was established for piano students. It was given by Murray and Loretta Mathis of Murfreesboro, TN in memory of their daughter. The growth of endowed scholarships was a great help as the School grew and needed to attract talented musicians.

In February of 1991, Tammy Dellmore (BM '93) and Alice Griffith (MME '92), piano students of Robert Marler's studio, placed first and second in the Jackson Symphony Orchestra League's Mid-South Piano Concert Competition. Tammy Dellmore's first-place win carried with it a performance with the Jackson Symphony Orchestra.

Six months later, in August 1991, the School of Music purchased 25 new Baldwin pianos (15 grand pianos and 10 uprights) to upgrade and enlarge the School's piano holdings. This purchase allowed the School to dispose of several old pianos (some from Ward-Belmont days) and to provide new grand pianos for teaching studios and upright pianos for practice rooms. This capital expenditure was made possible through a new source of funds provided through the Belmont budgeting process. Revenue from Academic Enrichment Fees was given to the various academic units for expenditures on resources that directly impacted teaching and learning resources. This boost in academic spending helped the School of Music greatly in years ahead, allowing for the acquisition of instruments, teaching equipment, and technology.[67]

On March 15, 1991 the Belmont Orchestra performed a concert for the Tennessee Music Educator's Association convention in Nashville. After only six years of existence the orchestra was chosen through blind audition for this honor.

New Position of Public Relations Assistant

In January, 1991 Karla Graul began working in the School of Music as its first Public Relations Assistant. With the growth in the School of Music, a staff person was needed to publicize events, to develop materials for prospective students, and to help plan events that would bring people to campus. With a degree in Mass Communications from Towson State University in Baltimore, Graul had previously worked for the Gospel Music Association. She immediately developed a Music Events Line, which the public could call for concert information. With her editing, the *Belmont Music News* became a more attractive and professional newsletter for alumni and friends. Graul's creative ability to write, design, and plan helped develop and present a new image for the School of Music in the Nashville community and beyond.[68]

Dean Jerry Warren Becomes Vice-President for Academic Affairs

After 21 years of service as Dean of the School of Music, Dr. Jerry Warren was appointed by President Troutt as Vice-President for Academic Affairs, beginning in May 1991. Warren had worked cooperatively with Dr. Troutt and had wholeheartedly adopted Troutt's quality improvement approach to administration, bringing its concepts into action in the School of Music. Dr. Warren's leadership of the School of Music had brought about impressive growth and change. When Jerry Warren came to Belmont in 1969, there were 45 music majors. In 1991 there were 257 undergraduate and 25 graduate music students, which placed the School of Music within the top 20 music units among private institutions in the country. With over 180 concerts per year, the activity and influence of the School of Music had become immensely important in Nashville. As an active scholar and musician, Dr. Warren had impacted the lives of hundreds of music majors over the years and was recognized as a leader in the American Choral Director's Association. As he moved to his new role in upper administration, he continued to maintain his music interests and conducted Oratorio Chorus for the first several years that he was Vice-President for Academic Affairs.[69]

Dr. Cynthia Curtis is Appointed Acting Dean for the School of Music

With Dr. Warren's new position of Vice-President for Academic Affairs, Dr. Cynthia Curtis was appointed to be Acting Dean while a search was conducted for a permanent Dean for the School of Music. Dr. Curtis was Director of Graduate Studies and had served on the Music School faculty since 1980, teaching courses in Music Education and Music History. For five years she was campus coordinator for the Tennessee Arts Academy for arts teachers, sponsored by the Arts Education Department of the State Board of Education. She accepted the appointment with enthusiasm: "I am excited about the challenge of serving as Acting Dean. The Belmont School of Music has a large, diverse and respected program that points to nothing but possibilities for the future."[70] As a highly organized and motivated administrator, she did not see the interim position as a strictly caretaking role. Rather, she took the job of Acting Dean with the purpose of moving the School of Music forward in any way possible during her term. She was a quick learner because of her active leadership in the School, and she moved into the role enthusiastically.

Belmont College Becomes Belmont University

It was not surprising that President Troutt led Belmont to become a university. An earlier administrative reorganization already divided the College into several schools. By 1991 Belmont had become one of the largest private institutions in Tennessee, second only to Vanderbilt University. Belmont's enrollment for fall 1991 was 2,821 with a growing graduate enrollment. The date chosen for officially becoming a university was September 4, 1991, 101 years after the 1890 opening of Belmont College for Young Women. A campus-wide convocation celebrated the event, with speeches given by Dr. Troutt, Chancellor Gabhart, State Senator Doug Henry, as well as representative students.

Belmont University's "World Premiere Celebration" was planned for Friday, September 6, 1991. Over 3,500 spectators attended an out-of-doors concert by the Nashville Symphony Orchestra, conducted by Brian Groner. The orchestra was placed in front of the Bell Tower with the audience seated in the amphitheater and up the lawn toward the Belmont Mansion. One of the highlights of the concert was the performance of Professor William Pursell's "United Electric Railway, 1890" from his *Heritage Symphony*. *Cellephone* by former Music School student Lee Gannon was also performed. In addition, Dr. Deen Entsminger, Professor in the School of Music, arranged an orchestral version of the Belmont Alma Mater for the concert. The grand finale of the concert was the performance of Tchaikovsky's *1812 Overture*, complete with a large fireworks display going off in the nearby gymnasium parking lot. Belmont's two carillonneurs, Beverly Buchanan and Richard Shadinger, furnished the bell part to the composition from the Tower. With this enthusiastic celebration, Belmont had moved into a truly new era 101 years after Misses Heron and Hood began a small girl's college on the campus.[71]

PART V
THE SCHOOL OF MUSIC UNDER CYNTHIA CURTIS (1991–1997)

Sam Wilson (center) is awarded the School of Music Applause Award for 1993. Pictured with Wilson are from left: President William E. Troutt, Dean of the School of Music Cynthia Curtis, and Dr. and Mrs. James Cotham.

CHAPTER ELEVEN

Building Blocks
(1991–1997)

Cynthia Curtis' Term as Acting Dean

Dean Cynthia Curtis recalls that soon after she was appointed to be Acting Dean she was introduced to a prospective student as "Acting Dean Curtis." This student responded that she was "really interested in acting and was pleased to meet the Dean of that area." Dr. Curtis' move to this position was more than "acting." She was very perceptive and quickly began to see a number of areas where she could improve the School of Music and meet the needs of students:

- She wanted to find a way of hearing the concerns and opinions of music students. Therefore, one of her first acts was to establish the Dean's Advisory Council to serve as a contact between students of the School of Music and the School of Music administration. The first student members of this council were Allan Hall, Angela Brownell Smith, Clay Price, Jamie Wigginton, Mark Brasher and Keith Martinson. The size of the council grew as enrollment grew and the Council became an effective sounding board when making decisions affecting students. In addition, the Council began to sponsor "snack breaks" during exam week and social events for students such as the annual dance held after "Christmas at Belmont" performances.
- To meet the needs of a growing Commercial Music Major a new choir called Belmont Pops was begun in 1991, under the leadership of Jeannine Walker. This large mixed vocal ensemble performed a wide range of choral repertoire including vocal jazz, popular standards, show tunes, current pop music, and gospel music.
- In the fall of 1991 Belmont's student chapter of the Music Educator's

National Conference launched a program to provide music education experiences at Rose Park School, an inner-city elementary school in the Edgehill community near Belmont. Music Education major, Lauren Wilkerson (Baker) (BM '93) was leader of the project. This important venture provided music experiences for students at a time when Metro Nashville Public Schools did not provide elementary music teachers and it provided excellent experience for Belmont's future music educators.

•   For the fall of 1991 the Faculty Concert Series became an organized series of concerts that could be promoted as a whole. For many years, School of Music faculty often performed solo recitals, without attention paid to variety or scheduling. Dr. Robert Gregg chaired a committee charged to organize the series. Faculty who wished to be in the series submitted proposals for the following year. The committee planned a varied and carefully scheduled series which could be promoted as such. The result was a series that provided a balance of classical and commercial faculty members, as well as a balance of vocal and instrumental concerts scheduled throughout the year's concert calendar. In the first year it was fortunate that the Faculty Concert Series was sponsored by Kraft General Foods who provided publicity and program support. Several of the concerts were performed at Tennessee State University as community outreach related to the Kraft grant. This gave the tradition of the Faculty Series an excellent start and helped it to become an anticipated series in the School of Music Calendar. The first year the Faculty Concert Series programs included Robert Marler and William Pursell, piano; Jeannine Walker and Bruce Bennett, vocal jazz; Julia Tanner, cello; John Pell, guitar with Jeff Kirk, flute; Marjorie Halbert, soprano, Keith Moore, baritone with Robert Marler, piano; Keith Ellis, trumpet with Richard Shadinger, piano and organ; Shirley Zielinski, soprano and Czeslaw Zielinski, baritone with Robert Marler, piano; Daniel Landes and Mark Putnam, synthesizers with Carolyn Binkley, soprano; Elisabeth Small, violin; John Arnn and William Pursell, jazz piano; Ted Wylie, tenor; and Michael Harrington, composer. Four of the concerts were chosen to be videotaped for broadcast on WDCN, the Nashville Public Broadcasting System affiliate. This series of twelve concerts showcased the remarkable variety and skill of the music faculty of 1991-92 school year.[1]

Belmont Camerata Presented on WDCN

In 1991-92 the Belmont Camerata was chosen to record a series of concerts to be broadcast on WDCN, the local Public Broadcasting System affiliate. After only three years of concerts, the Belmont Camerata had become an important fixture in the arts community with a loyal following of concert goers. Positive critical reviews in *The Tennessean* helped to build its reputation as a talented group performing cutting-edge repertory. The element which added to the strength of the programming was the performance location, the Belmont Mansion, which provided the ideal environment for chamber music. The beauty of the space, its fine acoustics, and historical heritage combined to make chamber performances by Camerata special. The WDCN videotaping was done in the Mansion which was technically quite a task, given the limitations of the Mansion for lighting and electrical supply. Later, several tapings were done at the WDCN studios to make it easier to handle the technical requirements. The television publicity of the 1991-92 Camerata season led to corporate sponsorship by the Nissan Motor Corporation for the 1992-93 season.[2]

In December, 1991 Belmont School of Music students were honored by *Billboard Magazine* by being chosen to participate in the annual Billboard Song Contest. Twenty-five School of Music students went through training in order to evaluate song entries. Belmont was one of three schools chosen for this event. In addition to Belmont, other colleges involved in the judging process were The Berklee College of Music and the Afro-American Institute of Music at the University of Pittsburgh.[3]

Classical Singers Concert

The voice faculty felt that there was need for extra performance opportunities for outstanding classical singers and consequently developed the concept of the Classical Singers Recital, which began in 1992. Teachers from each voice studio had their outstanding students audition for the privilege of singing on the concert. An outside judge, recognized as an experienced voice teacher, was selected each year to choose the singers for the concert. The selected students were then presented in the Classical Singers Concert presented in a formal setting on a Sunday afternoon. The concert became a way to provide an extra formal opportunity to perform, while it provided parents, fellow students and outside guests an opportunity to hear the outstanding classical vocal talent of the School of Music.

Sam Wilson Becomes a Benefactor of the School of Music

On October 19, 1992 University President William Troutt came to the School of Music faculty meeting to deliver the news that Sam A. Wilson was giving his entire estate (over $2,000,000) to the School of Music for the purpose of providing new music instructional space. The news was delivered in small Stride-Rite shoe boxes because Mr. Wilson had operated a shoe store in downtown Nashville and fitted shoes for young Nashvillians for decades. Sam A. Wilson, age 91, was a firm believer in higher education and wanted his gift to help young people. Speaking about the gift he said "It is ironic that someone who can't carry a tune in a bucket has decided to support music as a way to contribute to the development of young people. I'm very impressed that Belmont's School of Music ranks in the top 20 of all private schools in the country." In receiving the gift Dr. Troutt responded "Belmont University is grateful to Sam Wilson for making a dynamic difference on our campus. It will be an honor to pay tribute to his family by making our new music building a standing reminder of his impact on the education of our students."

Acting Dean Cynthia Curtis assured Mr. Wilson that with 275 music majors and over 60 faculty members the gift would touch many lives. "This gift will make possible what has only been a dream for us for many years – a new music building."

In making this gift, the devoted family man wanted to pay tribute to his deceased father, mother, wife, and sister. Historically, Mr. Wilson had a connection to the Belmont campus because before the turn of the 20th century his grandmother taught at Ward Seminary, and for many years he came to the Ward-Belmont campus to fit shoes for the young women.[4]

The New Wilson Music Building

The gift of Sam Wilson was to be used to totally renovate the Williams Library building to make it suitable for music instruction. The library soon was to move to its new Lila Bunch Library, leaving the Williams Library free for renovation. The old library building included much open space and the potential was there to provide a good number of rooms for music instruction. Dr. Curtis appointed a Building Study Group comprised of School of Music administration, faculty and staff to look at the needs of the school and to determine how the Wilson Music Building could best be configured to meet those needs. When the architect firm of Hickerson-Fowlkes was chosen for the project, their representative, Jim Thompson, worked closely with the faculty to gather maximum input for the architectural design.

The Wilson Music Building was designed for optimum use of space. The architect's plan provided for 15 practice rooms, 22 teaching studios, 4 offices, 6 classrooms (including one for class piano), 2 music technology labs, 2 conference rooms and a large area for the music office. The teaching and practice spaces were designed by an acoustical consultant to be as soundproof as possible. Double walls and floors with sound insulation and an electronic sound-masking system were included in the design. Faculty input was valuable in making many of the decisions for the building. One request from faculty was to provide plenty of window space for the outside walls, which provided lots of natural light. The faculty also wanted to provide a space with vibrant and interesting colors to mark the space of a creative discipline. This input resulted in a color palette with yellow and gold walls, bright red accent walls, green carpets and muted purple trim. Bold contemporary artwork, coordinated with those colors, was placed throughout the building. Construction began on the Wilson Building in the summer of 1993 with occupancy occurring in June of 1994.

Mr. Wilson's relationship with the School of Music was a special one. He lived alone in his condominium at Arden Place not far from the campus. When it was discovered that one of his greatest needs was for someone to provide him a meal each evening, the School of Music decided to begin a daily ritual of taking dinner to him each evening. A schedule was worked out in which faculty members or students volunteered to go by the University dining hall, pick up his dinner, and take it to his home. Often his new Belmont friends would stay for a visit, providing Mr. Wilson with some much appreciated social contact. On his 93rd birthday the School of Music held a birthday party for Mr. Wilson at the Arden Place clubhouse, which originally had been his home. On March 13, 1993 Mr. Wilson was honored at the President's Concert with the Applause Award. A visual presentation about the life and gift of Sam Wilson was shown, and afterward he was given a long and enthusiastic standing ovation by students, faculty and friends attending the concert. On June 9, 1993 the groundbreaking for the construction was held, a time when Mr. Wilson dedicated the building to the memory of his family members. Mr. Wilson did not live to see the official opening of the building he provided for the

School of Music. His health began to fail and he passed away on June 6, 1994, a few days before faculty members began to move into the new building. Ultimately the estate of Sam Wilson brought $3,500,000 to the School of Music.

The faculty moved into the Wilson Building in June, 1994, but the official open house and dedication for the building was held on Tuesday, September 13. The University community was invited to tour the building from 3:30-5:30 while the outside community visited between 5:30 and 7:30. Karla Graul, the Music School Public Relations Director, planned an interesting way for guests to tour the building. Each office and studio was graced with an item which had belonged to Mr. Wilson. Each faculty and staff member had the opportunity to choose one of his belongings to display in his office. Visitors to the building went on a scavenger hunt to see "The Sights of Sam." It was in every way a celebrative event. At the ribbon cutting Dr. Cynthia Curtis paid tribute to Sam Wilson and his cousin Professor James Cotham, who helped secure the gift, for their contributions to Belmont and the School of Music.[5]

As the 1994-95 school year began, the School of Music was excited about the new space. Private teachers had spacious studios and the classrooms were bright and well-equipped with everything needed for classroom music instruction. The office staff benefitted from a spacious office with a pleasant reception area. Dedicated spaces for piano lab and music technology existed on the lower level. New office furniture was placed in all offices and studios. Compared to the old Music Annex, the Wilson Music Building was truly a dream come true.

New Music Library in the Lila Bunch Library

As the School of Music was planning for the new Wilson Music Building the new Lila Bunch Library included wonderful new facilities for the study of music. With the move of the library to its new building across the street from the Wilson Music Building, extensive space was provided for the Music Library under the leadership of Music Librarian, Tim Gmeiner. Most of the third floor of the library was given to music and media materials. The music library space included a large Music Reference area with reference materials and collected editions of composers, a spacious stacks area with music scores and books on music. Plenty of space was reserved for student study and reading, including study carrels. An area was provided for browsing current periodicals. A Media Listening/Viewing Center provided space for viewing and listening, drawing from Belmont's extensive collection of recordings and videos. Other amenities included group listening/viewing rooms, a Music Special Collections room and facilities for accessing journals on microfiche and on-line. The statistics for Music Library use went up substantially with the new facility because of a growing graduate program and increased emphasis on research in music courses. The growth of the Music Library and its new space was noted as a very strong asset of the School of Music by NASM visiting evaluations committees.

Cynthia Curtis Is Named Dean of the School of Music

On June 1, 1992, Dr. Jerry Warren, formerly Dean of the School of Music and for one year Vice-President for Academic Affairs, was appointed to be the first Provost of the University. Soon thereafter, he appointed a search committee to recommend a permanent Dean for the School of Music. A national search brought over 70 applicants and several excellent candidates were interviewed. In the spring of 1993 the search committee recommended to the Provost and President that Dr. Cynthia Curtis be appointed the Dean of the School of Music. The appointment was announced in a special called Music Faculty meeting on April 30, 1993. During Curtis' almost two years as Acting Dean she had begun a number of important initiatives which had strengthened the School of Music. She possessed an ambitious vision for the School and had already made changes which were positive steps for that vision. She was viewed as an enthusiastic and energetic leader for the future. In addition, she had successfully led the music faculty through the planning process for the new Wilson Music Building.[6]

Dean Curtis Sets Goals for the School of Music

Upon her appointment as Dean, Cynthia Curtis soon developed a list of priorities of areas for growth and improvement for the School. She wanted to strengthen the administration by developing a strong Administrative Group made up of the primary administrators of the School, including the Associate Deans for Performance and Academic Studies and the Director of Graduate Studies. While the persons in these roles changed from time to time, the School of Music Administrative Group became the support group for the Dean's work, meeting weekly to envision, plan, or to solve problems.

The Administrative Group began to lead in developing documents that gave guidance to the overall workings of the School of Music. Over time the School developed an Administrative Handbook, A Committee Handbook, A Decision-making Process, a Staff Job Description Document and an Adjunct Faculty Handbook. The documents were reviewed periodically and updated as changes took place in the School. This process developed formalized means through which the work of the School could advance with organized, collaborative decision making.

In one important way Dr. Curtis came to the deanship at a fortuitous time. Belmont had recently begun to award much larger capital budgets to the academic units because of a new source of revenues called Academic Enrichment Fees. The funds, to be used for budget items which enhanced instructional programs, were allocated to Schools of the University based on enrollment and credit hours produced. Compared to the miniscule budgets of the 1980s, this was a leap forward for funding School of Music needs. The new capital funds provided for classroom equipment, sound equipment, instruments, music stands, lighting equipment and pianos. In addition, it enabled the School of Music to develop an orderly plan of replacement of equipment and instruments. This budgetary supplement helped to meet many of the goals in the years ahead, particularly providing adequate instruments and equipment. Under Dean Curtis' leadership an organized process for budget planning emerged which carefully considered the equipment, instruments, and program needs of the School of Music.

Dean Curtis viewed long range planning as an essential part of moving the School of Music forward. She appointed a Long Range Planning Committee to develop a five-year plan of goals. The committee sought faculty input through extended meetings and retreats. The committee took faculty ideas, and built a prioritized plan through consensus of the faculty. The Five-Year Long Range Plan then became a guiding document for administrative priorities. The goals were categorized in several sections (curriculum, facilities, faculty, enrollment and equipment, etc). Each year the plan was examined to note progress on the goals and the progress was shared with the music faculty. At the end of the five years a report on the results led to the development of a plan for the next five years. Each Five-Year Long Range Plan was flexible in order to encompass unexpected challenges or new possibilities which emerged. Almost every successful major initiative in the school was a result of the Long Range Plan. Goals could be small and simple, or large and complex. The long range planning process became a regular and accepted way for the faculty to be involved in decision making and for all to be held accountable for making progress toward the goals.

All these organized processes ultimately were necessary to build a collaborative and supportive faculty. As the School of Music grew it was easy for faculty to become so involved in their own discipline of the School that it was possible to lose a collegial attitude toward faculty teaching in other areas. Dr. Curtis wanted to build a faculty where there was a sense of mutual respect for all. This was not a goal which could be achieved quickly, but through involving all music faculty members and listening to everyone, healthy collegial attitudes were improved and over a number of years a supportive, cohesive faculty emerged, working together with purpose and cooperation.

Dean Curtis saw the need for greater community support for the School of Music. The School had made great strides in recent years, but the Nashville community did not seem to recognize that fact. An article in *The Nashvillian*, (December 5, 1991) by Belmont Alumnus Wheat Williams was entitled "Belmont: A best-kept secret." The article extolled the School of Music for its many concerts, its highly-regarded Camerata chamber music series, its recent Camerata broadcasts on WDCN's *Recital Hall*, its unique jazz and pop music offerings and its recently released *Kaleidoscope* recording featuring a wide array of Belmont's ensembles. Williams went on to say that he was not writing about Vanderbilt's Blair School of Music, rather the Belmont University School of Music, the largest Music School in a private institution in the South.[7] The article raised the question for Dr. Curtis – why was Belmont considered a best-kept secret? A look at the early 1990s reveals how the School of Music responded to this lack of a public image. The School had a creative Public Relations Director in Karla Graul and her work was vital in this effort. Consistent press releases were sent to the media about music events and contacts were made with the local media. An Events Phone Line was established and publicized for concert information. The Applause Award was established to honor major supporters of the arts in Nashville. Donna Hilley, CEO of BMI, was the first recipient of the award. She sponsored the production of the *Kaleidoscope* recording which had great public relations value. The donation by Sam Wilson of over $2,000,000 for the Wilson Music Building was publicized widely in the Nashville media. The President's Concert became a favorite community event, bringing supporters of the School of Music to campus. Curtis presented the idea of formalizing a support group for the School of Music to raise money for scholarships. This explosion of PR activity began to pay off as the community was faced with adequate information and news about music at Belmont.

A significant need for the School of Music was space for teaching and rehearsal. With tremendous growth, there was a constant need for space and equipment. Dean Curtis was Acting Dean when Sam Wilson provided money for a new music facility and she immediately set out to make the space the best it could be. The planning by faculty committees and consultation with the architects, all under the leadership of Dr. Curtis, made the Wilson building an attractive and highly useable space. Not long after the Wilson Building was completed, however, she set her sights on the renovation of Massey Auditorium, a space which had seen much use since 1968 and badly needed a major update. This project became a part of the long range plan as a goal for the near future.[8]

Accomplishment Highlights of 1992-93

While the School of Music was occupied with the logistical planning and construction for the new Wilson Music Building, important achievements were being made by Belmont students and faculty. Significant events in the School of Music for the 1992-93 year are represented in the following list:

- Six concerts of the Belmont Camerata Musicale were broadcast over WPLN radio 90.3 on Friday evenings, beginning March 13, 1992.
- The Nissan Motor Corporation continued a second year of sponsorship for the Belmont Camerata 1992-93 series.
- With the fall semester, 1992, the School of Music began to offer instruction in playing the carillon by Beverly Buchanan, one of only a few schools in the country to do so. This instruction was made possible by the addition of a practice carillon keyboard, provided through gifts from Ward-Belmont alumnae.
- Beginning in April, 1992 Belmont ensembles were invited to perform in the lobby of the Tennessee Performing Arts Center prior to the concerts by the Nashville Symphony Orchestra. Two of the first groups

to do this were Jazzmin, directed by Jeannine Walker and the Belmont Bluegrass Ensemble directed by Dr. Daniel Landes.

- On April 20, 1992 the Nashville Children's Choir under the direction of Marilyn Shadinger and Madeline Bridges performed a concert at Carnegie Hall in New York City.
- On October 31, 1992 Belmont cello major Bo Peng, a student of Julia Tanner, won first place in the Tennessee Music teachers Association String Auditions.
- Kraft General Foods sponsored the Faculty Concert Series again for the 1992-93 concert year.
- On February 24-26, 1993 WDCN, Nashville Public Television taped a series of concerts in the Belmont Mansion for broadcast over Channel 8 for the spring of that year.
- On March 25, 1993 the Belmont Chorale performed a concert for the Tennessee Music Educators Association convention in Nashville.
- In June of 1993, Gordon Mote, recent commercial piano graduate of Belmont, was chosen to tour as pianist with Lee Greenwood. Gordon's guide dog Atlas accompanied him on tours.[9]

Study Abroad Opportunities Expand

Belmont's opportunities for study abroad were meager in the early decades of the school, mostly connected to mission trips or concert tours by music ensembles. This situation began to change in 1993 when Wallace Rasmussen, a philanthropist with interest in international connections, offered to fund the beginning of a strong study abroad program. With the recent opening up of Eastern European countries, it was an exciting time for developing possibilities for study in new territories. The School of Music jumped quickly at the new possibilities for music students to study overseas. Dr. Jerry Warren, Provost, Dr. Robert Simmons, Dean of the School of Humanities and Dr. Steve Simpler, Chair of the Department of Religion had already made an extensive journey to Eastern Europe to make contacts for study possibilities in Germany and Russia. Their visit to Moscow paved the way for Belmont's first music connection in Russia. March 21-22, 1993 the School of Music hosted officials from the Russian Academy of Music in Moscow (The Gnessin School) who visited to discuss possible exchanges between the schools. The visitors from Moscow were Sergey Michaelovich, Rector of the Academy, Irina Michelovna, Vice-Rector and Nicholaevich

Sayamov, Vice-Rector. The discussions were fruitful, and progress was made on agreements between the schools. This first meeting of counterparts from Moscow involved opportunities for the Russian guests to see how American music schools function and to experience, for a short time, American culture. They sampled classes in the School of Music and heard performances which ranged from the Belmont Chorale to the Belmont Bluegrass Ensemble. During this meeting, agreements were signed between the two schools and plans were made for Belmont representatives to visit The Russian Academy of Music in May, 1993. The Russian guests were shown some of the sights of Nashville, including the wide array of consumer products at the Mall at Green Hills. Irina Michelovna remarked that the Belmont campus "seemed more like a vacation resort than a university."[10]

From May 11 to June 1, 1993 seven faculty members representing the School of Music, along with faculty from other disciplines, and a group of Belmont students journeyed to Dresden and Moscow to finalize agreements with music schools in those cities. The timing was perfect because the recent opening of previously communist countries made it possible to make these connections. The faculty members representing the School of Music were Jerry Warren, Provost, Cynthia Curtis, Dean, Richard Shadinger, Performance Studies Chairman, Paul Godwin, Academic Studies Chairman, Robert Gregg, Director of Graduate Studies, Ted Wylie, Vocal Department, and John Arnn, Commercial Music Coordinator. A number of music students were included in the School of Music entourage. At the Dresden Hochschule für Musik Belmont guests were invited to visit classes and private lessons. Meetings were held to forge an agreement between Belmont and the Hochschule. Time was provided for sightseeing, including a tour of historic Dresden, the Palace, the Frauenkirche and the Semper Opera House. In free time members of the group had the opportunity to visit Dresden's Baroque art gallery, Der Zwinger, and several of the music group were fortunate to acquire tickets to see Wagner's *Parsifal* at the Semper Opera. Excursions outside the city included a cruise by boat on the Elbe River to the mountain castle of Königstein and the country palace at Pillnitz. The visit to Dresden gave the music faculty a good sense of the possibilities for overseas study for Belmont students. (Jerry Warren relates the following account from the visit to the Hochschule für Music in Dresden: There was some concern about how the administrators of the Dresden Hochschule, a long-established European conservatory, would

143

view the possibilities of forming connections with a music school from a small university in Tennessee. The Belmont delegation was invited to sit in on a rehearsal of the school's jazz ensemble. By happenstance, the jazz ensemble was being led by a guest clinician, well-known American jazz trombonist, Jiggs Whigham. Jerry Warren and John Arnn were well acquainted with Whigham through his visits to Belmont for the International Trombone Workshop. He immediately interrupted the rehearsal to introduce Warren and Arnn to the group. John Arnn was invited to sit in at the keyboard with the ensemble. This connection with Whigham instantly gave the Belmont music program credibility with the administrators of the Hochschule).[11]

The next leg of the journey involved train travel from Berlin through Poland to Moscow. The border crossing into Russia in the middle of the night was an experience the group won't soon forget. Russian soldiers with rifles entered all the train compartments, carefully checking every passport and visa. It seemed as if for a few moments that the iron curtain was closing again as the Belmont group tried to enter the country. The visit to the Russian Academy of Music in Moscow gave the faculty a chance to see classes in action as well as an impressive presentation of students performing Russian folk music and dance. The leaders of the Academy provided an elaborate banquet for the Belmont guests during which agreements were signed for exchanging students. There was time to see important sights in Moscow including the Kremlin and the Pushkin Museum. Concerts attended included the Moscow Chamber Orchestra at Tchaikovsky Concert Hall, with famous Russian pianist Evgeny Kissin, performing a concerto by Mozart. On the second night the Belmont contingent were given choice seats for Tchaikovsky's opera *Iolanthe* at the Bolshoi Opera. After the Moscow visit another train excursion took the group to St. Petersburg, which was the historic and artistic highlight of the trip. Beautiful churches, the tombs of major Russian composers, The Tsar's palace at Pushkin and the Hermitage Museum were on the agenda. A cruise up the Neva River to Lake Ladoga took the Belmont group to recently reopened monasteries and ancient, enchanting Kizhi Island. When the Belmont contingent returned to Nashville, preparations were made for the first exchange students to come to Belmont in the fall of 1993.[12]

Dr. Ted Wylie was appointed Coordinator of Study Abroad in Music, overseeing students in exchange programs and directing an annual music study trip to Eastern Europe. Eventually, music study opportunities for music students expanded to Angers in France and Florence, Italy. The interest in language study increased because of students' plans to study abroad. The experiences of Belmont students who studied in Dresden or Moscow were life changing, adding to the cultural awareness of those students.

The first Belmont music students to make the exchange to study in Moscow, including Meredith Maddox, violin and Maria Keinanen, mezzo-soprano, were outstanding performers who benefitted greatly from the rigorous conservatory experience. They were the first of many Belmont music students to experience the broadening experience provided by overseas study. From Russia the first students to come to Belmont were Misha Stefanuk, jazz piano and Polina Efimenko, piano. Misha, a gifted jazz pianist and composer, wrote about his experience of arriving in the U.S. and knowing very little English. He was confused about how to answer the constant question "What's up?" When he was invited by Professor Jeff Kirk to come and play with the Jazz Ensemble, he was frightened by his lack of communication skills, but when he heard Kirk use the words "key" and "blues," he knew what those meant and immediately joined in the music making at a high level. As his language skills increased, he was appreciative of the caring attitude of faculty and fellow students.[13]

Over the years there was an active exchange of faculty members between Belmont and the Dresden Hochschule. Belmont faculty members who participated in the exchange for either short visits or an entire semester included Paul Godwin, Jerry Warren, Keith Moore, Shirley Zielinski, Cynthia Curtis, Madeline Bridges, Elisabeth Small, Kris Elsberry, Chris Norton, Jeff Kirk, and Robert Gregg. These exchange visits usually included guest performances, guest conducting, lectures on American music, class observations, and informal exchange of ideas and teaching approaches.

The Richard Miller Vocal Institute

In May, 1993 the School of Music began the annual Richard Miller Vocal Pedagogy and Performance Institute, under the guidance of Belmont voice professor, Dr. Shirley Zielinksi. Dr. Miller, one of the country's most respected vocal pedagogues, was in great demand for workshops and master classes. Because of Dr. Zielinski's close association with Miller, the Richard Miller institute continued for eight years, attracting singers and voice teachers from all over the country. The workshops were held in May after most colleges had completed their school year, and were designed to be a perfect mixture of pedagogical lectures, question and answer sessions, demonstration lessons, and master classes. After Richard Miller was unable to continue the workshop for health reasons, the Institute continued with the use of other important vocal pedagogues from across the country.[14]

The Vocal Arts Laboratory

Under the guidance of Dr. Shirley Zielinski in the early 1990s, Belmont began to establish a Vocal Arts Lab based on a similar facility at Oberlin College. Richard Miller, Oberlin voice professor and internationally known vocal pedagogue, had taught vocal master classes for Belmont vocal students in October of 1990. When Belmont began to present The Richard Miller Vocal Institute in 1993, the availability of the Vocal Arts Lab enhanced the offerings of the institute. The technology improved over the years and budget funds were made available to replace equipment as more advanced technology became available. In addition to recording equipment, video players and microphones, more specific vocal technology was available. Voice students had the ability to record and make a "voiceprint" which showed pitch, resonance, vowel quality and vibrato speed. Under the guidance of a teacher, the voiceprint could reveal to students elements of their sound which they were not able to hear. The lab also included Blue Tree Software, an interactive computer program that teaches students vocal anatomy, breathing and vocal health. For teachers of voice or vocal pedagogy there is a software program which can provide a synthesized voice with various qualities to illustrate aspects of the voice. The lab also includes models of the human torso, lungs and the larynx to be used in classes or by students to study the vocal anatomy. In addition, there is a human skeleton model which shows the ribcage for vocal anatomy. A library of books on vocal pedagogy is available for students who are researching vocal pedagogy subjects. Computer programs are available to assist vocal students with the International Phonetic Alphabet, as well as French, German, Italian and Spanish diction.

Numerous ways of using the lab developed over the years. Graduate Assistantships were awarded to Vocal Pedagogy Majors who worked regular hours to keep the lab open. It is used extensively by students in the Masters Vocal Pedagogy Major for their course work and research projects. Voice teachers may bring individual students to the lab for a voiceprint or to use other software or models. Student teachers in Vocal Pedagogy find the lab useful for their own students. Vocal Seminars or other classes may find it useful to visit the lab. Students in Aural Skills classes find the software on pitch matching to be useful. Students from neighboring universities have often visited the lab to become acquainted with its capabilities. When Dr. Shirley Zielinski retired from teaching in 2001, the lab was named "The Shirley McGaugh Zielinski Vocal Arts Lab" in her honor for the work she had done in establishing this unique center for vocal study at Belmont.[15]

Belmont Chorale 25th Anniversary Reunion

On March 24-25, 1995 the Belmont Chorale celebrated its 25th anniversary with a reunion on campus with a large number of alumni in attendance. A reception began the event with a display of pictures, programs and other memorabilia from the history of the Chorale, followed by a banquet. On Saturday Chorale members met by eras to sing selections from their years in the group. Dr. Jerry Warren, founder of Chorale and then Provost of the University, led the group from his 14-year tenure with the choir. Mrs. Sherry Kelly, director of Chorale after Dr. Warren, led the later group. A concert of the 1995 Chorale concluded the event. The Chorale, along with Chorale alumni, performed several pieces together to end the festive weekend reunion. The success of this alumni event started the practice of periodical reunions for targeted ensembles to bring more music alumni back to campus.[16]

Changes in Graduate Music Programs

In the fall of 1995 the School of Music invited Dr. John Werner from the Cincinnati College-Conservatory of Music to serve as a consultant for re-evaluation of the MME degree. The Master of Music Education had been in existence for eight years and it seemed to be an appropriate time to determine if there were ways in which the degree could be strengthened. At the time the MME had some required course work in the Department of Education. It was decided to move the responsibility of the degree totally into the School of Music and change the nomenclature of the degree to MM with a major in Music Education. This consultation paved the way for planning other majors under the MM degree. Now that the MM degree

147

was the offering of the School of Music other majors were possible and the faculty began planning degrees to be offered in Church Music, Music Performance and Pedagogy.[17]

Media Attention for the School of Music

For several years in the 1990s the Belmont Camerata Concerts had been well publicized in the local media and *The Tennessean* regularly printed reviews of the Camerata concerts. The reviews written by Alan Bostic, Arts Editor, and later by Jerome Reed, were almost always positive with only occasional minor negative comments. The reviewers praised the inventive programming, the musicianship of the performers, and the lovely setting of the Belmont Mansion. This attention helped to build audiences for the concerts, often leading to standing room only audiences.

For the November 19, 1995 issue of *The Tennessean* Alan Bostic wrote a lengthy article with pictures about the growth and importance of the Belmont School of Music. The article titled "Belmont Sharpens Up as Music City's Music School" went into extensive detail describing the excellent facilities of the new Wilson Music Building, its expansive classrooms, and modern technology labs. The article also gave information about the School of Music's wide curricular offerings, its extensive concert schedule, and its important place in Nashville's music world. The article also promoted upcoming Belmont concerts including, Elisabeth Small, violin, The Rock Ensemble, Oratorio Chorus and the Belmont Camerata.[18]

Beginning with 1996 the School of Music began using an annual theme with a consistent artistic look as a way of marketing concerts. Karen Litterer, Public Relations Director, helped to establish the theme and look of the artwork for each year. The theme for 1996-97 was "We Bring Music to Life." The artwork for this theme was a painting by Belmont Alumnus Ron York featuring several musicians performing in a colorful, stylized setting.[19] The theme for 1997-98 was "Enchanted Evenings" with graphic artwork picturing a cello. The theme for 1998-99 was "Sound Adventures" with a modern representation in cubist style of a violinist. The artwork, created by Belmont Art Instructor, Lanie Gannon was titled "Itzhak." The use of the themes and artwork on brochures, posters, news releases and program covers helped to bring a consistent and sophisticated image to the concert offerings of the School of Music. The concert theme for 1999-2000 was "Music of the City" and the theme for 2000-2001 was "Flights of Fancy."[20]

Founding of the Friends of the School of Music

Dr. Curtis knew that in order to meet goals she had for the School of Music, a strong support group would be necessary. She imagined a board of supportive individuals who knew and cared for Belmont, who also had connections to numerous facets of the musical and business community. On October 19, 1995 she called together a group of supporters from among alumni, faculty and community to form the first Friends of the School of Music Board. Committees were appointed to work on by-laws and to nominate officers. The officers chosen for the first year were Ronn Huff, President; Michael Omartian, Vice-President; and Steve Smith (BA '70), Secretary-Treasurer. One of the Board's first projects was to plan a celebrity concert for the following fall. Stormie and Michael Omartian served as the Co-chairs for the celebrity concert.[21] In the second year Michael Omartian was elected President. Ronn Huff served a second term as President in 1997-98. Jamie Dunham was President in 1998-99. Patricia Bullard, who served two terms as President 1999-2001, was responsible for a major gift to provide lighting equipment for Massey Concert Hall, as well as an endowed scholarship for a Commercial Music Major. In 2001-02 Sigourney Cheek provided able leadership as President and in 2002-04, Ann Lauterbach, whose support for FOSOM was long-lasting, served two terms as President.[22]

In its first year FOSOM developed an annual fund raising drive with appeals sent to alumni, parents of students, arts supporters in the community and past donors. The goal for the first year was $30,000 with an expanded goal of $50,000 in the second year. Soon the Friends organization took on the President's Concert and Dinner as a major fund-raising project. It was realized that the attraction of a wonderful concert performed by students preceded by a dinner on the campus was a winning combination for gaining support for the School of Music. The Board actively invited friends of the School of Music to "buy" a table at the dinner as a way of adding to the endowment for scholarships. The Board also saw one of their major roles as supporting major concerts on campus. Certain concerts such as the Commercial Music Showcase, the Classical Performer's Concert and the Fall Choral Festival were chosen for support through attendance or involvement in the planning of the event. The board also developed the idea of hosting luncheons prior to Sunday matinee performances of opera and musical theater productions as a way of building support for these programs.

From the FOSOM group also emerged specific scholarships. Board member Randy Smith donated $25,000 for a scholarship for a talented performer. Ronn Huff, the first president of FOSOM, was honored by his friends who presented an endowment for a scholarship to be awarded to a composition major to celebrate Huff's service to the Nashville musical community. In 2000 the Board set a goal to endow a substantial scholarship in honor of Cynthia Curtis, Dean of the School of Music. Over the years, the FOSOM Board was responsible for the raising of well over $1,000,000 for scholarship endowment.[23]

The Immanuel Baptist Church established the Richard C. Shadinger Scholarship in September, 1996 to honor their organist, Richard Shadinger on his 15th anniversary as organist. Shadinger had been on the music faculty of Belmont University since 1974. The church set up the endowment fund with funds donated for that purpose. Members of the congregation continued to add to the scholarship over the years until a substantial endowment was reached. The scholarship fund was specified to be awarded to a talented organist or pianist.[24]

With the reorganization of the University into Colleges in 2003, the School of Music became a part of the College of Visual and Performing Arts. With that change, The Friends of the School of Music enlarged and transformed into the Friends of the Arts at Belmont with an expanded board representing Music, Art and Theater and Dance.[25]

Curtain Call Award Is Established

In 1995 the Curtain Call Award, recognizing accomplishments of graduates in the field of popular music, was established as the first award to honor alumni for their achievements. By the mid-90s there were many Belmont Commercial Music graduates who were active in live performance, recording, and songwriting, and the award sought to recognize these alumni. The first recipient of the award was Chris Rodriguez (class of '83), an outstanding guitarist who had built an active career as a recording artist and guitarist for a number of important country artists. Guitar Instructor John Pell, Chris' teacher at Belmont, presented the award to Rodriguez.[26]

The second recipient in 1996, Tammy Rogers, was not actually a Commercial Music graduate of the School of Music, though she had become a world-class performer in bluegrass music. Tammy Rogers was a

Violin Performance major at Belmont who had served as concertmaster for the Belmont Symphony Orchestra. From East Tennessee, Rogers had strong experience as a bluegrass fiddler and after graduation from Belmont had formed a bluegrass group called "Dead Reckoning" which had become commercially successful. She and the group were featured in a full-page article in the *Nashville Banner* on May 30, 1996 as they were preparing to be headline performers for Nashville's "Summer Lights" Festival.[27]

Louis Nicholas Honored by the Belmont Voice Faculty

Louis Nicholas (1910-2006) was one of Nashville's most important and beloved music teachers and performers. He served on the voice faculty of George Peabody School of Music from 1944 to 1979, teaching hundreds of singers at Peabody during his tenure. His knowledge of vocal literature was impressive, and almost every year he performed a vocal recital of totally new repertoire. He served as the president of the National Association of teachers of Singing and was respected in vocal circles throughout the country. In addition to his teaching at Peabody, he directed church choirs at West End United Methodist Church and Vine Street Christian Church. In 1982 he wrote a biography of Thor Johnson, Conductor of the Nashville Symphony Orchestra from 1967-1975. For many years he was the Music Editor and Critic for *The Nashville Tennessean*. His knowledge of musical events in Nashville was all-encompassing. When the Peabody College closed its School of Music in 1979, Nicholas taught vocal diction at Belmont for several years and continued to be a regular attender of Belmont concerts.

On February 13, 1996, the Belmont vocal faculty honored Louis Nicholas with a concert of vocal music. Seven teachers from the voice faculty, including Ted Wylie, Shirley Zielinski, Sherry Kelly, Marjorie Halbert, Lawrence Bond, Keith Moore and Carolyn Binkley, performed a wide range of vocal literature including three works commissioned by Nicholas for his own performance. The final selection on the recital was an arrangement of "How Can I Keep from Singing" by John Carter, performed by all the singers together.

Mr. Nicholas left an important part of his music library to Belmont to be housed in the Belmont Music Special Collections. Called the Louis Nicholas Song Collection, it contains over 2500 songs collected by Nicholas throughout his career. In addition, the collection includes opera scores and

151

historical materials related to music at Ward-Belmont College. The contributions of Louis Nicholas to music in Nashville and Belmont were extremely important and the Belmont Voice faculty's tribute through song was a most appropriate way to recognize a man whose life was dedicated to the art of singing.[28]

National Association of Schools of Music Re-accreditation

The 1996 NASM accreditation visit on October 29-31, 1996 found the School of Music in the midst of growth and between the completion of the Wilson Music Building and the renovation of the Massey complex. The document enumerates many achievements of the previous ten years as well as plans to meet current needs. It was really a document which described the School of Music as a School in transition from a medium size unit to something much more significant. At the writing of the NASM Self-Study Document in 1996 the undergraduate music enrollment was 331 students with an additional 34 graduate students, compared to 213 students 10 years earlier in the NASM document (1986). The report enumerated goals, which also reflect the enrollment growth:

- To balance vocal and instrumental music and commercial and classical majors
- To consider capping growth in order to meet the needs of students
- To grow majors with smaller enrollments (Church Music, Piano Pedagogy and Instrumental Performance)
- To grow the instrumental area
- To develop a plan to meet equipment needs (through use of Academic Enrichment funds)
- To grow scholarship funds
- To develop dedicated rehearsal space without having concert halls double as rehearsal spaces
- To develop a new performance space between the size of Harton Recital Hall and Massey Auditorium
- To expand the majors in the graduate program through the MM degree.

The goals were well stated along with possible ways of reaching the goals. The School of Music was shown to be a well-organized, academically strong Music School with a well-educated, caring faculty. The visiting committee recommended the renewal of Belmont NASM accreditation with only minor comments and concerns.[29]

New Majors under the Master of Music Degree

One of the aims for the music graduate program at Belmont, as stated in the 1996 NASM Self-Study document was the addition of majors to the MM degree. This idea had existed for some time. Since the MME degree was changed to the MM, the possibility of building other majors under the same degree was possible. The need for graduate music programs in the Nashville area was clear since few music graduate programs were available in the area. Belmont's faculty had grown sufficiently to manage the course load for the new majors. The new majors proposed under the Master of Music degree were Performance, Church Music and Pedagogy. The planning for these majors was completed in 1996-97 with the entry of students in the new majors beginning in the fall of 1997. Statistics show that the new majors were attractive because the enrollment of active graduate students doubled within the next two years. The addition of the three majors brought a larger cohort of graduate students without affecting the School's emphasis on undergraduate music education. The addition of students interested in performance, pedagogy and church music broadened the interests of and enriched the overall experiences of graduate students in the School of Music.[30]

Church Music Activities

With the retirement of long-time faculty member Sherry Kelly in 1996, the School of Music conducted a search for a choral director for the Belmont Chorale who would also lead the Church Music program. The person chosen for the position was Belmont alumnus Dr. Timothy Sharp (BM '76). Dr. Sharp completed graduate work at The Southern Baptist Theological Seminary School of Church Music, and was an experienced choral conductor, college professor, and church music scholar. When he arrived in the fall of 1997, he instituted the Center for Church Music which was designed to be an umbrella for church music activities at Belmont. He edited a monthly journal called *Church Music News and Review,* which informed church musicians about major happenings in the world of church music, in addition to reviewing new music and materials available for use in churches.

In February of 1998 Dr. Sharp conducted a conference in England called "World Church Music Symposium," sponsored jointly by the School of Music of Belmont University and The Royal School of Church Music, meeting in Coventry, Cambridge and London to "address the challenges of Church Music Leadership in the 21st Century." The Coventry portion of the symposium included worship services, lectures, and an evening concert by the Coventry Cathedral Chapter House Choir conducted by Paul Leddington Wright. In Cambridge, the group experienced a Eucharist Service at King's College Chapel, followed by Evensong services at the various college chapels. Following this musical feast, the group gathered for dinner at St. John's College where they were joined by Sir David Willcocks, Stephen Cleobury, John Rutter, and other Cambridge church musicians. The following day Sir David Willcocks presented a session on "Cambridge Composers of Church Music" and John Rutter led a choral music reading session. The Symposium's London segment began at the Royal Festival Hall with a forum featuring Christopher Finzi (The son of Gerald Finzi) and Jonathan Willcocks, whose "Great is the Glory" was to be premiered that evening by the Bach Choir and the London Sinfonia. Between forum sessions the group was allowed to sit in on rehearsals with Sir David Willcocks and the Bach Choir. The significance of the evening was heightened by having David and Jonathan Willcocks collaborating in the concert. This was Sir David's last regular concert with the Bach Choir, as he retired in the spring after his long tenure with the choir. The final day of the symposium began at St. Margaret's Church with Martin Neary, Master of the Choristers at Westminster Abbey, speaking on the music of John Tavener which figured prominently in the funeral of Princess Diana. Following the lecture, the group worshiped at Evensong at Westminster Abbey.[31]

Belmont Academy Established

Belmont started a small Piano Preparatory Department in 1977 for the purpose of teaching pre-college piano students. This program provided a place for Piano Pedagogy majors to receive experience in teaching under the supervision of piano faculty members. In 1996 the concept was greatly enlarged and re-named the Belmont Academy, a pre-college division of the

School of Music providing instruction in a wide range of instruments and voice under the guidance of experienced teachers. It also became the umbrella under which the Nashville Children's Choir and Nashville Youth Choir operated. It provided a platform in which faculty members of the School of Music could teach pre-college students through the University. The Belmont Academy also provided teaching opportunities for graduate students in the MM degree in Pedagogy. The Academy had its own director, the first being Donna Stokes-Rogers, a recent graduate of the Belmont's graduate music program. In 2006 Amy Hodge, another graduate of the MM program, became Director of the Academy. The Belmont Academy had an oversight committee made up of representatives from the School of Music and Academy faculties to which the Director reported. The Academy developed a thorough handbook including goals, policies and procedures. The Belmont Academy taught most lessons in the late afternoon and early evening, conveniently teaching in the Massey Building after most adjunct teachers in the School of Music vacated studios. The Belmont Academy represented an important goal of the School of Music – to reach out to the community, providing instruction for young musicians.[32]

Cooperative Ventures with the Music Business Program

The Belmont School of Music and the Belmont Music Business Program jointly sponsored a Celebrity Benefit Concert at the Grand Ole Opry House on September 9, 1996. The event called "Driven by the Music" was chaired by Michael and Stormie Omartian, members of the board of the Friends of the School of Music. The all-star list of performers included Lisa Bevill, Steven Curtis Chapman, Christopher Cross, Amy Grant, Little Texas, Michael McDonald, Larry Stewart, Donna Summer, and Trisha Yearwood. Bevill, Chapman, Stewart and Yearwood were all graduates of Belmont. One guest appeared who had not been previously announced; Garth Brooks performed near the end of the concert as a guest of Trisha Yearwood. At the time he was the best-selling artist in country music. Especially exciting to the audience was the hard-driving performance of Donna Summer. The event raised $75,000 for the two sponsoring programs.[33]

In 1996 the Mike Curb Music Business Program established Acklen Records as the recording arm of the Music Business program. The purpose of this venture was to give students in the Music Business Program opportunities to see the production of a compact disc from its inception, through the recording process and ending in the release of the final product. Acklen Records was headed by Robert Mulloy, music graduate of Belmont (BM '57), and now the head of the Mike Curb Music Business Program. The first CD produced by Acklen Records was "Christmas at Belmont," featuring a wide range of School of Music ensembles including the Belmont Chorale, the Belmont Chamber Singers, the Nashville Children's Choir, the Belmont Symphony Orchestra, Collegium Musicum, Guitar Ensemble, Belmont Band, Company, Phoenix and Jazzmin. The CD was released on November 20, 1996 with a ceremony held in the Massey School of Business courtyard. The recording process was an excellent learning experience for students in both programs. Students from the Mike Curb Music Business Program worked in the development, recording and production of the CD, while music majors gained the experience of working in the new recording studio in the School of Business.[34]

CHAPTER TWELVE

High Aspirations
(1997–2000)

Renovation of Massey Fine Arts Building

One of the goals of Dean Curtis was to follow up the completion of the Wilson Music Building with the renovation of the Massey Fine Arts Building originally built in 1968. The Massey building had been used heavily and needed refurbishing, but more than that, it did not totally meet the needs of a growing music program in terms of modern lighting, sound equipment and stage facilities. The renovation was made possible by a generous gift from Barbara Massey Rogers, the daughter of the original donor, Jack Massey. She wanted to honor her father by providing an updated and attractive space for the current School of Music. Her gift of $1,900,000 provided much of the money needed for the project.

The Auditorium had several serious needs: improved acoustics, new seating, larger stage, a modern lighting system, and a sound system worthy of the commercial music performed in the space. Artek Acoustics provided the acoustical design for the room. The ceiling was removed to add to the volume of the space. The proscenium above the stage was made acoustically transparent to improve flow of sound from the stage. The balcony was extended to the sides to provide a wrap-around balcony for improved acoustics. The stage was extended by 15 feet to provide more space for large ensembles with orchestra and large musical theater productions. The enlarged stage required the orchestra pit to be moved forward as well. The opening of the ceiling allowed for greater variety of lighting placement and catwalks for reaching the lighting for moving and setting fixtures. In the back center of the hall a booth for the sound board was built below and in front of the balcony. Lighting booths were provided behind the sound booth. A follow spotlight booth was provided in the ceiling area. The generosity of Patricia Bullard, President of the Friends of the School of Music Board at the time, provided funds for the improved lighting for the room. She led the fund-raising campaign for sound and lighting equipment, providing $750,000 for equipment. In 2001 Bullard was given the Applause Award for her service to the School of Music. New state-of-the art Sony sound equipment provided new speakers, adding to the clarity of sound.

Visually, Massey Concert Hall was improved through the careful choice of colors, with the gold and greens, connecting the space with the look of the Wilson Building. New seating and a new stage curtain in a deep green color added to the sophisticated look. The enlarged stage and the new sound and light space slightly decreased the seating capacity for the concert hall. The improvements in the concert hall made it much more useful to the School of Music with its needs for a greater stage space and modern sound and light technology.

The lower level of the Massey building received a major overhaul. The three classrooms on this level remained as before, but were refurbished. The remainder of the lower level was rebuilt to provide as many teaching studios and practice rooms as possible, so extensive reconfiguring of the smaller spaces took place. The most complicated change took place in Harton Concert Hall. There had been no door where a performer could enter directly to the stage. By changing the height of the stage and reversing the stairs, it was possible to make this change. A totally new stage was built in Harton and new placement of doors provided two entrances with sound and light locks to block sound from the hallways surrounding the room. Curtains around the Harton stage provided adjustable acoustics from very live to much more dry acoustics. Harton's appearance was improved with a gold color for the side walls and a deep red for the back of the stage area. Coordinated colors for seating and carpet added to the finished and sophisticated look of Harton Recital Hall.[35]

During the year while construction was taking place, the School of Music was forced to be inventive in arranging teaching, rehearsal and performance space, because almost half of the school's space was affected by the renovation. Much of the teaching, rehearsal and performance space was moved to Belmont Heights Baptist Church, but other arrangements beyond that had to be made. Some classical student recitals were performed in the Leu Art Gallery. Commercial student recitals were held in "The

Rafters" in the Barn and in what was called the "Aquatorium," a space which had been built over the old swimming pool in the student center complex. Some programs were moved to churches or schools. Company and Jazzmin performed their spring concerts at local high schools. The Commercial Showcase was performed in a tent in the middle of campus during a week of school-wide talent shows. The Spring Awards Ceremony for the School of Music was held outside in the Atrium in rather cold temperatures. The Musical Theater production for spring, 1997 was held on a stage at West End United Methodist Church. In the school year of 1996-97 the Belmont School of Music was literally "on the road." The arrangements were not always ideal, but cooperation among School of Music faculty, staff and students, along with some good humor, helped the school get through the year.

The work with the architectural and acoustical consultants and input from the faculty made the building function much better for students and faculty. As the renovation was proceeding, it was decided to change the name of the space to "Massey Performing Arts Center," with the larger performance space becoming "Massey Concert Hall" instead of "Auditorium." Harton Concert Hall was changed to "Harton Recital Hall" to fit better with the small-scale programs held there. The completion of the Massey Performing Arts Center brought an end to four years of planning, dislocation, and building with the result being two modern buildings for music instruction and performance linked together by a pleasant shady courtyard. To further utilize the atrium as the School of Music's "outdoor living room," outdoor tables and chairs were purchased to encourage its use as a gathering place.

The opening of the Massey Performing Arts Center occurred on October 6, 1997 with a worship service of dedication entitled "When In Our Music...". Anthony Lombardi from the Literature and Languages Department was commissioned to write a poem entitled "Quod amor fecit (What Love has Made)" for the event, which he read during the service.[36]

The President's Concert was performed on October 11, 1997, delayed from its usual spring date. The concert was entitled "Celebration" to note the gladness with which the School of Music inhabited its new and improved performance hall. The concert was especially festive with the new décor, lighting, and sound of the room. Barbara Massey Rogers was honored with the Applause Award for making the renovated space possible.[37]

During the renovation of Massey Concert Hall the wiring and other electrical components of the Wicks pipe organ had been damaged, delaying the return of the organ to the hall. Since the organ console, built in 1968, had antiquated technology, it was decided to rebuild the console as well. The Wicks Organ Company, the original builder of the organ, was chosen for the project, which included new wiring, new electrical contacts, new keyboards, a solid-state combination action, and a movable platform for the console. The restoration brought the organ back to like-new condition for future teaching and concerts. The inaugural concert of the newly-refurbished organ was on March 6, 2000 in a program featuring organ instructor Andrew Risinger with the Belmont Faculty Brass Ensemble.[38]

John Rutter Choral Festival

Belmont had an annual choral workshop/festival beginning in 1981 with composer and conductor, Jean Berger. A variety of well-known choral directors visited Belmont each year to work with choral groups and to conduct a concert with Belmont ensembles. Dr. Tim Sharp wished to increase the profile of this annual workshop by inviting internationally known musicians to campus, and then encourage church musicians to come and be a part of the workshop. The School of Music invited well-known composer and conductor John Rutter of Cambridge, England for the 1998 Choral Music workshop. While at Belmont, Rutter worked with the individual choirs of Belmont, conducted a choral music reading session, led in an Evensong service at the Scarritt College Chapel, and rehearsed for a public concert of Belmont choirs. Because of the popularity of John Rutter's music, the workshop attracted a large number of church musicians. The public concert on October 30, 1998 packed the newly renovated Massey Concert Hall to standing room only. The John Rutter festival brought attention to Belmont like few other events of that time.[39]

Christmas at Belmont

Belmont established a Christmas tradition in the late 1960s called "Hanging of the Green" performed in the Belmont Mansion by Belmont Choirs. In 1974 the concert was called "Christmas at Belmont and Hanging of the Green." In 1974 and 1975 this program was taped for broadcast over WSM Channel 4. In 1978 the School of Music began offering a concert called

"Christmas Festival," which continued until 1988. The Christmas concert lapsed for a time because it appears that the academic calendar ended so early that there was hardly time to perform a Christmas program in December. In addition, the Oratorio Chorus often performed a major work on a Christmas theme which some years substituted for a Christmas Concert. On December 2, 1997 the School of Music provided an elaborate Christmas Concert with six ensembles entitled "Celebrate the Blessed Season of Joy." It was a program of all sacred music with readings interspersed with the musical selections. The response to the festive concert was so positive, that it was decided to have a similar concert the following year.

The 1998 concert on December 5 was titled "Christmas at Belmont" and a tradition was born. Planned and directed by Dr. Tim Sharp, the concert again featured all sacred music. The concert was done in the form of a lessons and carols service with scripture readings by international students reading in their native languages. The 1999 "Christmas at Belmont" broadened the ensembles to eight and the concert was all sacred music interspersed with scripture readings. One commercial ensemble, Belmont Pops, was included in the concert, though they sang a sacred composition. The 2000 "Christmas at Belmont" took on the format of varied styles which would characterize the concert for future years. The 2001 Concert included a scene from O. Henry's "Gift of the Magi" presented by students of the Theater Department in addition to the musical numbers. By 2002 "Christmas at Belmont" had come of age with a wide variety of ensembles, 12 in all, and superb production values. WSMV Channel 4 taped the concert for broadcast on the evening of December 2, 2002. Some of the segments were filmed at earlier times in the Belmont Mansion and the Ocean Way Studio and then spliced into the final TV broadcast. The local Nashville response to the WSM broadcast was positive, paving the way for future broadcast possibilities.[40]

With "Christmas at Belmont" an established tradition, the School of Music began to annually market four Christmas events on the campus as "Belmont's Christmas Gift to Nashville," helping to build support for concert events at the end of the fall semester. The four concerts included in this promotion were "Christmas at Belmont," The Nashville Children's Choir Concert, "A Camerata Christmas," and the Christmas Eve Carillon Concert played by Richard Shadinger. In addition, President Fisher used a compact disc of Christmas music from Belmont each year as a Christmas greeting to alumni, donors and friends of the University, bringing further attention to Belmont's seasonal Christmas offerings.

161

New Faculty in the 1990s

With continued growth in the School of Music a number of new faculty arrived during the 1990s. These faculty members with their teaching areas and places of terminal degree were as follows: Sandra Dudley, commercial voice (MM, Eastman School of Music); James Kimmel, music education and Company (MME, Northwest Missouri State University); Dr. Timothy Sharp, church music and Chorale (DMA, The Southern Baptist Theological Seminary); Dr. Madeline Bridges, music education (Ed.D, University of Alabama); Keith Mason, music technology (MM, University of Miami); Henry Smiley, commercial voice and ensembles (MM, University of Tennessee); Dr. Emily Bullock, classical voice and opera (DMA, University of Colorado).

Dr. Madeline Bridges joined the faculty in the fall of 1998 as Director of Graduate Studies and Professor of Music Education. Having worked for the Tennessee State Department of Education, and having taught previously at Middle Tennessee State University, she brought considerable administrative and teaching experience to her position. She was already familiar with Belmont because she had been co-director of the Nashville Children's Choir since 1990. As she began her task as Director of Graduate Studies there was much to be done because the School of Music voted to add three majors to the MM degree in the previous year. Policies for all the programs needed to be developed and recruiting for the new majors was a priority. She immediately went to work on graduate program issues and soon enrollment increased. Organization of curriculum, the mentoring process, and a schedule for graduation deadlines kept the program running smoothly. Moreover, as an author and national authority in areas related to music education for children, Dr. Bridges brought significant expertise to the courses she taught in undergraduate as well as graduate Music Education.

Music Technology Advances in the School of Music

With the completion of the Wilson Music Building in 1994, there was finally a dedicated space for Music Technology studies. With the growth of the Music Technology Emphasis Area under the Commercial Music degree, the establishment of a permanent Music Technology Lab on the lower level of Wilson was an important step forward. In 1998 Music Technology came under the direction of Professor Keith Mason, who brought years of professional music tech experience in the music industry to the School of Music. Under his leadership the School of Music developed a new Music Tech Lab which was used to teach a course entitled "Introduction to Music Technology." The National Association of Schools of Music recommended that the school find a way to meet technological literacy for all music majors. This course was designed to help students in all music majors handle the basics of music technology by learning computer based music production. While meeting the needs of the average musicians, Mason also made sure that the advanced tech lab for Music Tech students was state-of-the-art. Funds were made available to keep the equipment current, so graduates learned with the prevailing technology before going into the music industry. Approximately 30 Music Tech Emphasis students keep the lab busy throughout the day with classes and projects. In addition to Commercial Music Majors, the skills of film scoring, synthesis and computer based music production are of interest to majors in Music Composition, increasing the importance of the Music Technology courses. The digital audio workstations available in the lab teach music tech students and composers how to become "digital desktop musicians." Philosophically, Keith Mason said that Belmont has the ideal set-up for music technology. Areas of Recording Technology and Sound Reinforcement are taught through the Mike Curb College of Music Business, allowing the School of Music to focus on the creation of music through technological means. Mason observed that some colleges try to cover all of the areas through their music department, thereby neglecting the music creation components of Music Technology.[41]

Partnership with the Nashville Ballet

In January, 1999 a new partnership with the Nashville Ballet was unveiled as a children's ballet was performed in Massey Concert Hall, danced to the music of a Belmont composer. There were several unique aspects of this partnership. First, it was designed to be an outreach concert for children, and as such it was supported by a grant from the Metropolitan Nashville Arts Commission and the Tennessee Arts Commission. Secondly, the concert was performed on a Sunday afternoon in January, a slow time in the community arts calendar, and therefore attracted large audiences. Thirdly, the ballet was to be short, matching the attention span of the young audience. Fourth, the ballet was to be based on a children's story or folk tale which suggested possibilities for dance. Fifth, the music was to be composed by a Belmont faculty composer, providing an outlet for Belmont's large and creative composition faculty. The first concert was based on an African folk tale "The Singing Tortoise," with music composed by percussion faculty member Todd London and played by the Belmont Percussion Ensemble. The success of the first ballet led to a second ballet on January 30, 2000. Based on a Mexican folktale, "Borreguita and the Coyote" was composed by Belmont guitar instructor, John Pell and performed by students from the Belmont Guitar Ensemble. The 2001 Ballet was "The Emperor and the Nightingale" with music composed by Todd London and performed by the Belmont Percussion Ensemble. With its excellent dancing, exciting new music and a hundreds of enthusiastic children, this partnership became an annual event reaching an important audience in Nashville.[42]

A Nashville Premiere: Performance of *Pierrot Lunaire*

Arnold Schoenberg's *Pierrot Lunaire* from 1912 Vienna is considered to be one of the most significant and revolutionary compositions of the early 20th century. This extremely challenging work had never been performed in Nashville, and a group of Belmont faculty, with assistance from community players, decided that it was time for Nashville to hear the work live. The performance of *Pierrot Lunaire*, held on May 3, 1999 in Massey Concert Hall, was the School of Music's first concert to be broadcast live by video streaming on the internet. The musicians for the event were: Shirley Zielinski, Soprano (Sprechstimme); Bruce Christensen, violin/viola; Steve Drake, cello; Ann Richards, flute/piccolo; Paul Martin Zonn, clarinet/bass clarinet; and Robert Marler, piano. Timothy Sharp was the conductor. Three short spoken essays by faculty members prefaced the performance. David Ribar, from the Belmont Art Department, spoke on "Art and Expressionism." Lynne Eastes, from the Theater Department, spoke about "Theater and Expressionism." Timothy Sharp, School of Music, spoke on the topic of "Music and Expressionism." Six Belmont students in various styles of "Pierrot" costumes performed pantomime representations of the 21 songs from the cycle. It was an innovative and creative first presentation of the work for Nashville and a triumph for the performers.[43]

Belle Voci is Established

Dr. Jerry Warren, Provost and formerly Dean of the School of Music, kept his interest in choral conducting strong after leaving the School of Music. In 1999 he was asked to begin a choral ensemble to involve alumni, graduate students and community singers. The name chosen for the group was "Belle Voci" (Beautiful Voices). The choir rehearsed one night per week and typically performed two concerts each year. For several years Belle Voci sang an Advent Lessons and Carols Service at the Wightman Chapel at Scarritt College on a Sunday afternoon in December. The repertoire for the choir was wide ranging, often featuring a major work or varied programs on a theme. Belle Voci frequently performed in venues throughout Nashville which were appropriate to the music being performed. The choir was in existence from 1999 until Dr. Warren's retirement in 2007. In that time, many alumni and community singers participated in the ensemble, fulfilling an important part of Belmont's goal to provide outlets for musicians of all ages.[44]

Representative Alumni from the 1990s

Alumni from the 1990s reflected the higher profile of the School of Music. More college and university professors are found within their ranks, in addition to numerous teachers and church musicians. Belmont's status as a leader in commercial music is also reflected in a larger number of active performers in the world of popular music. Representative music alumni from the decade are: Janet Clowes Ivy (1990), actor/author/TV personality; Tim Lauer (1990), pianist/recording artist/songwriter; Dr. Kristi Whitten (1990), Professor of Voice, Belmont University; Grover Baker (1992), Music Librarian, MTSU; Stephen Z. Cook (1992), concert organist/teacher; Travis Cottrell (1992), contemporary Christian singer/songwriter/recording artist; Will Denton (1992), drummer/recording artist; Kelly Garner (1992) jazz singer/teacher/song writer/Professor at Belmont University; Dr. Alfredo Colman (1993), Musicology Professor, Baylor University; Jeff Cox (1993), bass player/recording artist/bass teacher, Trevecca University; Dr. Craig Filar (1993), Director of International Studies, FSU; Gordon Mote (1993), pianist/ performer/recording artist; Dan Muckala (1993), song writer/performer; Lauren Wilkerson Baker (1993), elementary music educator; Dr. Jeffrey Kirk (1994), saxophonist/performer/arranger/Music Professor, Belmont University; Michael McLain (1994), blue grass artist, banjo/guitar instructor at Belmont University; J.L. Nave (1994), Manager, Ft. Wayne Symphony Orchestra; James Wigginton (1994), singer/vocal coach/voice teacher at Belmont University; Julie Partin Cox (1995), opera singer/music educator; Kathryn Wolfe Zahn (1994), opera singer/teacher; Misha Stefanuk (1995), jazz pianist/composer; Eric Jones (1996), minister of music; Dr. Tina Milhorn Stallard (1996), Professor of Voice, University of South Carolina; Dr. Timothy Powell (1996), choral conductor/Professor at Martin Methodist College; Ginny Owens, contemporary Christian singer/songwriter; Russell Terrill (1996), first call recording session singer; Margie Landgrave Yankeelov (1998), oboist/teacher at Belmont University; Reid Greven (1998), pianist/performer/recording artist; Jennifer Matheny (1998), singer/teacher; Kenneth Moore (1998) church musician/composer; Jill Phillips (1998) contemporary Christian artist; Chris West (1998), saxophonist/jazz musician; Dr. Mark Whatley (1998), Voice Professor, Belmont University; Melinda Doolittle (1999), Gospel singer/recording artist; Denver Bierman (1999), trumpet, director, Denver and the Mile High Orchestra; Sandra McCrackin (1999), singer/song writer; Rick Padgett (1999), music educator.

Progress in the 1990s

Throughout the 1990s dramatic changes took place in the School of Music. Dr. Cynthia Curtis became the new Dean with an energy and purpose which made a positive difference in almost every area of life of the School. Enrollment grew to new heights with a total of 412 Music Majors by the end of the decade. A Long Range Planning process became the driving force for positive change. The School of Music's reputation in Nashville and beyond was beginning to bring more interest from prospective students and donors. The academic and musical profile of entering students was higher than ever. An increasingly large and strong faculty was working in a collegial manner to improve all aspects of the instructional program. The most visible aspect of the changes in the School of Music during the 1990s was the facilities growth and improvement with the completion of the Wilson Music Building and the total renovation of Massey Performing Arts Center. The building blocks were in place and great things were on the horizon for the new Millennium.

PART VI
A New Millennium:
The Music School Comes of Age
(2000–2012)

Full-time School of Music Faculty before Spring Commencement, May 2015

CHAPTER THIRTEEN

The Foundation of The College of Visual and Performing Arts

School of Music Becomes a Part
of the College of Visual and Performing Arts

In 1999 Belmont reorganized into Colleges, resulting in the following divisions: College of Arts and Sciences, College of Business Administration, College of Health Sciences, University College, and the College of Visual and Performing Arts. The College of Visual and Performing Arts (CVPA) included The School of Music, The Department of Art and The Department of Theatre and Dance, with Dr. Curtis becoming the Dean of the newly-organized College.[1] A College Council, consisting of the administrators from all three areas, was formed to deal with curricular matters and other business within the College. The entire CVPA faculty began to meet three times each year for the purpose of dealing with curriculum proposals. An important outgrowth of the unification of the arts under one College was better acquaintance, cooperation, and support among faculty members in the arts with similar interests.

One goal of CVPA was to work toward better facilities for the Theatre and Dance Department. While Music and Art had recently acquired new spaces, the Theatre Department was still laboring in less than ideal space in the old and inadequate Little Theater. In time, the Theatre Department would move into the new Troutt Theater, bringing all areas of the arts into adequate teaching spaces. The new College encouraged collaborative activities in which the arts could work together. The first major collaborative event was the Kurt Weill Festival in the fall of 2000. In addition, in the spring of 2004 CVPA hosted a major exhibit of the art works of Frederick Hart with the Music and Theater areas developing performances which related to Hart's Classical approach to modern art. The entire semester was promoted under the themes "The Creative Spirit" and "Belmont Celebrates the Arts." The development of the College of Visual and Performing Arts allowed the School of Music to engage with the other arts on campus in many creative ways.

The School of Music at the Year 2000

The year 2000 was met with great fanfare the world over. In addition to gigantic celebrations, there was also fear that our computerized technology would crash when expected to move digitally to the number 2000. The various media published many retrospects about the last century and the last millennium. Major events and famous people of past eras were highlighted and celebrated. January 1, 2000 passed with few blips on computer screens, and life lurched onward into the beginning of the next millennium. In the great sweep of history, Belmont's history as an educational institution seemed small indeed.

In 2000 Belmont as a coeducational institution was nearly 50 years old. As the new Millennium began, the School of Music had come of age as a large, mature, strong and nationally-known school. Statistics for the 2000-2001 show that the School of Music had grown from 222 students in 1990 to 444 in 2000 (100% growth over the decade). Some of the growth came from increased graduate offerings, but even without the graduate program growth the undergraduate enrollment increase was an impressive 90%. While the number of faculty had grown, it had not kept pace with enrollment, leading to an increased use of adjunct teachers. While facilities had improved tremendously in the 90s with the new Wilson Music Building and the renovated Massey Performing Arts Center, the School was again "bursting at the seams" and new space was being located increasingly at Belmont Heights Baptist Church with hopes that the space could be renovated for more efficient use. Impressively, while Belmont and the School of Music grew numerically throughout the 1990s, the academic profile of its entering students grew consistently at the same time.[2] Goals

169

for the new decade were important ones: more space and more faculty to meet the ambitions of a nationally-recognized School of Music.

To celebrate the new Millennium, the School of Music presented a special concert on May 1, 2000, when the Oratorio Chorus, under the direction of Timothy Sharp, performed Beethoven's Fantasia for Piano, Soloists, Chorus and Orchestra, Op. 80 with Dr. Robert Marler as the featured pianist. To end the program the Oratorio Chorus and Orchestra performed the 4th movement of Beethoven's Symphony No. 9 in D minor, Op. 125, based on Schiller's "Ode to Joy." Soloists for this landmark work were Katie Zeager (BM '99), soprano; Dr. Emily Bullock, mezzo-soprano; Dr. Ted Wylie, tenor; and Dr. Lonnie Bond, bass.[3] The rousing Beethoven "Ode to Joy" was a festive way to celebrate the beginning of a new era in history and exciting time for the School of Music.

Dr. Robert Fisher Comes to Lead Belmont

Dr. Robert Fisher became the fourth President of Belmont University on April 1, 2000. With a new president, a new decade and a new millennium, hopes were high in the Belmont community. Fisher brought a new personality and a bold administrative style, unlike any of the past presidents. He seemed to be the right presidential leadership for a new era. Appropriately, one of his first official duties as President of Belmont was attendance at the President's Concert on April 8, 2000. While the President's Concert officially honored composer Ronn Huff for his support for music at Belmont, the event also gave the School of Music an opportunity to welcome and honor its new President. Dr. and Mrs. Fisher seemed to be genuinely overjoyed to have landed into a position surrounded by such a high level of music making. Fisher's official Inauguration took place on Friday, September 29, 2000 in the Kitty Bugg West Amphitheater. Fisher's four main goals stated at his Inauguration were: enrollment growth, increased diversity of the student body, intensified fund raising activity, and the construction of a new student center. The School of Music was involved in the music for the Inaugural events, providing a student string quartet for the Inaugural Reception at the Belle Meade Country Club and a large brass ensemble of faculty and student players for the Inauguration Ceremony.[4] The change brought by Dr. Fisher would be felt early in his tenure as enrollment began to grow at a faster pace and visible changes on campus were soon seen.

Alumni Achievements in Fall 2000

Belmont Music Alumna, Ginny Owens (BM in Music Education, '97) was named "Outstanding New Artist of the Year" by the Gospel Music Association at the 31st Annual Dove Awards in Nashville. Upon her graduation from Belmont, Owens had immediately developed an active career as a recording artist and live performer. Because of her success as a recording artist, in 2003 she was presented the Curtain Call Award by the School of Music.[5]

On October 6, 2000 Josh Turner, a Commercial Music Major, performed his junior recital on which he sang publicly for the first time a song he composed titled "Long Black Train." Within a few years Josh Turner became a top young country artist with "Long Black Train" rising to the top of the country charts. Eventually, Turner's video of "Long Black Train" was named by Country Music Television as one of the top country videos since 2000. This was not the first nor last time that student creativity within the academic program would lead to national recognition of a Belmont alumnus.[6]

Kurt Weill Festival

The School of Music began the first fall semester of the new millennium with two blockbuster musical events: A Kurt Weill Festival, celebrating the 100th anniversary of the birth of Kurt Weill, followed by a Choral Festival conducted by internationally known British conductor Sir David Willcocks.

In commemoration of the 100th anniversary of the birth of Kurt Weill, the School of Music's Kurt Weill Festival began on October 16, 2000 with a concert of performers from New York City, presenting a wide variety of songs from Weill's operas and musicals. Ruth Golden, soprano and Michael Philip Davis, tenor were the featured performers of a variety of arias and songs by Weill. Regina Resnik, internationally renowned operatic soprano who had worked with Weill and premiered many of his operas, was the narrator for the concert. The concert was supported by the Kurt Weill Foundation and the Metro Nashville Arts Commission and drew a large audience from the community. In an extensive article in *The Tennessean* (October 8, 2000), entitled "Weill, Weill, Weill," Arts Editor Alan Bostic promoted the series of events and

171

complimented Belmont for putting together this wide-ranging and cutting-edge festival.

At the same time, as part of the Kurt Weill Festival, the Art Department mounted an exhibition in the Leu Gallery of paintings by Arbit Blatas, representing scenes from Kurt Weill's stage works. Regina Resnick, widow of Blatas, introduced the exhibit in a lecture in the Leu Gallery on October 15. Film screenings related to Weill, *The Three Penny Opera* and *M*, were shown on campus during the festival. The Kurt Weill Festival concluded in November with a performance on November 10-12 by the Belmont Opera Theater of Kurt Weill's opera *Street Scene*. This opera, directed by Dr. Emily Bullock, brought a new level of production values to opera at Belmont. Musically, it was a challenging work, but the large cast and orchestra rose to the challenge. In terms of staging it was the most elaborate opera production to date.[7]

Choral Workshop with Sir David Willcocks

After the successful choral festival under the leadership of composer and conductor John Rutter in 1999, the School of Music built on the momentum in October of 2000 with the visit to Belmont of the renowned British conductor Sir David Willcocks, one of the most famous choral conductors in the world. Eighty-one years old at the time, Willcocks exuded energy and a strong musicianship that was captivating to the students. The schedule of events at Belmont was packed with rehearsals and performances, but Willcocks led the pace with enthusiasm. On Thursday, October 26, Sir David conducted Belmont's Belle Voci choir in an Evensong Service at West End United Methodist Church. The choir sang masterpieces of British choral literature accompanied by Belmont's organ instructor, Andrew Risinger. The service was followed by a dinner at the church during which Sir David gave an entertaining account of his illustrious career, illustrated with slides from places and events in his life. On Friday, October 27 rehearsals were held for an evening performance of Vaughan Williams' grand Christmas oratorio *Hodie* (This Day). The concert began with British choral selections sung by the Belmont Chamber Singers, Men's Chorus, Women's Choir, and Belmont Chorale. The Oratorio Chorus and Nashville Children's Choir with the orchestra performed *Hodie*. Because Sir David Willcocks was the organist at the first performance of *Hodie* in 1954 under the direction of the composer, the performance at Belmont had special significance and gave performers a connection to a great British composer.[8]

Beginning of the Musical Theatre Major

For decades the School of Music had presented a spring musical theater production which was an anticipated event each year. Even when there was no major in musical theater, music students enjoyed the experience and the productions were often remarkably strong, though done with rather small budgets. Planning for a new major in Musical Theatre began in 1997 with the first students entering the program in the fall of 1998. Mrs. Marjorie Halbert was designated as the coordinator of the program. The School of Music chose to make the major a strong academic program, and therefore planned the curriculum within the guidelines of the Bachelor of Music degree. The curriculum required a large area of coursework in theatre and dance. Along with the music core and the general education requirements, it was a major designed for talented and hardworking students. To assure that the program would be a strong one, the audition process was carefully planned to test all aspects of the students' talent. In addition to singing, the auditioning student was asked to perform a short dramatic monologue and a dance audition. In order to keep the number of Musical Theatre Majors manageable, a limit of ten students entering per year was set. This number allowed students to have adequate opportunities for roles in the musical productions while in the program. The limit also increased the possibility of balancing male and female singers in the program, an often difficult task.

The productions of 1998-2000 immediately showed the impact of the presence of majors in Musical Theatre. The fall production of 1998, *Sweeney Todd*, took the Musical Theatre program into new territory with its dark comedic plot. With each production (*The Wizard of Oz, Seven Brides for Seven Brothers*, and *The World Goes 'Round*) the impact of a growing body of talented singers and dancers was evident. The spring production of 2000 of *Into the Woods* showed heightened production complexity as well as excellent singing and acting.

In October, 1999, the Musical Theatre Department began an annual tradition of visiting New York in October during Fall Break to see Broadway shows and to meet Belmont alumni working in New York. The itinerary included two musicals which the entire group of faculty and

173

students would see. The students had an opportunity to see another production of their choice while in the city. An important part of the agenda was a dinner where Belmont students could meet and visit with Belmont alumni who were performing in New York, giving students an introduction to the New York musical theatre scene.

Musical Theater majors were required to perform both a Junior and Senior Recital. The Junior program was a 30-minute program with the student performing accompanied only by piano. The Senior Recital required the student to plan and execute a concert involving dance, singing and staging. The students were creative in coming up with themes, and building the programs around them. The senior program could involve costumes, as well as extra players and singers. As a total performance, it clearly showed the talent and maturity of the student.

As the Musical Theatre program developed, it was clear that freshman students would not likely be chosen for major roles in productions their first year. However, they often had chorus roles or worked technical aspects of the productions. Eventually, the idea of having a "Freshman Showcase" as a forum for showing the talent of new students developed. Held in the Black Box Theatre and other venues, it showed the potential of the freshman Musical Theatre majors and gave them a chance "to shine" apart from the upperclassmen.

In 2008 the Musical Theatre program reached a new milestone with its production of *Ragtime*, coinciding with Belmont's focus on *Debate 08*; the Presidential Debate between John McCain and Barak Obama brought the national spotlight to Belmont that fall and *Ragtime* was part of an effort by the College of Visual and Performing Arts to present a yearlong focus of concerts and productions focusing on the American experience. *Ragtime* was particularly daunting challenge with a complicated story, large cast and demanding staging. The production benefitted from having a new full-time faculty member, David Shamburger, to serve as Stage Director in partnership with Marjorie Halbert as Musical Director.

The faculty for the Musical Theatre grew as the program developed greater demands, more students and higher expectations. In 2007 Nancy Allen, an experienced musical theatre performer in the Nashville area, joined the faculty to teach voice to Musical Theatre majors. In 2010 Jo Lynn Burkes came to Belmont to teach Musical Theatre courses and to assist with the musical and orchestral directing for productions. As the Musical Theatre faculty grew, the group came to be known as "The Dream Team"

174

because of their individual talents in all the specialized areas of musical theatre production.

In spring, 2009, the Musical Theatre program began presenting a Senior Musical Theatre Students Showcase in New York City. Using the Laurie Beechman Theatre on West 42nd St., casting agents and directors in New York were invited to hear Belmont Senior Musical Theatre majors in a showcase setting. The Showcase was one of the reasons for the success of Musical Theatre graduates in finding performance opportunities. At the 2011 Showcase on April 11, Alumni staff from Belmont went with the Musical Theatre group to help establish a New York chapter of the Belmont Alumni Association because of the large number of Alumni working in various fields of music in the city. Over 40 alumni met the Belmont group with interest in establishing a Belmont link in New York City.

The success of the Musical Theatre program became evident in the number of outstanding graduates becoming active in New York theatre, touring Broadway shows, regional theatre, and television. A survey of Musical Theatre graduates after 2000 showed that almost all graduates were active in theatre in various venues across the country. Jeremy Parrish (BM '03) performed in the chorus of the Metropolitan Opera. Rebecca Covington (BM '05) performed in the Broadway hit *Motown*. Matthew deGuzman (BM '06) performed in *Follies* on Broadway with Bernadette Peters. Emily Fitzpatrick (BM '07) had success in national Broadway touring shows, commercials and film. Lauren Turner (BM '10) performed with the national touring company of *Grease*. These students were representative of the success of students from the Belmont Musical Theatre program.[9]

New General Education Program at Belmont

Belmont's approach to general education in its early decades had always been discipline oriented. Students were required to take certain courses from a set list of areas with some choice within the disciplines. Several attempts to update the general education program failed during the 90s, with only minor modifications taking place. In 2002 the new Provost, Dr. Dan McAlexander, called the faculty together once again to work on the issue. A General Education Study Committee representative of Colleges in the University was given the challenge of totally revising Belmont's approach to general education. Through many hours of hard work, tough choices and negotiation, a plan emerged which was solid, innovative, vertical and equitable. It was presented to the faculty through a number of information sessions and approved by the faculty, changing the way general education takes place at Belmont. Called the BELL Core (The Belmont Experience: Learning for Life), the program focused on a number of important academic areas and skills: writing and communication skills, arts, humanities, natural sciences, social sciences, critical thinking, and a wider view of the world.

Several important common experiences were included in the curriculum, a First Year-Seminar, a second-semester Learning Community Course, a Junior Cornerstone course involving experiential learning, and a Senior Capstone.

The College of Visual and Performing Arts was asked to develop a menu of arts "experience" courses in music, theater, art and dance to replace the traditional music, theater and art appreciation courses. The School of Music also took this opportunity to revise its Music History curriculum for Music Majors, establishing an Introduction to Music History to be taken in the freshman year. The Introduction to Music History course also joined the general education program by being part of a "Learning Community" in which freshmen would take two courses together as group to explore the interconnections between disciplines. This change was in line with the BELL Core which emphasized verticality of courses. Music faculty members became more active in teaching non-music students through the First Year Seminar and Junior Cornerstone, both of which offered courses in a wide range of disciplines. Finally, the BELL Core provided a Senior Capstone course in each major, giving the School of Music a course which could help music students reflect over their college experience and plan for the future after graduation. When *U.S. News and World Report* ranked Belmont in the Top Five among institutions in the Southeast, one of the reasons given was Belmont's innovative general education program which fostered critical thinking in a creative approach to the curriculum.[10]

New Merit Pay System Impacts Faculty

One of President Fisher's early initiatives in 2001 was to establish a merit pay system for faculty with a goal of improving faculty salaries. Dr. Fisher was aware that salary improvement was a major factor in attracting top-notch faculty members in the future. Each College was expected to develop its own process for determining merit pay. Dean Curtis set up a

Compensation Committee made up of representative administrators and faculty from Art, Theater and Music. The committee developed a handbook with criteria and a calendar for merit pay decisions. While the committee did not make decisions about who received various levels of merit pay, it was instrumental in developing the processes and the manner of allocating categories of merit pay. The process required each faculty member to annually present individual goals for the following year, followed by a portfolio showing how goals were attained. Another component of the pay system was the development of equity pay increases for faculty members whose salary lagged behind national averages for their rank and discipline. While the new merit pay process met with some concerns by faculty in the beginning, the result in general was significantly increased salaries over a period of several years. Statistics kept by the School of Music indicated that through this ongoing process most music faculty members had salaries which grew to equal or exceed salaries of peer institutions. The annual portfolio each faculty prepared each year for merit pay consideration also dovetailed with the portfolios required for faculty who were approaching promotion and tenure applications. Another result of the new plan was an increased ability of Belmont and the School of Music to attract and hire outstanding faculty members when new positions became available.[11]

Music and Discourse Series

Soon after the new millennium, Dr. Rick Hoffman and Dr. Paul Godwin proposed the idea of inviting guests to campus to present music academic lectures. The first guest lecturer was Dr. Dana Wilson from Ithaca College, who gave a lecture on "African Roots of American Music" and led a workshop on group improvisation. When Dr. Kenneth McLeod (PhD from McGill University) joined the faculty as Assistant Professor of Musicology in 2002, he brought renewed interest in developing a regular lecture series on musicology and theoretical subjects. McLeod, along with Hoffman and Godwin, saw the need to bolster the academic offerings of lectures to balance the already strong concert life of the School of Music. Out of their meetings the concept of Music and Discourse (MAD) emerged. The series started with faculty presentations, giving faculty an opportunity to share research and sabbatical projects. With Dean Curtis' support, budget funds were developed for inviting guest lecturers; the faculty planned for one guest lecturer each semester with faculty

177

presentations to complete the MAD series. The spring guest lecturer was usually presented in a "residency," in which the visiting scholars could speak to classes, present a convocation lecture, and make other presentations to targeted groups of music majors, depending on the expertise of the visiting scholar. As the series developed, a wide range of nationally known scholars visited Belmont, speaking on theory, popular music, jazz, music history, ethnomusicology, music education and church music, enriching the academic programs of the School of Music.

Representative visiting lecturers since the inception of Music and Discourse were: Dr. Ron Pen (University of Kentucky), Appalachian music specialist; Dr. Yvonne Kendall (University of Houston), dance scholar and African-American music specialist; Dr. Angela Mariani (Texas Tech University), early music performer and NPR host; Dr. Joan Tower (Bard College), composer; Sounak Chattopadhyay (Kolata, India), Classical Indian performer; Kofi Mawuko, African drumming specialist; Dr. Elliot Antokoletz (University of Texas), Bartok scholar; Dr. Annegret Fauser (University of North Carolina, Chapel Hill), musicologist; Dr. Paul Richardson (Samford University), hymnologist and church music scholar; Dr. Patricia Shehan Campbell (University of Washington) music education specialist and ethnomusicologist; and Dr. Alfredo Colman (Baylor University), ethnomusicologist. Belmont was especially pleased to bring Dr. Colman, a Belmont alumnus (BM '93), to present lectures in September, 2012. During his visit Colman, a nationally recognized scholar in South American music, was presented the Encore Award for his outstanding service to the field of ethnomusicology through his teaching, writing and lecturing.[12]

Alumni Achievements of 2002

Several Belmont music alumni brought honor to the School of Music through significant awards:
* The School of Music claimed its second Fulbright Scholar when Anne Marie Padelford, a Piano Performance Major (BM '06) was selected to teach German in Austria. She minored in German at Belmont in addition to her major in piano performance, and participated in the School of Music's Study Abroad Program by studying for a year in Dresden at the Hochschule für Musik. Her language skills and overseas study experience contributed to her strong application for the Fulbright Scholarship.

- Timothy Powell (BM '96 and MM 2000) was chosen in 2002 for a Fulbright Scholarship in Romania. He was completing his DMA in Choral Conducting at the University of South Carolina when he received the honor. In Romania he conducted research on the choral music Romanian composer Dobri Hristov. In an article in *The Belmont Circle* (Spring, 2003) he credited his Belmont Professors Tim Sharp, Daniel Landes, and Richard Shadinger, for their effectiveness in leading him to become a scholar.[13]
- Commercial Music Alumna, Marcie (Moe) Loughran (BM '93) won the Coca Cola New Music Award and was presented in a performance of her song on the American Music Awards show on national television, winning the competition out of more than 1000 entries.

CHAPTER FOURTEEN

National Recognition

"Christmas at Belmont" is Broadcast Nationally

In 2003 Nashville Public Television approached the School of Music about the possibility of taping "Christmas at Belmont" for broadcast over the National Public Television network. With funding provided by the Beaman Family Foundation, plans moved forward for the production for December, 2003 with Brenda Lee chosen to be the celebrity host for the concert. As a well-known country and pop singer, Brenda Lee was an excellent choice to host the concert. She was a charming presence on stage and her rendition of "Rockin' Around the Christmas Tree," accompanied by Belmont students, was a show stopper. The rehearsal and technical preparation for a program to be broadcast nationally required an immense effort by faculty leaders and student performers alike. The result was a polished product broadcast over 150 PBS affiliates across the country on December 23 and 25, 2003. The School of Music had gained priceless national exposure on a major network broadcast.

The 2003 production of "Christmas at Belmont" was re-broadcast during the Christmas season of 2004 with plans for a new production in 2005. The celebrity host for the 2005 concert was Belmont alumnus and country recording artist Josh Turner (BM '01), an important emerging young artist with a first album which had gone Platinum. He had recently been nominated as Top New Artist by the Academy of Country Music. The 2005 concert involved performances by 14 School of Music Ensembles. The staging of a concert for broadcast involved much planning and hard work by many people, including dozens of music faculty and staff along with NPT staff working together to make the concert a success. Especially important was the hard work and musicianship of the over 300 student performers led by capable directors of the ensembles. The total viewership nationwide for the 2005 Christmas program was 826,563.

In 2007 the decision was made to move the "Christmas at Belmont" concert and TV taping to the magnificent new Schermerhorn Symphony Center in downtown Nashville. The space was acoustically perfect and visually beautiful, a perfect place to showcase Belmont talent. However, there were financial issues, which were solved by major funding from Beaman Family Foundation. Logistical issues of transporting over 300 performers, instruments and equipment downtown, providing food during all-day rehearsals, as well as ticketing processes made this move challenging. The host for the 2007 performance was Melinda Doolittle, Belmont Alumna (BM '99) and runner-up for the 2006 "American Idol" show on Fox Television. Before "American Idol" Melinda Doolittle had developed an active career as a back-up singer for Nashville recording sessions. She won the hearts of America on the TV show and New York Times described her as "a phenomenally gifted, stylistically adroit Gladys Knight-Tina Turner hybrid who brings a compelling honesty to every phrase she sings." The guest conductor for the concert was Paul Leddington Wright, well-known conductor from Coventry, England, who had directed Belmont's choirs in 2004 in a concert of works by William Walton. Melinda Doolittle was an engaging host and helped propel the broadcast into becoming a national tradition. The 2007 "Christmas at Belmont" was replayed during the Christmas season of 2008. The number of viewers for the 2007 broadcast jumped significantly to 1,461,000, almost twice the viewership of the 2005 broadcast.

The 2009 production of "Christmas at Belmont" was again at The Schermerhorn Symphony Center. The logistical issues were somewhat easier this time because many of the problems involved in moving the concert downtown had been worked through two years earlier. The guest host for 2009 was country music star and recording artist Trisha Yearwood, a Belmont Alumna of 1990. With 12 albums and 20 top-10 hits, she was one of the most successful country music artists of modern times. Her vocal style and personality added an important presence to the 2009 "Christmas at Belmont." The viewership of "Christmas at Belmont" continued to climb with 1,535,000 viewers across the country.[14]

181

Growth in the School of Music

Under the leadership of President Fisher, Belmont moved into an era of remarkable growth. Belmont's rise in rankings such as the *U.S. News and World Report* college rankings and the national attention of Belmont's success in NCAA basketball helped propel national interest in the University. However, it cannot be overlooked that at the same time the School of Music was making a national name for itself through the graduation of outstanding alumni in many fields of music and through its annual national broadcasts of "Christmas at Belmont" on the Public Broadcasting System. These factors caused the School of Music to grow as well, sometimes without adequate space. The enrollment of music majors in 2000 was 433. By 2005 the number was 525, a growth of almost 100 in five years. The School of Music needed space, and rooms at the Belmont Heights Baptist Church, owned by the University, became the source of teaching space. The Dynamo Room, a separate building at the church location, was already in use for jazz ensembles and percussion practice, and the church sanctuary often served as a concert venue and organ teaching space. The guitar area was located in a suite of rooms that met their needs quite well for the large number of students in the guitar program. Sound-proof Wenger modular rooms were put into use for percussion practice and teaching. Rooms were designated as teaching studios for faculty members in percussion, strings, woodwinds and brass. Rehearsal spaces were found to accommodate large ensembles such as Orchestra and Wind Ensemble. With the expanding concert schedule, the church sanctuary came to be used more often for performances. In effect, the Belmont Heights location was gradually becoming a secondary site for the School of Music, housing most of the instrumental teaching and rehearsals.

Company and the Music City Show Shoppe Festival

Company, Belmont's show choir, had a history of successful and award-winning performances from its beginning in 1979 under the leadership of Marjorie Halbert. Beginning in 1995, under the leadership of James Kimmel, Company continued this tradition of creative choreography and musicality. Professor Kimmel often focused on a cappella singing by Company as a way of developing strong musicianship, bringing strong recognition to the group by the American Choral Director's Association, which invited Company to perform at five conventions over a period of several years. In 2004 Company performed for the Southern Regional ACDA Convention. One year later, 2005 Company was invited to Los Angeles to perform for the national ACDA convention, giving Company the unprecedented opportunity to perform concerts in several Los Angeles area high schools as part of their tour that year. In 2006, 2008, and 2010 Company was again invited to perform at three consecutive Southern Regional ACDA conventions.

Since 1996, Company has hosted the Music City Show Shoppe Festival, which invites outstanding show choirs from throughout the South and Mid-west to Belmont. The February event includes approximately 15 high school show choirs. The Festival is unique in the amount of assistance received by the participating choirs. Each choir performs on stage in Massey Concert Hall with helpful critique given by experienced judges. Well-known clinicians present workshops for the groups and their leaders. For example, Timothy Shew, well-known Broadway performer has participated in the Show Shoppe Festival several times. The top choirs are awarded a place to sing on the final concert. Belmont's Company presents a concert for all the students present during the weekend. In addition to the choral performances, soloists are invited to perform for judges, with the winning singers presented in one of the public performances. An award is given for the group with the best band, the best choral sound, and the best choreography. Company members serve as staff for the festival, providing assistance throughout the weekend, gaining experience in the administration of the event. The School of Music found that the festival was an excellent recruitment event for singers. With Jim Kimmel's strong standing in the world of show choirs and the excellent planning of the event, Music City Show Shoppe became one of the most acclaimed music festivals of its kind in the nation.[15]

Summer Music Camps

Summer music camps are viewed as a good way to provide summer music enrichment for high school students, while also recruiting talented students for the School of Music. The camps give high school students the opportunity to live on Belmont's campus and study with outstanding faculty members in their area of interest. Belmont's own students assist as camp counselors, giving the chance for high school students to know what it is like to study music in a college setting. Dr. Barry Kraus serves as the coordinator of the summer camps for music students.

The first music camp, held in the summer of 2004, was for string students. When Celeste Myall joined the faculty as instructor in violin, she became coordinator of the camp. The string camp was called "Triple Threat" String Camp because of Belmont's strength in all three styles of classical, jazz and bluegrass. Later the name was changed to "String Crossings" Camp, using a play on words relating to string technique and crossover of music styles. The camp utilized Belmont's strong roster of string teachers, supplemented by guest teachers. The camp provided a variety of experiences including private lessons, master classes, faculty performances and ensemble experiences led by Belmont faculty conductors. Belmont string students assisted as organizers and camp counselors. The string camp eventually expanded the styles taught to include swing, rock and celtic.[16]

The Belmont Invitational Piano Camp began in 2008 under the leadership of Dr. Kristian Klefstad. The piano camp capitalized on the acquisition of Steinway pianos and the potential for performing in the new McAfee Concert Hall. The camp allows piano students to choose either a classical or jazz track with choices of classes in music theory, sight-reading, technique and improvisation. Faculty members present a faculty concert during the week. Students study privately with Belmont faculty and participate in master classes and a student recital.[17]

The Summer Youth Wind Symphony Camp began in 2010 under the leadership of Dr. Barry Kraus. The first summer the enrollment was 35 students and by 2012 it had grown to 63. The students are given the opportunity to perform in wind ensemble, jazz band and chamber ensembles under the guidance of Belmont faculty. In 2013 the band camp was renamed "Summer Winds Band Camp."[18]

In the summer of 2016, Belmont began a summer camp for singers called Belmont Summer Vocal Arts Intensive. Planned and directed by Dr. Lesley Mann, the camp provided students experience participating in singing solo, small ensemble, and large choral ensembles. Elective courses included conducting, diction, and dance. Twelve Belmont choral faculty provided leadership with assistance from Belmont music students who served as counselors. For the first year the enrollment was 95 students, reaching the maximum size planned for this new summer camp.

In addition to developing their music skills all of the music camps give the high school students an opportunity to experience campus life and to have fun with peers with similar interests. The School of Music has found that the camps serve as a great way to connect with young students and to encourage their application to Belmont when the time comes.

Belmont Chorale International Tours – England and China

The Belmont Chorale, under the direction of Edgar Scruggs, renewed its tradition of touring internationally in the summer of 2004 by attending the International Church Music Festival in Coventry, England. Faculty members travelling with Chorale were Dr. Jane Warren, Assistant Conductor and Dr. Richard Hoffman, who taught a Study Abroad course for students participating in the tour. The Chorale began its trip in England by singing for a broadcast of BBC's *Daily Service* on Radio 4. The recording of the broadcast was done in a church in Manchester and then patched into the live service broadcast over BBC the following day. The International Choral Festival in Coventry featured the Belmont Chorale and the St. Michael's Singers from Coventry in a special concert on the second evening of the festival. On the final evening of the festival the Chorale joined choirs from the UK, the USA, Poland, the Czech Republic, Slovakia, and Moldova to perform a concert with all choirs under the direction of Paul Leddington Wright.[19] Belmont's connection with Paul Leddington Wright was a strong one. He visited Belmont twice to conduct major events: On October 25, 2002 he was guest conductor of Oratorio Chorus celebrating the centennial of the birth of composer William Walton in a performance of Waltons' *Te Deum* and *Beshazzar's Feast*. In 2006 he returned to conduct the mass choir/orchestra works for "Christmas at Belmont" at the Schermerhorn Symphony Center. Leddington Wright also provided several of the choir/orchestra arrangements for the 2006 "Christmas at Belmont" concert.

The Belmont Chorale carried the name of Belmont University into the Orient for the first time on its tour during May 14-May 25, 2007. Dr. Jane Warren was the Director of Chorale for this adventure into a very different culture. Coming just one year prior to the Olympic Games in Beijing, there was heightened interest in American culture in China. Within their first two days in Beijing the Chorale performed concerts at the Forbidden City

Concert Hall and Renming University, one of China's most prestigious universities. After sightseeing in Beijing, including the Great Wall of China, the Chorale travelled by train for the second leg of the journey to the city of Qingdao, where the Chorale sang two concerts as part of the Qingdao Choral Festival. The concerts in both Beijing and Qingdao were held in large impressive concert halls with enthusiastic crowds of eager Chinese listeners. The Chorale sang a selection of American choral music, including spirituals and Appalachian folk music, which were especially appreciated by the audiences. One highlight was an Appalachian folk song arranged by Chorale member Mollie Skaggs (BM '07) daughter of country music legend, Ricky Skaggs. It seems that Ricky Skaggs was known to the Chinese audiences and this selection brought special applause. The Chorale also learned several popular Chinese folk songs. Each time they began these songs the audience erupted in applause and joined in singing with the Chorale. During the Qingdao Choral Festival, Dr. Warren appeared at a press conference where she gave greetings from the United States, Tennessee, Nashville and Belmont University. As a part of this speech she had the opportunity to share information about Belmont and its musical programs.

The Chorale travelled to Nanjing where they again received a warm welcome at their concert in the Music Hall of the Nanjing Arts Institute. A special event in Nanjing was a concert at the Nanjing Seminary. In this visit, hymns were sung with the Chorale in English and the Chinese Christians in their own language, bringing a strong connection between the two cultures. Another meaningful encounter was at the House of Blessing, a residential center for mentally challenged adults. The Chorale sang for the residents and then in exchange, the residents performed a program of welcome for their American guests. The Belmont Chorale made a strong impression on the audiences in China and, in addition, the Belmont students were enriched by the experience in this far-away country.[20]

Nashville Opera Fellows

In 2006 the Nashville Opera established the Nashville Opera Fellows program in partnership with Belmont University. This program was designed to provide singers in the master's program in vocal performance valuable experience with a professional opera company. Fellows gain experience by performing in Nashville Opera's chorus and singing roles in the touring productions, as well as performing in the company's main productions. The fellows also can develop their careers through participation in masterclasses and career development workshops. Fellows receive scholarship funds from Belmont with the possibility of further compensation from the opera company. The fellows are chosen through auditions with the Nashville Opera and Belmont University School of Music. Since the beginning of the Fellows program numerous Belmont graduate vocalists have received experience which helped them begin their own opera careers.

New Heights for the Belmont Symphony Orchestra

As the Belmont Orchestra moved toward its 20th anniversary, the name of the orchestra was changed to the Belmont University Symphony Orchestra, signifying the orchestra's change from a small college orchestra playing small works to a 90-piece ensemble performing major works of the symphonic repertoire. Because of the Orchestra's status among universities in Tennessee it was invited to perform at the Tennessee Music Educators Association conventions in 2005 and 2009. The 2005 performance featured Elisabeth Small, Belmont Instructor of Violin, in Vaughan Williams' *The Lark Ascending*. One of the advantages of being in a large music school is the strong talent among the faculty to perform in orchestra concertos. Faculty members featured with the orchestra have been Robert Marler, piano; William Pursell, piano; John Pell, guitar; Mario DaSilva, guitar; Joel Treybig, trumpet; Richard Shadinger, piano and harpsichord; Kristian Klefstad, piano; Sarah Cote, viola; Elisabeth Small, violin; Roy Vogt, electric bass, and Tracy Silverman, electric violin. Silverman, America's most important electric violinist, had previously performed with the Los Angeles and Nashville Symphonies before appearing on his home stage with the Belmont Symphony Orchestra, performing his own Concerto for Electric Violin. When Gregg was asked about some of his proudest moments of the orchestra's recent performances, he mentioned the outstanding performances of major works such as Beethoven's Symphonies No. 5 and 7, Elgar's *Enigma Variations,* Dvorak's Symphony No. 9 (*From the New World*) and Tchaikovsky's Overture-Fantasy *Romeo and Juliet*. In addition, Gregg was pleased with the level of performances by students in the concerto-aria concert each spring. For most of these students it was their first opportunity to perform with an orchestra, and they rose to the challenge.[21]

To celebrate the 25th anniversary of the Belmont University Symphony Orchestra, on February 27 and 28, 2009 the School of Music held a reunion of orchestra players from years past. Julie Thomas from the Belmont Alumni Office assisted in contacting alumni about the event. A Friday night banquet gave an opportunity for alumni to visit, renew acquaintances, and to peruse photographs, programs, and other memorabilia from the previous 25 years. Over 40 orchestra alumni joined with the Symphony Orchestra for a concert on February 28, 2009. The gala concert included Rossini's Overture to *The Thieving Magpie* and Mozart's Sinfonia Concertante, K. 364 featuring soloists Elisabeth Small, violin and Sarah Cote, viola. The finale of the concert was a performance of Respighi's *Pines of Rome*, bringing the event to a rousing conclusion.[22]

Belmont Percussion Ensemble Performs for Percussive Arts International Society Convention

On November 11, 2004 the Belmont Percussion Ensemble reached an important stage in their growth as an ensemble when they performed a concert of new music for percussion ensembles at the convention of the Percussive Arts Society International meeting in Nashville. When Dr. Chris Norton joined the music faculty in 2001 he led the Percussion Ensemble to a high level of performance through active recruiting of strong players and through careful development of their skills. The ensemble also benefitted from the acquisition of new and improved percussion instruments, including the very best brands of marimbas, timpani, cymbals, and drums. The Percussion Ensemble concerts became a favorite event every semester, drawing large audiences.

Bruin Blast and Belmont Fight Song

When Belmont University joined the NCAA in 2004, moving into the Atlantic Sun Conference, the need for a larger and more dynamic pep band became apparent. With the completion of the large state-of-the art Curb Event Center used for basketball games, the new pep band became known as the "Bruin Blast." Under the leadership of Dr. Gary Schallert the band became larger, and took on a larger role in building Belmont team spirit. Graduate assistants were chosen to help with the leadership of the band. At about the same time, stipends were paid to students, providing greater consistency of instrumentation at basketball games. Bruin Blast is a dynamic presence at all home basketball games and other school spirit events. The group has also travelled to perform at NCAA national tournament games at locations across the country. Approximately 75 students perform with Bruin Blast. While many are music majors, the group draws from students in various majors across the university. In 2008, Dr. Barry Kraus took over leadership of Bruin Blast, which continues to be an integral part of a thriving Belmont Athletic Program.

In 2007 Tyler Ewing (BM 2007), a Music Composition Major, wrote Belmont's new fight song. This catchy, spirited song has become a strong tradition and is played by Bruin Blast at the beginning and end of all basketball games. In 2012 a clever text was added to the tune, written by several members of the Belmont community (Samantha Beringer, Nathan Griffith, Laura Guenther and Ryder Lee). Belmont now had a universally loved fight song which became a tradition in short time.

Friends of the School of Music and Music Scholarship Progress

Adequate scholarships for music students had been a major need for the School of Music for decades. In long range planning and in fundraising this issue was always uppermost on the needs list, because it was clear that a strong music school could only be built through the ability to attract the best student scholars and performers. Several factors helped to improve the scholarship situation over time. The University itself responded by budgeting more funds for music scholarships with regular annual increases. Special scholarship funds were targeted toward attracting instrumentalists to support the growing instrumental program. Belmont University was also offering substantial academic scholarships which helped many academically strong music majors. While the University was gradually giving more toward scholarships, aggressive fund raising was conducted by the School of Music to increase the number and amount of endowed music scholarships.

In 2004 the Friends of the School of Music (FOSOM) was transformed into Friends of the Arts at Belmont (FAB). With the bringing together of Music, Art, Theatre and Dance under the umbrella of the College of Visual and Performing Arts, it was decided to enlarge the organization by adding board members who could serve as supporters for all the arts programs in the college.[23]

By the year 2011 the School of Music had scholarship endowments in the amount of $3,500,000, providing scholarships for a large number of music majors.[24] In 2013 the combined amount of scholarships awarded from both

189

the endowed scholarships and budgeted music scholarships was nearly $1,000,000.[25] As a comparison, 25 years earlier in 1986, the total amount of music scholarship awarded was $32,000. This comparison is dramatic, but scholarships remain a high priority because of higher tuition costs and competition from schools who have large scholarship budgets. Belmont always keeps growth of scholarship funds on the long range plan to assure that the School of Music remains competitive in attracting talented students.

The Steinway Initiative

Dean Curtis was known for identifying opportunities to make situations in the School of Music better. If a choice was to be made, she tried to take the path which most improved the learning environment for the School. The problem of inadequate pianos was a long-standing one, and with a growing student body and faculty, simply keeping enough pianos was a challenge. Over time pianos were becoming less dependable, and needed replacement. In 2004, with Dr. Curtis' leadership, the School of Music investigated the possibility of becoming an All-Steinway School. The prospect seemed unlikely without a major donor in the wings. Working with Bill Metcalf from the Steinway Piano Gallery of Nashville, the School of Music began using capital funds to purchase a few Boston and Steinway pianos each year to upgrade the instruments and move in the direction of the All-Steinway designation. A detailed replacement plan was drawn up, replacing pianos where they were most needed, and progress began to be seen.[26]

As the plans were developing to replace pianos, it was also noted that the school's old Sabathil harpsichord, in use for 40 years, was in need of replacement. A search was conducted to find the best harpsichord available to meet the needs of performance at Belmont, resulting in the purchase of a harpsichord built by Richard Kingston of Mooresville, NC. Kingston was known for building harpsichords of superb quality, using traditional building techniques of builders from earlier centuries. The harpsichord was modeled after a French single-manual instrument of the 1700s. The harpsichord arrived in May, 2005 and found much use in Camerata chamber concerts as well as faculty and student programs. Dr. Richard Shadinger played the inaugural recital on the new Kingston harpsichord in the Belmont Mansion on April 3, 2006 as part the Faculty Concert Series.[27]

190

Merrydale Woods' Bequest to the School of Music

Merrydale Sutherland Woods (1915-2007) decided in 2006 at age 91 to leave a bequest to the Belmont University School of Music. She was married 68 years to her "soulmate," Hunter Woods, who had a business relationship with Belmont benefactor Jack Massey early in his life. Later he invested wisely in the stock market and the Woods' estate grew. Mrs. Woods had no children and decided early that she wanted her own career – to pursue her passion for music through teaching piano in her home. Over the years hundreds of young people benefitted from her teaching and many of them kept in touch well into their adult lives. She was fond of Mozart and Beethoven, but she could also play popular and jazz favorites as well. When she made the decision to include Belmont in her will, Mrs. Woods said "I hope the endowed scholarship fund will help others enjoy the music making I've enjoyed over the years. If you end up loving music it is wonderful because you can share it with someone else. When I was young there were many people who helped me along the way. I now know that my life has had a greater purpose – that after my death there will be young people at Belmont who will be able to pursue their passion for music – and that makes me feel good."[28]

Merrydale Woods' bequest amounted to over $1,000,000. Half of the amount was placed in an endowed scholarship fund known as the Woods Piano Scholarships. These awards are given annually to outstanding incoming piano students who audition for the School of Music. The other half of the bequest was used to help Belmont realize its dream to become an "All-Steinway School."

With the funds from Merrydale Woods' estate in hand, the School of Music moved forward with the purchase of Steinway and Boston pianos. The prospect of having Steinway pianos in all piano practice rooms, classrooms, piano faculty offices and concert halls was exciting. Representatives of the piano faculty travelled to the Steinway Showroom in New York City to choose Steinway pianos for Massey Concert Hall and Harton Recital Hall. Massey was the recipient of two nine-foot concert grand pianos and Harton, as a smaller room, was to have two seven-foot Steinway grand pianos. As a part of the transition to higher quality pianos, the School of Music also developed a new piano maintenance plan, providing systematic tuning and maintenance for all pianos.

Belmont Hosts 102nd Annual Convention
of the United Sacred Harp Musical Association

On September 9-11, 2005 Belmont School of Music hosted the United Sacred Harp Convention for its 102nd annual meeting. The coordinator of the event was Dr. Richard Hoffman assisted by Dr. Kenneth McLeod and Dr. Richard Shadinger. The first day of the conference consisted of scholarly papers on shape-note singing presented by foremost scholars from across the country. For the conference Shadinger prepared an extensive collection of historic shaped-note hymnals from his own collection which were displayed in the Leu Art Gallery. On Saturday and Sunday, the Convention met in the Neely Dining Room to sing from the Sacred Harp book. A large group of enthusiastic singers participated in the singing; the Neely Dining Room with its open spaces, wooden floors and live acoustics provided the perfect environment for hearty singing. The successful event was important because it showed that Belmont was capable of hosting and supporting a meeting of a national group interested in the academic side of Sacred Harp singing.

2006 National Association of Schools of Music Reaccreditation

To the Dean of Music and music faculty it seemed that the ten-year NASM reaccreditation process came more often than ten years. With constant annual reports, the NASM processes seemed to be never-ending. Dean Cynthia Curtis had become active in NASM affairs as Chair of the Ethics Committee of the Association. In addition, she served two terms on the National Accreditation Commission and became an evaluator of schools of music, serving as chair of evaluation committees. Dean Curtis' experience with NASM was helpful as the faculty entered the 2006 self-study process. At least a year was needed to prepare the Self-Study Document, a particularly daunting task because of the growth in the number of students and faculty, the addition of new programs such as Musical Theatre, and the growing complexity of the School of Music. Therefore, the 2006 NASM Self-study document was massive in size and scope. The basic report numbered 307 pages with a book of appendices which was even longer. In addition to the reports, all School of Music documents, concert programs, faculty minutes, recruitment materials, audition documents, alumni surveys, CDs, and videos etc. were gathered and placed in a documents room for the visiting team of evaluators. The report was written over a period of a year with faculty committees responsible for the various sections. Statistical data on all aspects of the school's enrollment were provided in the reports. The NASM documents were important because they showed how the School of Music fulfilled rigorous NASM standards.

The NASM evaluators were present October 22-24, 2006, during which they interviewed various faculty, students and administrators. They also visited a sampling of classes, rehearsals and private lessons throughout the time. A concert representing a cross-section of School of Music students was presented for the visiting team. The result of the visit was positive with no points of deferral out of all the areas in Belmont's large and complex school. The report noted a long list of strengths and a much smaller list of areas for improvement. The areas of strength noted were:

- Clearly stated, well-developed mission, goals and objectives
- Strong faculty and staff
- Experienced and collaborative leadership
- Excellent, well-planned instructional program
- Strong, stable enrollment
- Good facilities and upkeep
- Excellent equipment
- Outstanding music library
- Excellent interaction with the community
- Good national visibility
- Excellent record keeping.

Some of the areas for improvement given were:
- Need for additional scholarship funding
- Need for enrollment balance between majors
- Need for additional practice rooms and rehearsal space
- Need for additional support staff.

On June 28, 2007 the School of Music received the official notice of continuing in good standing with the National Association of Schools of Music. The notice requested a progress report on the development of the Belmont Heights site for music instruction. On April 28, 2008 Dean Curtis responded with a Progress Report to the NASM Commission on Accreditation, noting progress made through the completion of the Troutt Theatre, and the plans for phase II with fund-raising for renovation of the sanctuary space as a concert hall. The Progress Report was accepted by the commission, successfully ending the accreditation renewal process.[29]

CHAPTER FIFTEEN

Accelerated Change

Faculty Transitions

After 2000 several long-time faculty members retired after many years of contributions to the School of Music. John Arnn, Assistant Professor of Commercial Piano since 1981 retired in 2006. Shirley Zielinski, Professor of Voice since 1984, retired in 2006. Linda Ford, Assistant Professor of Piano and Coordinator of Piano Pedagogy retired in 2006 after 30 years of service. Jerry Warren retired in 2007 after 38 years of service as Dean of the School of Music, Provost, Interim President and University Professor. Dr. Paul Godwin, Professor of Theory retired in 2009 after 36 years of teaching in the School of Music. The retirement of long-term faculty members left a void within the school that would be replaced by younger faculty.

On April 13, 2007 the School of Music celebrated the retirement of Dr. Jerry Warren, Dean of the School of Music from 1969 to 1991, after which he became Provost of the University, a post he held until 1999. From 1999 until April 2000 he served as Interim President between the terms of Dr. Troutt and Dr. Fisher. While he was Provost he continued to conduct Oratorio Chorus for several years. In 2000 he was named University Professor and provided leadership in the planning of the First Year Seminar for the new BELL Core. He continued to teach First Year Seminar, several music classes, and to direct Belle Voci, Belmont's community chorus. Upon his retirement he had served Belmont for 38 years in a variety of important roles. For the retirement ceremony, former Belmont Chorale members were invited to return and sing under his direction. Warren chose to lead the Chorale and alumni in Brahms' "Create in Me a Clean Heart" and Beryl Vick's "When I Survey the Wondrous Cross," which he had commissioned Vick to compose for the Belmont Chorale in 1969. Tributes were given by former President Dr. William E. Troutt, President Bob Fisher, Dr. Cynthia Curtis, Dean of the School of Music, and alumna Susan Smith Cauley (BM '73). The 2007 Belmont Chorale under the direction of Edgar Scruggs sang a tribute to Warren. Following the ceremony in Massey Concert Hall a reception was held in the Belmont Mansion. Assisting in the planning was Julie Thomas (BM '77), who arranged a historical display of Warren's time at Belmont.[30] Upon retirement, Dr. Warren served for a time as interim Executive Director of the American Choral Directors Association in Oklahoma City, and continued to serve as Minister of Music at Immanuel Baptist Church in Nashville.

The number of incoming faculty members during the same time period outpaced the number of retirements because of the growth in the number of music students. The new faculty, with superb credentials and excellent teaching experience, represented a bright future for the School of Music. Faculty additions after 2000 with their teaching area and school of their terminal degree were: Dr. Richard Hoffman, Theory (PhD, University of Kentucky); Dr. Christopher Norton, Percussion (DMA, Louisiana State University); Dr. Kristi Whitten, Voice (DM, Indiana University); Dr. Kenneth McLeod, Musicology (PhD, McGill University); Bruce Bennett, Commercial Voice (MM, New England Conservatory of Music); Dr. Jennifer Coleman, Voice (DMA, University of Kentucky); Dr. Joel Treybig, Trumpet (DMA, University of Texas Austin); Dr. Bruce Dudley, Commercial Piano (DMA, University of Colorado); Dr. Anthony Belfiglio, Commercial Piano (DMA, University of Texas Austin); Dr. Terry Klefstad, Musicology (PhD, University of Texas Austin); Dr. Kristian Klefstad, Piano (DMA, University of Texas Austin); Dr. Barry Kraus, Director of Wind Ensemble (DMA, Arizona State University); Dr. Peter Lamothe, Musicology (PhD, University of North Carolina); Elisabeth Small, Violin (MM, Julliard School of Music); Dr. Jane Warren, Choral Conducting (DMA, University of South Carolina); Dr. Kathryn Paradise, Commercial Voice (DMA, University of Illinois Champaign-Urbana); David Shamburger, Musical Theatre (MFA, University of Nevada Las Vegas); Dr. Mark Volker, Composition (PhD, University of Chicago); Dr. Clare Eng,

Theory (PhD, Princeton University); Dr. Mark Whatley, Voice (DMA, Rice University); Dr. Jeffery Ames, Director of Choral Activities (PhD, Florida State University); and Alex Graham, Saxophone and Commercial Instrumental Music (DMA, Eastman School of Music); In addition to excellent full-time new faculty members, the School of Music also provided full-time adjunct status for a significant number of long-term adjunct teachers who provided excellent supplemental teaching.

The administration of the School of Music underwent several personnel changes during the same time period. In 2002 Dr. Madeline Bridges became Associate Dean for Academic Studies, replacing Dr. Kris Elsberry who moved into full-time teaching in the theory and piano areas. At the same time Dr. Robert Gregg became Director of Graduate Studies, the role previously held by Dr. Bridges. In 2007 Dr. Richard Shadinger, Associate Dean for Performance Studies, relinquished that role for full-time teaching in the Music History area. Dr. Jeffrey Kirk, having recently completed his doctorate, took on the role vacated by Shadinger. Professor Henry Smiley stepped into the role of Coordinator of Commercial Music which had been previously held by Jeffrey Kirk. Belmont was fortunate to have qualified faculty members able to fill the administrative roles as needed, maintaining continuity and a strong administrative group.

Enlarged Carillon Brings National Attention

Belmont's 23-bell carillon built in 1986 was designed with a keyboard with the potential of accommodating 20 extra bells. In 2005 a grant from the Massey Foundation made it possible to add the 20 new bells, bringing the carillon to 43 bells with a range of 3 and 1/2 octaves. This addition allowed the carillon to become a true concert carillon with a range capable of playing much of the literature for the instrument. In June, 2007 the Guild of Carillonneurs in North America held their annual congress at The University of the South in Sewanee, TN. As a part of the convention, on June 22, 2007 the members travelled to Nashville to hear the Belmont carillon. Richard Shadinger presented a concert for the visitors and afterward members of the group enjoyed playing the instrument. After a picnic lunch on campus, the guest carillonneurs toured the Belmont Mansion before visiting other sites in Nashville.

The Belmont Tower had served as Belmont University's logo for a number of years, appearing on every official document and portrayal of the University. The Tower was connected to the history of Belmont since its construction in 1853 and was centrally located at the southern end of the University quadrangle in front of the Student Center and Curb Event Center. The Tower was in need of restoration and a fundraising campaign was begun soon after the addition of the new bells with the restoration to take place a few years later.[31]

New Theatre Facilities: The Troutt Theatre

The development of the Belmont Heights site as a complex for Music and Theatre advanced in 2007 with the completion of the Bill and Carol Troutt Theatre, replacing the old and inadequate Little Theater located in the basement of Hail Hall. The new theatre, named for former President and Mrs. Willliam Troutt, was built within the space of what was once the chapel of the church. With its lovely theatrical setting, large proscenium stage, elaborate scenery fly space, large orchestra pit, plus excellent lighting and sound equipment, it was the perfect space for of all types of student and professional theatrical performances. In addition, the theatre had elegant lobby spaces, as well a spacious scene construction shop behind the stage, and support/storage space on the lower level. An especially lovely touch in the new Theatre was the restoration of a large chandelier original to the space.

The Troutt Theatre immediately became the most desirable theatre space in Nashville, used often by community groups such as the Nashville Shakespeare Theatre, The Actor's Bridge Ensemble, The Nashville Children's Theatre, and The Nashville Ballet. In addition to the Troutt Theatre with seating for 300, a Black Box experimental theatre seating 150 provided a place for creative theatre in a variety of configurations. The School of Music often cooperated with the Theatre and Dance Department in a number of productions. The School of Music began to perform opera and musical theatre productions in the Troutt Theatre. The first School of Music productions held there were the opera production of November, 2007, Lehar's *The Merry Widow*, and the musical theatre production of *Thoroughly Modern Millie* in April, 2008. Both productions were enhanced by stunning sets and lighting made possible in the new Troutt Theatre. Set changes were much easier to facilitate because of the fly space and sophisticated rigging provided on the Troutt stage.

197

The Encore Award

The School of Music established the Encore Award to recognize Belmont music alumni who had achieved remarkable careers in the world of classical music, to work in tandem with the Curtain Call Award which was awarded to outstanding alumni in the world of popular music. The planning for the Encore Award began in 2008 with a recipient who was an obvious first choice. Clifton Forbis (BM'85) had gained international fame as an operatic tenor and the date for the award ceremony, March 31, 2009, had to be carefully worked around his touring schedule.

Clifton Forbis became a leading tenor in opera houses around the world including The Metropolitan Opera, Opera National de Paris, The Canadian Opera Company, Teatro alla Scala in Milan, Deutsche Oper Berlin, The Seattle Opera, and The Chicago Lyric Opera. He performed with the Chicago, Toronto, Pittsburgh and Boston Symphony Orchestras. Reviewer David Nice in *The Arts Desk* said that "Forbis has his finest moments in going further than any Tristan I've ever heard other than the incomparable Jon Vickers in expressing fathomless despair."[32]

Forbis actually made his operatic debut at Belmont on December 10, 1979 in a production of *Amahl and the Night Visitors* in which he sang the role of King Melchior. In awarding Forbis the first presentation of the Encore Award Dr. Jeffrey Kirk said "Clifton is a natural choice for this award. With performances with opera companies and symphony orchestras around the world, Clifton is one of our most distinguished alumni. He is a great example of what we hope all of our alumni achieve both personally and professionally." At the presentation event Forbis presented a master class for four Belmont vocal majors, using his performance insights to help them find a greater vocal presence on stage. In 2011 Forbis was named head of the Voice Department at Southern Methodist University.

On September 29, 2009 the second presentation of the Encore Award was made to Daniel Weeks, operatic tenor and faculty member of the University of Louisville School of Music. Weeks, a Vocal Performance and Church Music alumnus from 1989, sang with the Houston Symphony, the Dallas Symphony, the Pittsburgh Symphony, the Cincinnati Symphony, the Louisville Orchestra, the Florida Symphony, the Sioux City Orchestra, the Venezuelan Youth Orchestra, The Indianapolis Symphony and the Johnstown Symphony. He sang operatic roles with the Cincinnati Opera, the Kentucky Opera, the Florentine Opera of Milwaukee, the Austin Lyric

Opera, the Nevada Opera, and the San Francisco Opera. In receiving his award he expressed appreciation for his teachers at Belmont in both voice and academic subjects. He made the observation that Belmont provided many "firsts" for him saying, "the first time I ever heard an opera was when I was in one at Belmont." A well-rounded student, he was an excellent violinist and performed with the Belmont Orchestra in its formative years. In 2014 Weeks was appointed to the position of Professor of Voice at the Cincinnati College-Conservatory of Music.

The third Encore presentation was held on September 28, 2010 with the award going to two graduates, Dr. Sharon Lawhon and Dr. Daniel Lawhon. Sharon Lawhon is chair of the vocal-choral department of the School of the Arts at Samford University. She completed her BM degree from Belmont in Vocal Performance in 1979. She earned her advanced degrees at the Southern Baptist Theological Seminary where she was on the faculty of the School of Church Music before moving to Samford. She is an active recitalist, performer in oratorio and opera and a voice clinician. Daniel Lawhon, a 1983 Organ Performance Major from Belmont, earned his advanced degrees at the Southern Baptist Theological Seminary. He currently serves as organist-choirmaster at the Baptist Church of the Covenant in Birmingham. He served on the faculties of Samford University and the University of Alabama at Birmingham. The Lawhons were students at Belmont for a total of seven years because each one worked full-time while the other attended school. Their concert at Belmont Heights Church included vocal selections by Sharon Lawhon and solo organ works by Daniel Lawhon.[33]

Debate '08 Between McCain and Obama at Belmont

The national spotlight shone briefly on Belmont University in October, 2008 as in no other time during the Town Hall Presidential Debate between John McCain and Barak Obama. Held in the Curb Event Center on October 7, 2008, the debate was broadcast around the world, placing Belmont in the center of national politics only one month before the 2008 presidential election. Belmont chose as its slogan for the year "The race to the White House runs through Belmont University." The debate itself required that the Belmont campus become one large broadcast media center with tight security. Therefore, fall break was set for the week of the debate to clear the campus for media events.

The debate gave the Belmont community an opportunity to focus on national politics and what it means to be an American. During the 2008-09 academic year the campus theme was "The Art of Being Free." Belmont invited outstanding speakers to campus to cover various aspects of American life. Some of the important guest speakers were Dr. Tony Campolo, speaker on religion in America, Barbara Bradley Hagerty, religion correspondent for NPR, and Ken Burns, documentary filmmaker. The most distinguished guest in the series was David McCullough, well-known author on American history. McCullough's speech on March 19, 2009 brought a capacity crowd to the Curb Event Center.

Departments on campus were encouraged to present programs which reflected the year's theme and the School of Music responded with a number of concerts on American music including "American Popular Song" sung by the commercial voice faculty; "Classic American Rock," played by percussion teacher Zoro; "American Music for the Carillon" by carillonneur Richard Shadinger; "American Classics" including Copland's *A Lincoln Portrait* performed by the University Symphony Orchestra; "Classic American Jazz," by the Belmont Jazz Ensemble; and "American Music, Jazz and Beyond," performed by jazz pianist Bruce Dudley. In keeping with the year's theme, the Musical Theatre production for fall, 2008 was *Ragtime*. The 2008 Presidential Debate provided many opportunities for the School of Music to be involved in an important national event.[34]

Belmont Designated as "All Steinway School"

The Belmont University School of Music was listed as an "All Steinway School" in Steinway ads in the May, 2010 issues of *The American Music Teacher* and *Clavier*, joining a list of 86 colleges, conservatories and universities, including Julliard School of Music, The Curtis Institute, Yale University, James Madison University, Oberlin College, Columbia University, Tulane University, University of Florida, University of Georgia and Vasser College, to name a few.

The Steinway connection was officially celebrated on September 10, 2010 with the Woods Memorial Concert by Van Cliburn Silver Medalist Yeol Eun Son, Pianist. The concert was an opportunity to honor Merrydale Woods for her bequest of over $1,000,000, because her gift had made possible the purchase of Steinways and major piano scholarships. Representatives from the Steinway Piano Company honored Belmont with a plaque signifying that Belmont officially had joined the prestigious list of institutions known as "All Steinway Schools." Making the presentation was Sally Coveleskie, National Director of Institutional Sales and Tommy Edds, Regional Manager of Steinway and Sons. Bill Metcalf of the Steinway Piano Gallery of Nashville who had facilitated the purchase of pianos was present representing Steinway locally. Also recognized at the presentation was Tom McAfee, representing the McAfee Foundation, who on August 20 had announced a major gift to renovate the Belmont Heights sanctuary to become a new concert hall for the School of Music. Yeol Eun Son's brilliant concert of works by Schumann, Bach, Prokofiev and Moszkowski was an excellent tribute to Mrs. Woods and a perfect way to celebrate the "All Steinway" status of the School of Music.[35]

Historic Belmont Tower Undergoes Major Renovation

During the summer of 2010 the historic tower at Belmont University, housing its 43-bell carillon, underwent a major exterior restoration. As soon as the spring semester was completed, scaffolding went up around the tower and work began; the project was completed in August just before students arrived on campus for the fall semester. The roof of the 1853 structure was replaced and all deteriorating material at the top of the tower was replaced or rebuilt. Drainage off the top of the tower was improved to solve leakage problems. Loose mortar was removed from the brickwork and new mortar applied. The exterior of the tower received a water repellent coating. The windows of the tower were restored and repainted, retaining all of the remaining original glass. Little was done to the interior of the tower except for a new and much-appreciated central air conditioning system which replaced old and unattractive window units in the playing room and practice level of the tower. At the conclusion of the project a bronze plaque was placed in the prayer chapel in the base of the tower designating that the structure is listed on the National Register of Historic Places by the United States Department of the Interior.

The restoration cost was over $400,000 with lead gifts contributed by Helen Jarrett Kennedy (class of '55), Drew R. Maddux (class of '56), Virginia Frances Potter, and the Estate of James H. Moore. Over 800 Alumni, faculty and friends of the University made contributions to the project.

On October 2, 2010 (a perfect fall day) a celebration of the completion of the project was held at the tower. A 30-minute program of carillon music was played by Richard Shadinger, Professor of Music and University Carillonneur. Special guests for the event were alumnae of Ward-Belmont, who attended their reunion luncheon on campus prior to the dedication ceremony. Guests were welcomed by Dr. Bo Thomas, Vice-President for University Advancement and by Dr. Bob Fisher, President of the University. Mr. Drew Maddux, Class of '56, spoke of the importance of the tower and the carillon to the University. Mr. Maddux was the major donor of the 23-bell carillon in 1986 and was a leader in the fund-raising efforts to complete the instrument in 2003. Mr. Stephen W. Brown, President of Republic Construction Company, who completed the restoration project, spoke about the efforts to restore the structure while maintaining its historic appearance. Republic Construction Company had completed restoration projects on other historic buildings in Nashville, including the Tennessee State Capitol, The Hermitage, The Ryman Auditorium and the Belmont Mansion. Mrs. Vicky Tarleton, Director of Planned Giving and Major Gifts, recognized donors. Mrs. Helen Kennedy and Mr. Drew Maddux unveiled a plaque recognizing the donors to the project. The ceremony ended with remarks and a benediction by Dr. Todd Lake, Vice President for Spiritual Development. After the dedication program a number of guests toured the tower to see how the carillon is played.

On the following afternoon, Sunday, October 3, Richard Shadinger played a second concert celebrating the restoration of the tower as well as the 500th anniversary of the first carillon. To celebrate the event, Angela Brownell Smith (BM '92, MM '93) had been commissioned to compose a work for the carillon. Her work entitled "Restoration" depicted the activity of the restoration process. The composer was present in the large audience of Belmont students, faculty and friends from the community.[36]

The historic tower exists today after more than 160 years as a symbol of the history of the campus and the aspirations of the educational institutions associated with the location. The tower stands at the center of a modern growing university, serving as the symbol for the institution. The prayer chapel in the base of the tower is used frequently by student groups for worship and prayer services. The music from the carillon in the tower is an important part of the cultural and communal life of the University. The restoration preserves the integrity of the structure for future generations of Belmont University students and citizens of Nashville, who view the tower as an important historical landmark of Nashville.

McAfee Foundation Gift for New Concert Hall

For over a decade the School of Music had used the Belmont Heights sanctuary for concerts, rehearsals and organ teaching. The room had many good qualities: excellent acoustical properties, seating for over 1000, and a superb Aeolian-Skinner organ. As it currently stood, however, it was not an ideal concert space because the small stage, poor lighting, and a total lack of concert hall amenities such as storage, green room and support space. The room had a dark and dilapidated appearance and the organ was in need of restoration. For some time the School of Music had envisioned a renovated space which would enhance the already good properties of the room, providing an excellent environment for classical concerts. The space was brought to the attention of Mrs. Carolyn McAfee, a Belmont Trustee. Mrs. McAfee already had shown her support for the School of Music through a scholarship for students with a major in organ or classical music. As a musician and a former organist, she was impressed by the 55-rank Aeolian-Skinner and saw the possibility of showcasing it in a better concert environment. In 2008 she made a contribution which allowed architectural concepts to be drawn for the space. On August 20, 2010, a public announcement of a lead gift from the McAfee family was made in the sanctuary of Belmont Heights Baptist Church to a large assembly of Belmont faculty and staff, and community supporters.[37]

New Graduate Commercial Music Major

For some time the School of Music Graduate Council had discussed the possibility of offering a Commercial Music Major under the Master of Music degree program. Through surveying the academic landscape, Belmont discovered that there were relatively few places in the United States where a student with an undergraduate major in commercial music could continue graduate study in the same field. Most of the available graduate program appeared to be limited primarily to jazz studies. After extensive study and planning in 2008-09 by a committee chaired by Professor Keith Mason, a program was brought forth for approval, and the first class of seven students entered in August, 2010. The new Masters Degree in Commercial Music included two academic options: Performance and Composition and Arranging. The degree was designed primarily for those students who wished to teach on the collegiate level. For others it provided an opening into advanced performance and work in the music industry. There were several unique features to the curriculum. All students were required to take a course in Master Recording Techniques as well as a course called The Entrepreneurial Challenge. This second course recognized the fact that many graduates of the program will need to build their own careers through inventive initiative. All students in the program take part in an apprenticeship, which is more than the typical Internship experience; students are placed in an appropriate high-level work or leadership setting where they gain important skills which strengthen abilities for their work ahead.

It was decided to keep the Masters program in Commercial Music relatively small in order to give students the close mentoring which already characterized Belmont's other graduate majors. Entry to the program was selective because the curriculum was designed for very talented musicians with good backgrounds in popular style and strong potential for leadership in the field. The first class of seven graduate students entered the program in the Fall of 2010. Belmont had been a leader in commercial music studies for over 30 years and the expansion to graduate studies was seen as a logical progression of that leadership. With the growth in colleges offering studies in popular music, there was need for faculty members with graduate degrees in the subject area. It was predicted that Belmont would provide significant academic leaders in the collegiate world of commercial music.[38]

2010-11 Theme: Invention and Creativity

Each year Belmont University chose a theme around which programs, speakers and the First Year Seminar were based. The School of Music sought to find ways in which the University theme could be worked into the programming of concerts for the year. The 2010-11 theme of "Invention and Creativity" suggested many possibilities. A Commercial Voice faculty Concert was entitled was called "Creativity – Singer's Jam." A concert by the String Faculty was "The Creative Spirit – String Fling." A carillon concert by Richard Shadinger celebrated 500 years of the carillon with "500 Years of Carillon Creativity." The Belmont Symphony Orchestra played a concert of works by Beethoven and Brahms entitled "The Alpha and Omega of the 19th Century." The most extensive use of the theme came through the Belmont Camerata concert series in which the ensemble explored creative composers of chamber music throughout history with the following concerts:

- The Baroque Imagination: Fervor and Flamboyance (Dall' Bacco, Purcell, Corelli, Telemann, Bach)
- The Classical Ideal: Clarity and Grace (Haydn, Mozart, Beethoven, Mendelssohn)
- The Romantic Impulse: Passion and Virtuosity (Brahms, Dvorak, Debussy)
- The Modern Vision: Revolution and Transformation (Shostakovich, Bartok, Schoenberg, Berg, Crumb)[39]

Alumni Achievements

The flood of May 2 and 3, 2010 was one of the worst disasters in Nashville history. Two days of torrential rains caused the Harpeth and Cumberland Rivers to flood neighborhoods throughout Metropolitan Nashville, flooding important cultural centers such as the Schermerhorn Symphony Center and the Grand Ole Opry, causing many millions of dollars of damage. The Belmont campus suffered only minor problems, but many of the Belmont community were affected by the flooding of homes. Belmont, like many institutions, rose to the challenge to volunteer to help those in need after the rains stopped. The Grand Ole Opry was rebuilt in an amazingly short time and reopened on September 28, 2010. Belmont Alumnus, Josh Turner, performed as part of the first show on the Opry stage after the flood.

The Schermerhorn Symphony Center re-opened in January, 2011 following massive reconstruction made necessary by the flooding of the Cumberland River. Two Belmont Alumni performed with the Nashville Symphony Orchestra in its first performances after the reopening of the Schermerhorn Center. On January 13 Music alumnus Boh Cooper (BM in Piano Performance '04) performed piano and vocals with Grammy Award winning singer and songwriter Peter Cetera, appearing with the Nashville Symphony Orchestra. Three days later on January 16, Melinda Doolittle (BM '99) was the headline singer for the Nashville Symphony's Martin Luther King Day "Let Freedom Ring" Concert.[40]

On October 18, 2010 two Belmont Alumni, Travis Cottrell (BM '92) and Melinda Doolittle (BM '99) performed at Carnegie Hall in New York City with the New American Symphony Orchestra and Chorus, Eric

Knapp, conductor. Melinda Doolittle was also scheduled to perform with the Boston Pops Orchestra in their 2010-11 series.

On January 22, 2011 two Belmont student String Quartets participated in a concert at the Blair School of Music celebrating the "Year of Collaborative Music," sponsored by the Nashville Area Music Teachers Association. The Belmont String Quartets were coached by Belmont violin teachers Elisabeth Small and Tracy Silverman.[41]

Maestro Giancarlo Guerrero Visits Belmont

Maestro Giancarlo Guerrero became Conductor of the Nashville Symphony Orchestra in 2008, leading the Orchestra in very short time to three Grammy Awards, and bringing the orchestra to national prominence. He showed a strong interest in connecting with many facets of the Nashville musical community, and he was therefore enthusiastic about speaking to the Belmont music student body on February 25, 2011. His presentation for the students was humorous, informative, and inspiring. A native of Costa Rica, he spoke about how fortunate he was to have musical experiences in a third world country, and he encouraged students to be grateful for the wealth of their musical education. He also encouraged students to practice their craft with intensity and enthusiasm, taking advantage of every learning opportunity. His speech was warmly received by Belmont students and many took time to speak with him personally after the presentation. He was genuinely interested in each student and was an inspiration for music majors. The charisma of his conducting attracted numerous students to Nashville Symphony concerts, allowing them to take advantage of this important musical resource in Nashville.

Belmont Chorale 40th Anniversary

Jerry Warren, Chair of the Department of Music, founded the Belmont Chorale in the 1969-70 school year. Over 40 years the Chorale had five directors: Dr. Jerry Warren (1970-1984); Mrs. Sherry Kelly (1985-1998); Dr. Timothy Sharp (1998-2000); Edgar Scruggs, (2000-2007); and Jeffery Ames (2008-   ). In addition to annual tours in the U.S., the Chorale has travelled overseas to The St. Moritz Choral Festival in Switzerland (1974 and 1987), Czechoslovakia, Hungary, Romania, and Yugoslavia (1989), England (1999), China (2007) and Italy (2011). The Chorale has recorded albums of the works of Jean Berger, Jester Hairston, Daniel Pinkham, and Robert Ward.

The 40th Anniversary Celebration began with a reception on Friday afternoon, May 6, 2011 followed by a dinner of former Chorale members and directors in the Vince Gill Room. Pictures from historic Chorale events were shown on a screen before the dinner. Former Chorale directors Jerry Warren, Sherry Kelly and Timothy Sharp spoke about their memories, both profound and humorous, from their years with the Chorale. At the end of the dinner a group of alumni made an announcement that they were cooperating with the Office of Development to establish a scholarship in honor of Dr. Jerry Warren as Founding Director of the Chorale. The music alumni making the plans for this scholarship were Catherine Brown Byrd ('79), Darrell Wiley ('79), Chris Krause ('80) and Dr. Timothy Sharp ('76). Julie Thomas ('79), Chorale alumna and staff member of the Belmont Alumni Office, provided leadership in planning the reunion dinner.

On May 7 Chorale alumni rehearsed with the current Belmont Chorale preparing for the afternoon concert. At the concert all three returning Chorale directors led a choral selection performed during their time as director. The Chorale performed their spring concert as part of the reunion and also as a preview of their upcoming concert tour to Italy. The Chorale Reunion was a time of renewing friendships and connections with Belmont for those who returned to their Alma Mater.[42]

Belmont Chorale Tour to Italy (May 15-25, 2011)

The Belmont Chorale Italian tour was accompanied by Dr. Jeffery Ames, Director, and music faculty members Dr. Jane Warren and Dr. Richard Shadinger. Shadinger taught a course on "Music in Italy" for 14 of the students on the journey. The tour began in Milan with a day of sightseeing, included the Church of St. Ambrogia and the massive Milan Cathedral. Travel northward took the Chorale into the Italian Alps and its first concert in Trento at the Chiesa di San Francesco Saverio. Next was the city of Venice, which was a favorite of many of the students. A concert at the Chiesa di San Salvador was the climax of the stay in Venice. The art treasures of Florence were sampled by the Chorale before a concert at the Chiesa Santa Maria della Ricci. A stopover in Assisi on the way to Rome was a high point of the journey with its historic churches and its beautiful sunlit views across the Umbrian landscape. The stay in Rome provided a feast of historic sites and great works of art. Sights of Rome visited were St. Peter's Basilica, the Vatican Museum, the Sistine Chapel, the Roman Forum and the Pantheon. The final concert of the tour was sung in the grand Baroque church Santa Maria Montesanto. The churches were packed for all the concerts with enthusiastic audiences. Chorale members gained knowledge of art and history from the travel while serving as excellent musical ambassadors for Belmont University.[43]

Recording Projects

Earlier recording projects of the School of Music had included *Kaleidoscope* (1992), *Christmas at Belmont* (1996), and CDs by the Belmont Chorale (1990s). There had long been a need for a CD representing the wide range of student ensembles to use for recruiting purposes. In 2008 such a CD was released, entitled *Belmont University School of Music, Vol. 1*. The CD was produced by Professor Keith Mason and featured 15 ensembles from the School of Music. The CD was creatively packaged with a graphic design provided by students in the Department of Art. In 2011 Vol. 2 was released updating the concept with more recent performances of 12 ensembles, representing the wide variety of groups in the School of Music. The plan to provide regular updates of recordings was very productive in recruiting students.

Early in his tenure as President, Dr. Fisher began to send an annual Christmas CD to alumni, donors and friends of the University. Each year this short CD featured several selections of Christmas music by Belmont performance groups drawn from Christmas concerts and "Christmas at Belmont" telecasts, providing a unique and festive holiday greeting to the constituencies of Belmont. Beginning in 2003, a video was made from each televised production of "Christmas at Belmont" which was used for public relations purposes by the University and the School of Music. This video project was a natural way to build on the success of the national broadcasts and provided further publicity for the School of Music.

Debut of the New Concert Band and String Chamber Orchestra

The School of Music's woodwind and brass programs grew gradually over a decade and by 2009 the Wind Ensemble could not accommodate the increasing number of instrumental majors. Dr. Barry Kraus, Director of University Bands, led in the decision to form a new ensemble called the Concert Band to attract non-music majors and to provide a secondary ensemble for developing music majors. With the formation of the new ensemble, the Wind Ensemble had the ability to play more advanced repertoire, and to compete for invitations to perform for various music educators' conferences.

The growth of Belmont's string program over a period of two decades was remarkable. By 2010 the University Symphony Orchestra had grown to symphonic size, but could not accommodate all the string players who wished to perform with the orchestra. Dr. Robert Gregg, Conductor of the Symphony Orchestra, proposed forming a new String Chamber Orchestra to provide performance opportunities for students who could not play with the University Symphony. The new ensemble met several needs: a place for less experienced players; an opportunity for non-music majors to continue playing while in college; experience for future instrumental music educators; and ensemble experiences for music majors who played stringed instruments. In addition, the Chamber Orchestra gave graduate ensemble interns an opportunity for conducting experience and provided more opportunities for instrumental majors to perform concertos on their principal instrument.

The Belmont String Chamber Orchestra made its debut on October 7, 2011 in a noontime outdoor performance in the School of Music Atrium, the perfect fall weather providing a lovely environment for the orchestra's first performance. 32 string players played an engaging program consisting of *Andante Festivo* by Jean Sibelius, Violin Concerto in G Minor, Op. 12, no. 1 by Vivaldi and *St. Paul's Suite* by Holst. The soloist for the Vivaldi Concerto was Violin Performance Major Julia Johnson. An important new facet of the string program was now in place, providing a new performance option for string players.[44]

2011 "Christmas at Belmont" Broadcast on PBS

December 5, 2011 marked the third time that "Christmas at Belmont" was performed at the Schermerhorn Symphony Center and videorecorded for broadcast on the Public Broadcasting System. The celebrity host for 2011 was a Laura Bell Bundy, a young Broadway star and an emerging country music artist. Bundy had been a stage performer since childhood and had recently been nominated for a Tony Award for her portrayal of

Elle Woods in the Broadway musical *Legally Blond*. In 2008 she moved to Nashville to further her career as a singer, releasing her first country album in 2010 under the Mercury label. Her singing and dancing ability, along with her youth and stage presence, made her an excellent addition to the Belmont students with whom she shared the stage.

Since this was the third time that the concert had been presented and recorded at the Schermerhorn, the sound and visual aspects of the production improved with experience. The generous gifts from the Alvin and Sally Beaman Foundation and the Jack C. Massey Foundation once again provided funding for the production, which was broadcast on Thursday, December 22, 2011 with approximately one million viewers. This national exposure continued to give Belmont University and The School of Music incalculable public relations and recruiting presence across the country.

Music Librarian Tim Gmeiner Retires

Tim Gmeiner, Music and Media Librarian in Belmont's Bunch Library, retired from his post on December 16, 2011. Over his 33 years of service to the music library he provided stellar leadership in guiding the development of the collection to its current status as a comprehensive music research collection. When Gmeiner came to Belmont as the first full-time library faculty member devoted to the music collection, the music library held a bare-bones collection of basic books, reference works and recordings. Thirty years later the 2006 NASM visiting evaluating committee hailed the library music collection as the "crown jewel" of the School of Music.[45] Only careful, steady and strategic acquisitions by the music librarian could account for such a remarkable growth. Certainly one factor in this remarkable development was gradually increased funding for library acquisitions as Belmont grew as a university.

In an interview Gmeiner was asked about important events in the Music Library which stand out. One which immediately came to mind was the acquisition in 1989 of the Uttinger Collection of classical recordings. This collection doubled the size of the library's recording holdings, causing a big step forward in availability of recorded works to music students. One aspect of his work that demanded his attention over the years was the changing technology for accessing information. When he began his work at Belmont, there were still many 78 RPM recordings in the collection, although 33⅓ recordings were the standard at the time. For a while cassette recordings were popular before Compact Discs became the main format for recordings. Every change brought about new playback equipment and changes in housing the media. For many years music periodicals were usually bound for future reference or kept on microfilm rolls. Because of space issues microfiche began to replace bound copies and microfilms. In more recent times journal articles are available in on-line computer databases. Thousands of recordings and videos are now available on on-line databases and the Music Library subscribes to many of these at substantial cost. Every few years something changes in technology which brings new (and usually more convenient) ways of accessing printed and listening materials.[46]

The First Decade in a New Millennium

It seemed that the last notes of Beethoven's "Ode to Joy," sung by the Belmont Oratorio Chorus in May of 2000, had barely faded away before vast changes had occurred in the School of Music. The first decade of the next thousand years had brought about regular performances of "Christmas at Belmont" on the Public Broadcasting System, media attention for outstanding performances, enrollment growth, new technologies, successful fund-raising initiatives, and faculty transitions. In addition, all of these changes were happening in the context of a university on the move with constant building projects, and an increase of its national reputation. The fast pace of change was a challenge, but these were met with steadiness of purpose and careful long-range planning.

PART VII
A Trajectory for the Future
(2012–2016)

Dr. Cynthia R. Curtis, Professor of Music (1980-1991); Dean of the School of Music (1991-2016); Dean of the College of Visual and Performing Arts (1999-2016)

CHAPTER SIXTEEN

A High Profile
for the School of Music

The four year period from 2012 to 2016 was dominated by the anticipation, the construction, and the celebration of the new McAfee Concert Hall, undoubtedly one of the premiere events in the history of the School of Music. The potential for a space that could showcase student and faculty talent in a beautiful venue with superb acoustics brought much excitement. While the construction of the new concert hall was the dominant event of this period, it provided the backdrop for a time of remarkable accomplishments by students, alumni and faculty of the School of Music.

New Music Library Initiatives

In March, 2012 Lina Terjesen Sheahan came to Belmont as the new Media Librarian for the Bunch Library. She had earned the MLS in Library Science and an MM in Historical Musicology from the University of Buffalo, and had gained valuable experience as an intern at the Library of Congress where she archived the papers of important American composers such as Lucas Foss, Morton Gould, Roy Harris and Louise Talma. Prior to her appointment to Belmont, she served for one year as a music cataloger at Gettysburg University. As a new librarian, she immediately began to see ways of broadening the use of the Belmont Music Library and Media Center. In an effort to unify the music and media collections, she designed and brought about the "Popular Media Collection," relocating the existing collection from the first floor to the Media Center and expanding it with current holdings from the Media Center collection. By increasing the collection's browseability, she made it available to any student interested in award-winning CDs and DVDs. In addition, she began to evaluate many of the older media items (such as LP recordings) for weeding in order to provide space for new acquisitions, as well as back issues of music journals previously stored in Collection Management. With a desire to reach out to students and inform them about the resources in the Music Library, she started a Facebook page for the Music Library and began to embed herself in the Graduate Research courses and first-year Music History courses. Her outreach efforts extended to displays in and around the library, highlighting items in the Music Special Collections, as well as updates to the technology in group listening/viewing rooms. All of these initiatives had a direct impact on the use of the Music Library, and statistics show that the Music Library and Media Center are more lively and well-used than ever.[1]

Encore Award Recipient: Conductor Teresa Cheung

The fifth recipient of the Encore Award was Teresa Cheung, respected conductor and 1988 Belmont graduate in Piano Performance. Cheung was conductor of the Altoona (PA) Symphony Orchestra as well as resident Conductor of the American Symphony Orchestra in New York City. In addition, she directed the orchestra at Bard College and was Assistant Conductor for the Bard Music Festival and Summerscape. She served as a clinician for Lincoln Center's "Meet the Artist" program since 2007 and made a national name for herself as guest conductor for orchestras and opera companies across the country. As an opera conductor, she led the American premieres of Franz Schrecker's *Die ferne Klang*, Robert Schumann's *Genova*, and Marc Blitzstein's *Regina*.

The presentation of the Encore Award to Cheung occurred on February 14, 2012 when she conducted both the String Chamber Orchestra and the University Symphony. She communicated well, and led the Symphony Orchestra in a technically precise and passionate performance of Tchaikovsky's Overture-Fantasy *Romeo and Juliet*. In accepting the Encore Award she expressed appreciation to Belmont faculty for their thorough teaching and individual attention to her development as a young musician. She expressed special appreciation to Dr. Jerry Warren, her teacher in conducting and Dr. Robert Marler, her piano professor. She noted her astonishment at the growth in size and capability of the

University Orchestra, comparing the orchestra to many of the metropolitan orchestras she had worked with as guest conductor. She also provided encouragement to women students who aspire to become orchestral or choral conductors. While admitting that it is not an easy path to follow, Cheung stressed that perseverance pays off, and that there is a place for more women in her field. The presentation of the Encore Award capped off exciting performances by both orchestras.[2]

Milestone for Belmont's Graduate Music Program

On May 4, 2012, the School of Music held its spring Hooding Ceremony for candidates for the Master of Music degree. At this ceremony a record number of graduates, 14 in all, were recognized. Another important aspect of the event was the graduation of the first three candidates for the new MM in Commercial Music: Megan Gleckler Santi, Anna Grace Kimbrough and Nick Palmer. The following list of other graduates for 2012 indicates the breadth and variety of majors in the graduate program: Stephen Aber (Church Music), Haley Arrington (Vocal Performance), Melissa Edgington (Violin Performance), Amy Frederick (Piano Performance), Monica Gibbs (Vocal Pedagogy), Carrie Griffin (Music Composition), Michael O'Gieblyn (Violin Performance), Alan Puglisi (Percussion Performance), Amy Stennett (Cello Performance), Ryan Traub (Vocal Performance), and Cory Winters (Music Composition). In the Hooding Ceremony, the students were honored with words of appreciation from their committee mentors and were presented with their hoods to be worn at the university commencement ceremony. This intimate occasion for graduates, faculty and parents is a special time to recognize graduate students before the larger commencement later in the weekend.[3]

Music Faculty Members Perform
with the Nashville Symphony at Carnegie Hall

The Nashville Symphony Orchestra was invited to be a part of a May, 2012 Spring Festival in New York City featuring important American orchestras in concerts at Carnegie Hall. On May 12, 2012 the Nashville Symphony performed a daunting program of works by Charles Ives, Percy Grainger and Terry Riley. Belmont was well represented in the concert. Dr. Chris Norton, Professor of Percussion was one of five conductors for the complex *Universe Symphony* by American iconoclast Charles Ives. The orchestra was divided into five different ensembles, coordinating entrances with a click track and five conductors. Other Belmont performers were Dr. Robert Marler, Elena Bennett, and Andrew Risinger, pianos; Keith Nicholas, cello; Daniel Lochrie, clarinet; Dawn Hartley, bassoon; Radu Rusu, horn; Patrick Kunkee, trumpet; Alison Gooding, violin; Todd London, percussion; and Belmont alumnus, Alan Fey, percussion. Terry Riley, one of America's most important living composers, was commissioned to write a new concerto for electric violin and orchestra featuring Tracy Silverman, Belmont's instructor in jazz violin and the world's most accomplished performer on the instrument. Hundreds of enthusiastic Nashvillians attended the concert in New York, cheering the symphony in a triumphant performance.[4] Belmont's role in this important musical event with Nashville's cultural flagship performing ensemble was evident, indicating the importance of Belmont's place in the classical music world of Nashville.

Faculty Chamber Ensembles at Piccolo Spoleto

Belmont's Camerata Chamber Ensemble often performed string quartets as part of its annual concert series. On May 25, 2012, the Belmont String Quartet, consisting of Elisabeth Small, first violin; Gerald Greer, second violin; Sarah Cote, viola; and Keith Nicholas, cello, performed a concert during the first day of the prestigious Piccolo Spoleto Festival in Charleston, SC. The quartet performed two challenging works, Mendelssohn's String Quartet in F Minor, Op. 80 and Bartok's String Quartet No. 2.

In the following year, on May 28, 2013, The Belmont Organ Trio, made up of Andrew Risinger, organ, Carolyn Treybig, flute and Joel Treybig, trumpet, performed in the Piccolo Spoleto Festival. Their diverse program of music from the 18th and 21st centuries was performed in Charleston's historic Bethel United Methodist Church to a full audience.

Faculty Honors and Achievements

On January 16, 2012 Bruce Dudley, Professor of Commercial Piano, performed a piano concert entitled "Mostly Monk" at the Blair School of Music of Vanderbilt University. The concert was a unique "double quartet" performance, with four of Nashville's best jazz players plus a string quartet.

216

The performance was a concert version of Dudley's recent CD "Mostly Monk." Later in the year on August 12 Dudley presented a concert at the Steinway Piano Gallery as an event to celebrate the release of his new CD entitled "The Solo Sessions."

In February, 2012 Dr. Alex Graham, Assistant Professor of Saxophone, announced that Belmont students would be auditioned to work as musicians at the Grand Hotel on Mackinac Island, Michigan. Graham serves as Music Director at the iconic resort, planning and coordinating the extensive roster of musicians for the various evening entertainments and dances at the hotel. Seven Belmont students were chosen to perform during the summer of 2012 where they gained invaluable playing skills by rehearsing during the days and performing at night. This became an ongoing learning and employment opportunity for Belmont commercial music majors. In addition, Dr. Graham was a performer and lecturer for the North American Saxophone Alliance Bi-Annual Conference in March of 2012 at Arizona State University.

In February, 2012 Roy Vogt, Instructor in Bass, was featured in an extensive interview in the February issue of *Bass Music Magazine*. The article gave a detailed profile of Vogt, his career, and his philosophy of teaching. The article, entitled "From Bedroom to Business: How to Make a Living as a Working Musician with Roy Vogt," focused on his teaching techniques used with his large studio of bass students at Belmont. Additionally, in January of 2013 Vogt was presented in a video interview with Erica Cantrell posted on the website of the Mel Bay Music Corporation. The video was part a series of music videos featuring some of America's great jazz performers.[5]

Dr. Mark Whatley performed major baritone roles with opera companies such as Glimmerglass Opera, Nashville Opera, and Birmingham Opera. In 2011 he sang *Carmina Burana* for the Nashville ballet and the Fauré *Requiem* with the Houston Choral Society. In 2012 he served as cantor for a worship service for the national convention of the American Guild of Organists with the Westminster Presbyterian Church Choir. In the same year, he also toured France and Switzerland as baritone soloist with the Westminster Presbyterian Church Choir. In addition, he recorded his first CD with organist Phillip Kloeckner entitled "Exotic Variations" released in 2013.

Dr. Jeffery Ames was the guest conductor of the DODDS–Europe Honors Music Fest in Wiesbaden, Germany. Ames worked with 89 high school students from military families from throughout Europe for five days, culminating in a concert at Wiesbaden's Kurhaus on March 31, 2011. The concert was broadcast live on-line through the Defense Department website. In *Stars and Stripes* (March 31, 2011) Mark Patton quoted Dr. Ames as saying, "They are a wonderful choir to work with, very responsive."[6]

Dr. Madeline Bridges, Professor of Music Education and Associate Dean for Academic Studies, served as the national President of The Choristers Guild and was the Campus Administrator for the annual Tennessee Arts Academy. In 2011 she completed the compilation of *The Book of Church Songs and Spirituals* with music educator John M. Feierabend (GIA Publications, Inc.)[7]

On April 12 and 14, 2012 Dr. Keith Moore, Coordinator of Vocal Studies, performed the role of Larkens in the Nashville Opera's production of Puccini's *La Fanciulla del West*, prompting positive notice in *The Nashville Tennessean's* review of the production.[8]

Elisabeth Small participated in panels at two sessions at the National American String Teachers Association Conference. The first was "Kreutzer Cubed: A Trio of Pedagogues Share and Compare Teaching Strategies" with teachers from Indiana University and Penn State University. The second was "String Performance at the Heart of the University." Small also presented master classes and performances for the South Carolina American String Teacher's Association state conference, as well as the South Carolina Governor's School for the Arts string program.[9]

Zoro, Belmont's internationally known percussion teacher, published a book in 2012 entitled *The Big Gig: Big-Picture Thinking for Success* (Alfred Music Press), dealing with the vocational, personal, and spiritual aspects of achieving a successful music career.[10] In connection with the book, Zoro made numerous appearances on radio and television, including Fox News with Lauren Green and appearances on Glenn Beck's "Liberty Treehouse." Known for being the drummer for Lenny Kravitz and other legendary performers, Zoro was also honored at the nation's capital as part of The White House "Fatherhood Champions of Change Convening on Engaging Men." He was among a select group recognized for promoting responsible fatherhood and mentoring of boys.

The spring 2012 issue of *Fiddler Magazine* featured Belmont alumna and fiddle instructor Tammy Rogers in an extensive interview about her career as one of America's premiere fiddlers and teachers. A 1987 Belmont graduate in Violin Performance, she went on to complete the MM in Violin

Performance Pedagogy in 2010. She became known for playing fiddle and singing vocals with the popular bluegrass group, The SteelDrivers.[11]

On May 3, 2012 *The Nashville Scene* published a lengthy article about Belmont's electric violin teacher, Tracy Silverman, who has been called by the BBC as "the greatest living exponent of the electric violin." The six-page article, entitled "String Theory," reported on a new Concerto for Electric Violin composed especially for Silverman by Terry Riley, one of America's most important composers in the minimalist style. The concerto was performed by the Nashville Symphony Orchestra on May 3 in Nashville prior to a performance by the orchestra and Silverman at Carnegie Hall in New York City on May 12. The article included information about Tracy Silverman's busy teaching schedule for jazz/rock violin students at Belmont.[12]

Dr. Joel Treybig performed Anthony Plog's *Jocaan Trio*, on May 23 at the 2012 International Trumpet Guild Conference at Columbus State University. Additionally, Dr. Treybig continued to perform regularly as a trumpet player for several orchestras, including the Chattanooga and Nashville Symphonies.[13]

Dr. Robert Marler was named as permanent keyboard player for the Nashville Symphony Orchestra, performing on piano, celesta, and harpsichord. With a significant number of new compositions programmed by the orchestra, the piano and celesta played by Marler have been prominent in Symphony performances.[14]

Dr. Chris Norton was appointed in 2008 as Conductor and Artistic Director of the Nashville Philharmonic Orchestra, a volunteer community orchestra made up of high-level Nashville musicians. The mission of the orchestra is to bring great orchestral music to a wide audience through its free concerts. In addition, since 2002, Norton has performed and recorded with Alias, a Nashville chamber ensemble known for its cutting-edge repertoire and superior performances. In December, 2013 he conducted the Nashville Symphony Orchestra in its performances of The *Nutcracker* with the Nashville Ballet. He performs in the summer with the Peninsula Music Festival Orchestra in Wisconsin. Additionally, he performs regularly with the professional percussion quintet Sympatico, composed of outstanding percussion teachers from universities across the country.[15]

Dr. Terry Klefstad, a noted Shostakovich scholar, had two items published in 2012. She contributed a chapter "A Soviet Opera in America" to the book *Contemplating Shostakovich: Life, Music and Film* by Alexander Ivashkin and

Andrew Kirkman.[16] The second item was an article published in *Music and Politics* (Spring 2012) entitled "Shostakovich and the Peace Conference."[17] In addition, she began research and writing of a book about Bill Pursell, Belmont's nationally-known composer. Her research and writing has provided the basis for her Music and Discourse lectures in the School of Music.

Dr. Virginia Lamothe, Musicology, presented a paper at the national meeting of the American Musicological Society on November 12, 2011 in San Francisco. The topic of her paper was "The Cardinal-Patron as Saint: Opera and the Oratorio in Seventeenth-Century Rome." This presentation followed the publication of two major articles in musicology journals: "Dancing at a Wedding: Some Thoughts on Performance Issues in Claudio Monteverdi's 'Lasciate I monti' (*Orfeo*, 1607)" published in *Early Music* (November, 2008)[18] and "Fanning the Flames of Love: Hidden Performance Solutions for Claudio Monteverdi's *Ballo delle ingrate* found in Renaissance Dance," published in *Performance Practice, Issues and Approaches* (2009).[19]

Professor Sandra Dudley presented jazz vocal master classes at Middle Tennessee State University and Trevecca University in the spring of 2013. Her performances as a jazz vocalist included the Memphis Jazz Festival in 2012 and the Cookeville Jazz festival in 2013. She served on the board of the Nashville Jazz Workshop and created new jazz courses for the Jazz Workshop.[20]

Student Ensemble Achievements

On March 25, 2011 the Belmont Strings, Elisabeth Small director, performed Bach's Brandenburg Concerto No. 5 for *Bachanalia*, a Bach Festival held annually at Christ Church Cathedral in Nashville.

On April 13, 2011 members of the Belmont Guitar Ensemble, Robert Thompson, director, presented a concert on Nashville's Public Radio Station 91.1 on the program "Live in Studio C."

Travis Patton, Commercial Music Violin Major ('13), was the Senior Division Grand Prize Winner of the Eclectic String Festival. Patton also was the lead performer for the internationally-acclaimed string ensemble, Barrage. Other Belmont students performing with Barrage were Daniel Pentecost ('10) and Lindy Donia ('07). After a world tour, Barrage performed in Atlanta for the convention of the American String Teachers Association in summer, 2012. Barrage was featured on the cover of the

February, 2012 issue of *American String Teacher* prior to the Atlanta performance.

In March, 2012 the Belmont Chorale, Dr. Jeffery Ames, director, performed at the Southern Regional Conference of the American Choral Directors Association in Winston-Salem, NC. The concert was entitled "Singstunde," the traditional Moravian Love Feast. The concert was performed in the historic Home Moravian Church in Old Salem. In October, 2013, the Chorale performed in Nashville for the national convention of The National Association for Music Education (formerly MENC).

On April 6, 2011 the Belmont University Wind Ensemble, Barry Kraus, conductor, presented a concert on the opening night of the Tennessee Music Educators Association State Conference on the stage of the Grand Ole Opry House. This was the first time Belmont's Wind Ensemble had been chosen through a juried selection process to perform at this conference.

In September and October, 2012 Belmont student ensembles presented a series of Sunday afternoon concerts at Cheekwood Botanical Gardens and Art Museum. The six-week series began on September 23 and went through October 28. The groups performing were Bluegrass Ensemble, String Chamber Orchestra, Small Jazz Group, Woods Piano Scholars, Classical and Jazz String Quartets, and Student Brass and Flute Ensembles.

On November 4, 2012 The Belmont Bluegrass Ensemble under the leadership of Michael McLain performed at the Country Music Hall of Fame as part of the museum's instrument demonstration series. In the program each student talked about their instrument and demonstrated its sounds and capabilities. After this presentation the ensemble played a program together demonstrating the sound of the Bluegrass band.

Representative Alumni 2000-2014

In the new millennium the number of alumni increased dramatically as the enrollment of the school grew. With the tremendous talent among alumni of this era, the ones listed represent only a small percentage of the students who are working in various fields of music across the country: Brandon Fraley (2000), Songwriter/performer; Patrice Jegou (2000), opera performer; Christine Poythress (2000), music instructor, MTSU; Daniel Kirkley (2001), commercial singer in New York City; Josh

Turner (2001), award-winning country artist; Jeremy Fritts (2002), classical guitar performer/teacher; Christopher Gregg (2002), saxophonist, church musician; John Marc Mulkey (2002), church musician; Paul Nelson (2002), cellist, composer, arranger; Christia Starnes (2002), classical singer; Joshua Wright (2002), music educator; Rachel Fogarty (2003); composer, collaborative pianist; Mark Hagewood (2003), choral director; Lauren Lucas (2003), commercial singer, recording artist; Tyler Merideth (2003), orchestra conductor, Montgomery Bell Academy; Jeremy Parrish (2003), Metropolitan Opera Chorus; Emily Tello Speck (2003), musical theatre professor, Belmont University; Silas Stamey (2003), commercial singer; Amy Zigler (2003), musicology teacher; Samantha Barnsfather (2004), musicology teacher; Michael Berg (2004), music faculty, Baylor University; Boh Cooper (2004), commercial pianist; Chris Cropsey (2004), medical doctor; Andrew Greer (2004), Christian songwriter, performer; Steve Hyman (2004), concert pianist, medical doctor; Mallory Yerger (2004), elementary music teacher; Rebecca Covington (2005), Broadway performer; Derek Deakins (2005), country singer, fiddler; Ryan Greenawalt (2005), commercial/musical theater performer; Dr. Nathan Lambert (2005), Professor of Music (Strings and Orchestra), Berry College; Jeannette MacCallum (2005), music educator, church musician, conductor; David Madeira (2005), church musician, composer; Maureen May (2005), piano teacher; Lydia Mulkey (2005), children's choir specialist; Hans Nelson (2005), commercial pianist; Sam Allen (2006), Christian singer, recording artist; Alan Barnes (2006), bass player, music educator; Matthew DeGuzman (2006), Broadway performer; Kristina Siemer (2006), orchestral violinist; Ricky Braddy (2007), commercial singer, American Idol Finalist; Giacomo Fiore (2007), classical guitarist, teacher, San Francisco Conservatory; Craig Madole (2007), string music educator, conductor, Nashville Youth Repertory Orchestra; Molly Skaggs (2007), country singer, songwriter; David Edgington (2008), Head, music department, Nashville State Community College; Megan Gleckler Santi (2008), instructor, Belmont University; Mary Maples (2008), music educator; Melanie Parobek (2008), commercial violinist; Cara Pollock (2008), commercial pianist; Matthew Slemp (2008), church musician; Christopher Smallwood (2008), piano teacher, pianist for touring show Rain; Kyle Baker (2009), composer; Steve Mauldin (2009), composer/arranger/producer; Nicholas Palmer (2009), guitarist, instructor, Belmont University; Charity Callahan (2010), violin teacher, orchestra conductor, Greenville College; Monica Coombs (2010), administrator, Naxos Records; Randy Craft (2010), pianist/songwriter; Janelle Gansky (2010), choral music educator; Blane Howard (2010), country singer; Daniel Pentecost (2010), violinist, performer with Barrage; Gerald Senechal (2010), organist, church musician; Chester Thompson (2010), professional drummer, instructor, Belmont University; Lauren Turner (2010), Broadway performer; Deonte' Warren (2010), Broadway performer; Joshua Eric Wright (2010), Christian singer; Ben Laxton (2011), musical theater performer; Garrett Overcash (2011), violinist; James Wells (2011), church musician, assistant conductor, Nashville Children's Choir; Stephen Aber (2012), organist, church musician; Eric Bikales (2012), pianist, recording artist; Amy Fredricks (2012), pianist, instructor, Belmont University; Scott Hearn (2012), trombonist, Marine Bands; Michael O'Gieblyn (2012), orchestra violinist; Christopher Rayis (2012), pianist, composer in New York City; Eric Taylor (2012), music educator; Ryan Ogradny (2013), country fiddler; Elias Salazar (2013), music teacher, Ensworth School; Joshua Watkins (2013), percussion teacher, University of Trinidad and Tobago; Bill Alexson (2014), jazz/commercial pianist.

School of Music Embraces Technology

Website -Throughout the 1990s and into the new Millennium the use of website media became an increasingly powerful and important means of presenting information about the work and mission of the School of Music. Belmont embraced the University website as the primary means of getting its information out to the public, and the School of Music led the way in updates for its website, making it more sophisticated and user-friendly. At the present, the School of Music website is a state-of-the-art place where prospective and current students can find all the information they need concerning audition requirements, faculty information, curriculum information, and concert schedules. The website has the potential for an increasing number of video samples, including concert excerpts, a short documentary on Belmont's Jazz Ensemble, clips from "Christmas at Belmont," and a Steinway ad featuring Belmont and its new McAfee Concert Hall. A School of Music staff member keeps the website current.

Facebook – The School of Music maintains a Facebook page which reaches hundreds of friends, parents, students and prospective students. The page posts information about news and accomplishments in the School of Music and music alumni, upcoming events, and connects to YouTube videos of Belmont performances and events. It is perhaps the most current way to keep up with the pulse of School of Music activity.

Twitter – A Twitter account is used to post quick and recent information about events in the School of Music and responses to those events. It is one of the best ways to reach the current student generation.

E-Newsletter – The E-Newsletter is an electronic newsletter sent to a large constituency monthly with information about the concert calendar and news of the School of Music. The target for this medium is parents of students, alumni, faculty members and community friends.

CVPA 411 – CVPA 411 is a newsletter emailed every Monday during the academic year to all students in the College of Visual and Performing Arts. Its purpose is to remind students about concerts, exhibits, plays, lectures and events for the week, as well as deadlines, and important meetings. CVPA 411 is designed and written by a student worker in the Public Relations Office of the College of Visual and Performing arts.[21]

On-line Instruction – On-line instruction was slow to come to the School of Music since the "Belmont experience" stressed faculty and student interaction in a smaller classroom setting. However, there was the need in a growing university to provide optional course delivery possibilities for some classes. With this in mind, the School of Music planned for on-line instruction in several specific ways. The first was to provide an on-line study of Music Theory Fundamentals for entering freshman music majors. This sequenced study of theory was designed by Dr. Richard Hoffman to help entering students prepare for the Music Theory Placement Exam. The goal was to assist students to score high enough on the Placement exam to avoid taking the remedial Music Fundamentals course, enabling freshman music majors to go directly into Theory I, keeping them on track with the required freshman music classes. The second use of on-line courses was to provide sections of MUH 2000 (The Music Experience), a course that meets the general education Fine Arts requirement taken by a large number of non-music majors. The on-line delivery was expected to meet the needs of a large number of students. The first on-line courses began in the summer and fall of 2013.

Live Streaming of Concerts – In 2015 the School of Music began live streaming of concerts on-line. Times and lengths for streamed concerts were posted on the School of Music website. This availability was especially appreciated by parents of performing students.

Vital Role of Non-Tenure Full-time Music Faculty

Since the 1970s the Belmont School of Music has used a large number of adjunct instructors due to constant growth. In addition, adjunct faculty also met important teaching needs in areas where there were not enough students to warrant a full-time instructor, including certain instrumental areas such as oboe or viola. Belmont always benefitted from a cultural environment where there was a supply of talented performers and teachers due to Nashville's vibrant arts community and the music industry. It has often been noted that a school of music such as Belmont's could not have grown and thrived in a small or isolated musical environment. The establishment of full-time positions for adjunct teachers benefitted both the School of Music and the instructors. Belmont gained a consistent roster of experienced and talented teachers to help carry the large teaching load at Belmont, and to assist with advising and other important tasks of the school. For the faculty members the positions provided steady teaching employment with benefits and improving salaries. In this arrangement these faculty members became a vital part of the instructional program through their teaching, performance and interaction with students.

In the 2012-14 academic years the following instructors were teaching full-time, many of them having done so for many years: Stephanie Adlington, commercial voice; Nancy Allen, voice and musical theatre; Elena Bennett, piano and class piano; Dr. Lonnie Bond, classical voice; Dr. David Bridges, music theory and musicology; Jo Lynn Burks, musical theatre; Jocelyn Fisher, classical voice: Mary George, classical voice; Megan Gleckler Santi, Company and commercial music; Todd Kemp, percussion and music theory; Dr. Virginia Lamothe, musicology; Todd London, percussion; David McKay, music theory and piano; Emily Tello Speck, musical theatre; Roy Vogt, bass and electric bass and Jamie Wigginton, commercial voice and Phoenix.[22] In 2015 the full-time non-tenure faculty members were given the official title of "Lecturer."

School of Music Staff Contributions to the Success of the School

While talented and dedicated faculty are extremely important to the success of the School of Music, the support provided by staff members is the equally important, though less-visible, part of the team which makes the school run efficiently. The history of the music staff began back in the 1960s when the staff consisted of one secretary for the Department of Music. Music alumni from the 1970s and 80s remember Lila Boyd, who was the ultimate multi-tasker, providing secretarial support for the Department Chair, typing concert programs, as well serving as a receptionist and switchboard operator. Just about any process in the music area, from advising, recruiting, budget planning, and record keeping was either done by, or supported by, the department secretary. Over the years as the university grew, staff positions increased as well. Positions to support public relations and facilities supervision, as well as clerical positions, were among the new positions of staff support.

At the writing of this book the School of Music staff consists of 10 gifted and dedicated individuals who take pride in their work in the School of Music. Their professional and positive interaction with faculty, students and visitors adds immeasurably to the work of the School of Music. Joan Eakin, Administrative Coordinator, provides administrative support for the Dean, coordination of the office staff, as well as serving as the budget manager for the School of Music. April Simpkins, Receptionist and Secretary, is the friendly face of the School of Music Office and owns a number of duties, including assisting with registration and auditions, and supervising a talented group of administrative student workers. Scheduling Coordinator Caroline Scism provides administrative support for the Music Graduate Program and coordinates the complicated scheduling process for the school. Gina Lackore, Undergraduate Program Assistant, provides academic support for the Associate Deans and has the daunting task of designing over 200 printed programs every academic year. Sarah Davis, Director of Public Relations and Advancement for the School of Music, provides press releases, advertisements, brochures and other types of public relations materials and media. She coordinates all fund-raising events and initiatives of the School, and works with the Friends of the Arts at Belmont board. Maren Bishop, Coordinator of Admissions, CVPA, cultivates relationships with prospective students and plans auditions days. Her duties require much record keeping and communicating with the University Admissions Office as well as prospective students. Holly Yearout is the School's Adjunct Liaison and Web Coordinator, working with all of School's adjunct teachers and web media. Rusty King is the School of Music Production/Facilities Manager, overseeing the maintenance and use of School of Music facilities and equipment. He is charged with the production responsibilities for over 300 annual events in the School of Music. He is assisted by Music Facilities Secretary Sally Dodd and Thom Roberts, Music Facilities Assistant. Together they oversee a small army of student crew members who do a variety of tasks including concert stage set-up, concert recording, sound and lighting.[23]

Growth in Concert Presentations

As Belmont grew, the scheduling of concerts of all types became a complex process. With a limited number of performance venues and growing number of students, creativity was needed to make the concert calendar work. A Calendar Committee was formed to determine policies and priorities for making decisions about the concert schedule. The Committee approaches their task as if putting together a giant, complex puzzle in order to meet the needs of ensembles, students, faculty performers and guest artists.

Efficient use of performance spaces was necessary and new spaces were sought. In addition to Massey Concert Hall, Harton Recital Hall and the McAfee Concert Hall, some graduate and faculty recitals were held in the Belmont Mansion, which afforded a pleasant concert space. Junior Commercial Recitals were often performed in the Curb Cafe. The Concert Committee gives priority of evening recital times to student ensembles, major events, faculty recitals and guest artists.

Student Junior and Senior Recital were especially problematic because of the increasing numbers of students performing these events. These were usually scheduled on Fridays, Saturdays and Sundays, often with multiple concerts happening simultaneously. There is an attempt to schedule as many of these concerts as possible in the fall semester, but most of these concerts of necessity must occur near the end of the academic year. The School organized a convenient on-line scheduling process, so that this complicated schedule of concerts happens efficiently every year.

In the 2011-2012 academic year, the School of Music scheduled 244 concerts, broken down in the following categories: 157 undergraduate recitals, 21 graduate recitals, 19 faculty recitals, 57 ensemble concerts, 4 guest recitals and 5 major events. The number 244 did not include master classes and musicology lectures, which would add considerably to the number. The total number of concerts for the 2012-2013 school year was 248, slightly higher than the previous year. The importance of performance is uppermost in a major school of music because philosophically, performance is the outgrowth of music learning. Belmont goes to great lengths to make the performance calendar work efficiently for students because of the important place of performance in the music curriculum.[24]

2012-13 Encore Award: Dr. Alfredo Colman

Dr. Alfredo Colman, Assistant Professor of Musicology and Ethnomusicology at Baylor University, was the 2012-13 recipient of the Encore Award, Belmont's recognition for outstanding alumni in various fields of classical music. Dr. Colman received the BM degree in Church Music in 1993, followed by the MM at Baylor and the PhD in Musicology from the University of Texas, Austin. Dr. Colman is an active writer of articles and a lecturer with notable expertise in South American Music. Dr. Colman also teaches regularly at the Universidad Evangelica del Paraguay in San Lorenzo. His new book, entitled *The Paraguayan Harp: Colonial Transplant to National Emblem*, was published by Music Word Media just days after his visit to Belmont on September 6 and 7, 2012. Colman presented two lectures at Belmont, one on the Paraguayan Harp and one on Israeli folk music influenced by Latin American music. Dr. Colman's visit was enhanced by the presence of alumni who were his fellow students at Belmont.[25]

Back to School Alumni Concert – September 8, 2012

The 2012-13 school year for the School of Music started off with a rousing "Back to School Alumni Concert" on September 8. A group of Commercial Music alumni, under the guidance of Brooks Parker, volunteered to perform the concert as a kick-off for the new school year. Alumni performers included Shelby Baker (2009), Ricky Braddy (2007),

Krysten Terry Hill (2007), Blane Howard (2010), Shelly Johnson (2007), Alvin Love (2007), Daniella Mason (2012) Brooks Parker (2008), Ragdoll (Jason Cox, 2005), Cristina Taddonio (2007), Blake Brandenburg (2011), Chris Dunn (2008), Jason Dyba (2007), Cody Fry (2012), Jake Goss (2009), Melvin Lightford (2008), Jordan Kyle Reynolds (2011), and Paul Gregory Shearer (2006). Jason Dyba served as leader for the band. The concert was an excellent representation of recent graduates who are actively performing in the music industry. The preface on the printed program expressed pride in its alumni: "The School of Music is proud to present the Back to School Concert. As a tribute to the many talented School of Music graduates, alumni return to the stage a 'living proof' of the depth and quality of the Belmont University music program."[26] On September 7, 2013, a second "Back to School Alumni Concert" was performed with many of the same alumni participating. A highlight of this second performance was the surprise presence of guest performer, Amy Grant.

CHAPTER SEVENTEEN

A Year
of Celebration

With announcement on August 20, 2010 of the gift from the McAfee
Foundation to build a new concert hall in the Belmont Heights
Sanctuary, the planning process for the facility began in earnest. The
architect firm of Earl Swenson Associates began working on the details
of the design for the new space, consulting with music faculty members
who would use the space on how the hall was to be used, the size of
performance groups, and storage needs. The major contractors for the
project made up the Design Team: American Constructors, general
contractor; Littlejohn Engineering Associates, engineering specifications;
Ross Bryan Associates, structural engineers; I.C. Thomasson and
Associates, Inc., mechanical, plumbing and electrical design; Akustiks,
acoustical consultants; and Theatre Consultants Collaborative, theatrical
consultant. The Milnar Organ Company was contracted to undertake the
rebuilding of the Aeolian-Skinner organ. The architectural design was
completed by early in 2011 so construction could begin at the end of the
spring semester of 2011.

Two important concepts for the space began to emerge as design
planning for the hall began. First, was the discovery by the acoustical
consultant that the space had the same architectural footprint and volume
as the Tonhalle in Zurich, Switzerland, one of the most famous concert
halls in Europe, noted for its architectural beauty and acoustical
perfection. The second concept was that the new space resembled a
miniature version of the Nashville Symphony's renowned Schermerhorn
Symphony Center. In fact, the hall began to be referred to as "a miniature

Schermerhorn." Because the architect firm of Earl Swenson Associates and the acoustical firm, Akustiks, had both been involved in the Symphony Hall design, their expertise matched this project perfectly.[27]

The first stage of the project was actually a demolition process. By mid-summer 2011, the Belmont Heights sanctuary had been totally gutted with the exception of the balconies. The organ was removed, beginning its restoration. Pews were removed, and the ceiling had been demolished. The raw space remaining was impressively large and acoustically live. On August 1, 2011, Carolyn McAfee came to campus for a "kick-off" event in the hall, signifying the beginning of the construction phase of the space. A large group of faculty, staff and friends of the University gathered in the space to envision what it would become within the next year. To illustrate the sound of the room Dr. Robert Marler performed Debussy's "Reflections in the Water" on a Steinway Concert grand piano provided by the Steinway Piano Gallery of Nashville. At this event President Bob Fisher expressed his appreciation to the McAfee family, "We are very grateful to the McAfee family for this generous gift. Their commitment to the university and support for this project means that we will have a concert hall to match the high quality of our music programs, and one that will appropriately showcase the amazing talent of our performing arts students." Mrs. McAfee responded in her statement "My late husband Jim, my son Tom, daughter-in-law Julie, and I have always been enthusiastic about supporting Belmont as a leader in Christian education. Belmont's School of Music has earned a national reputation for the quality of its programs and the breadth of its vision. Our family is proud to kick off the fundraising efforts for the new concert hall which will match those high standards with a performance space suitable to the talents these programs attract."[28] The construction schedule moved forward at a fast pace since the goal was to complete the project by May, 2012 so the room would be available to accommodate performances for the National Convention of the American Guild of Organists in July, 2012.

Celebration Events Planned for McAfee Concert Hall

While the construction of the hall moved forward, a faculty committee was appointed by Dean Curtis to plan a series of events to showcase the new venue. The committee arrived at a theme for the events,

"A Year of Celebration," and began to plan a series of six concerts to illustrate the flexibility of the hall and its ability to accommodate a variety of acoustical performances. The University provided funding to support the events projected for the 2012-13 academic year:

October 6, 2012, 7:30 – A Celebration of Beginnings – This concert was designed to show a variety of classical ensembles in various combinations, serving as the gala dedicatory event for the new concert hall.

October 23, 2012, 7:30 – A Celebration of Community – A performance by the Grammy-Award-winning Nashville Symphony Orchestra to welcome the Nashville community to the new hall. Under the director of Associate Conductor Kelly Corcoran, the Nashville Symphony's program was designed to showcase the concert hall's excellent acoustics.

December 1, 2:00 and 8:00; December 2, 2012, 2:00 – A Yuletide Celebration – *Christmas at Belmont 2012*, celebrating the spirit of the season with a variety of School of Music ensembles and mass choir performances that show the diversity of Belmont students' talents.

February 15, 2013, 7:30 – A Celebration of Unity – Internationally acclaimed Mezzo-Soprano Denyce Graves and various School of Music ensembles present a concert celebrating the world's diversity with music that brings an awareness of tolerance, peace and unity.

March 25-26, 2013 – A Celebration of Learning - Dr. Richard Taruskin, internationally renowned musicologist and author of the *Oxford History of Western Music*, presents lectures on the history of Russian Music, drawn from a lifetime of musical research and writing.

April 20, 2013, 8:00 – A Celebration of Achievement – The 24th Annual President's Concert ends the year's celebration of the McAfee Concert Hall with music performed by numerous School of Music Ensembles and the presentation of the 2013 Applause Award.[29]

Music Faculty and Staff Preview of McAfee Concert Hall

On April 25, 2012, prior to the ending of the 2012 academic year, the music faculty was given the opportunity to tour the interior of the concert hall as it was nearing completion. Seeing the almost finished hall was exciting to the faculty after a year of anticipation. As the faculty toured the building, workers were finishing the painting, installing balcony seating, and giving the room a thorough cleaning. Many of the organ pipes were in place, but the major work of the organ installation was just beginning. It was obvious to the faculty that in addition to the superb acoustical environment, McAfee Concert Hall was a space of grandeur and beauty.

Two New Steinway Concert Grand Pianos for McAfee

At a Music Faculty meeting on April 23, 2012 Dean Cynthia Curtis announced that donors had been secured for two new Steinway concert grand pianos for McAfee Concert Hall. The donors for one of the pianos were longtime supporters of Belmont, Bill and Sharon Sheriff; Sharon Sheriff was finishing her year as President of the Friends of the Arts at Belmont. The second piano was given by the Andrea Waitt Carlton Family Foundation. Representatives from Belmont travelled to New York City to choose Steinways for the concert hall on June 13 and 14. Sharon Sheriff and Paul Moore from the FAB Board made the trip along with Dean Cynthia Curtis, Sarah Davis, Director of PR and Advancement, and Bill Metcalf of the Nashville Steinway Piano Gallery. Piano faculty members Dr. Daniel Landes and Dr. Robert Marler were present to play the pianos and make recommendations based on the tone and action of the Steinways available. When the pianos were delivered in the fall, it was clear that excellent choices had been made, because the pianos proved to be perfect for the hall.[30]

Restoration of the Aeolian-Skinner Organ

The pipe organ in Belmont Heights Baptist Church was a 55-rank, three-manual instrument built by the Aeolian-Skinner Organ Company in 1969, widely regarded as the finest organ company in America, building instruments for major churches, universities and concert halls. Mrs. Carolyn McAfee, trained as an organist, was intrigued by the potential of the organ as she considered giving toward the renovation of the space. The organ was a bold instrument, well-suited for a concert hall. Yet, by the time of the renovation it was in need of a major restoration in order to reach its full potential.

The Milnar Organ Company of Eagleville, Tennessee was contracted to undertake the rehabilitation of the organ. It was decided to leave the organ tonally unchanged, since it already possessed beautiful individual ranks and an impressive overall sound. The organ was removed from the premises before the demolition began, so the organ restoration could proceed while the concert hall was being constructed. The rebuilding of the organ included the following components: new electrical contacts and wiring for the entire instrument; new draw knobs for the console; a new Peterson ICS-4000 stop processing system; disassembly, cleaning and reassembly of all reed pipes; cleaning and lubrication of the chime system; revoicing of all mixtures and Festival Trumpet; addition of a new adjustable bench and music desk lamp; refinishing of the console to like-new condition; new metal grill for all openings of pipe chambers, and a new rolling platform for the console, providing easy movement to anywhere on stage. For maximum flexibility, the stage was equipped with six outlets where the organ console could be plugged in. By May, 2012, the Milnar staff was busy reinstalling the organ in the completed space. During the six-week installation, it became obvious that the organ benefitted from the new concert hall in several ways. With the improved acoustical environment, the organ sounded more clearly and boldly in the room. The new HVAC system provided a quiet environment, as well as stability of temperature and humidity ideal for the instrument. Visually, the organ was part of the stunning appearance of the new design of the hall, with the organ pipes soaring above and behind the large stage area. The organ installation was completed just days prior to its debut at the National Convention of the American Guild of Organists.[31]

American Guild of Organists National Convention Concerts at McAfee

From July 1-7, 2012 Nashville hosted the National Convention of the American Guild of Organists. While Nashville was the smallest city to ever host this prestigious convention, the Guild was impressed with the numerous fine concert venues and organs in the city. The convention took advantage of wonderful downtown organs, including those of the Schermerhorn Symphony Center, First Baptist Church, Christ Church Cathedral and West End United Methodist Church. One of the most highly praised concert venues was the new McAfee Concert Hall at Belmont.

Three concerts were held in the McAfee Concert Hall during the week. The first concert held on July 1 was called "Rising Stars" and featured three outstanding young organists who performed advanced organ repertoire. The audience included Mrs. Carolyn McAfee and numerous Belmont guests who were present to hear the first notes performed publicly in the hall. On Thursday, July 5 a concert (performed twice) was divided into two sections. The first part was a performance by the Nashville Chamber Singers (Angela Tipps, conductor) who performed two new works commissioned for the convention: an a cappella choral work, "There is a Flow'r" by Alan Smith; and a large work for choir and orchestra, "The Cry of Jeremiah," by Rosephanye Powell. The second half of the concert was a performance of Baroque masterpieces by an ensemble made up of Matthew Dirst, harpsichord; Colin St. Martin, flauto traverso; and Mary Springfels, viola da gamba. An observation made about this varied concert was that all of the various works on the concert sounded superb in the acoustics of the new hall. An article in the October, 2012 issue of *The American Organist* gave extensive reports on the events and concerts of the convention. The writer of the article on the concerts at Belmont stated "The auditorium is an attractive space, seating perhaps 800 – a fine addition to the variety of venues for the cultural events Nashville has to offer." In the article the McAfee Concert Hall is shown in a prominent picture of the Nashville Chamber Singers in concert.[32]

McAfee Concert Hall Description

The visual design for the hall draws from the great concert halls of Europe, with its shoebox shape, front featuring the organ, large arched windows, large lantern-style chandeliers, sophisticated colors and elaborate woodwork. Finishes include high quality woods for floors, stage surface, and seating. Heavy velvet drapes over the windows can adjust the acoustics for various types of ensembles. The elegant concert hall lobby is notable for its use of art work, fine furnishings, and floors of granite forming classical designs.

Acoustical design for the space was done by Akustiks of South Norwalk, CT with C. Russell Todd as the project manager. Acoustical volume of the room was enlarged 1.5 times the original space by opening up access to the attic above and by steeply raking and lowering the floor-level seating. This gives the room a 2 second occupied room reverberation time providing optimum blend of orchestral and choral sounds. The side balcony overhang was decreased in depth by adding side corridors that serve two purposes: allowing access to parterre (side) seating and providing appropriate side under-balcony geometry for supporting lateral sound reflection to the audience. The area under the parterre seating provides return air path, delivering air at very low velocity through return air tunnels. The attic supply air duct is round to provide acoustical diffusion and is sized to provide air at a very low velocity, so that no HVAC sound is heard. The angle of the rake of the orchestra seating provides excellent visual and acoustic sightlines to performers on the stage. The stage floor is resiliently mounted to serve as a soundboard for low frequency string instruments. The architectural ceiling is sound transparent to allow sound access to the attic above with the coffers providing acoustical diffusion back to the stage. The side pilasters beside the windows serve as enclosures for the heavy velour drapes used to adjust the room reverberation for rehearsals. The pilasters also serve as lateral reflections, returning the sound back into the room. The audience floor is a very hard wood, helping to retain optimum reverberation. The audience chairs have hardwood backs and fabric which resists sound absorption. The existing windows were upgraded to include 1-inch-thick interior glazing which isolates the room from exterior noise and reduces sound absorption in the room. All new interior wall spaces have multi-layer drywall construction for retaining low frequency sound reverberation. Doors to the audience chamber are all acoustical which reduce noise from front and back of house. Sound and light locks are present at entrances to avoid the intrusion of sound and light from exterior spaces. A new sound system is tailored to the room acoustics for voice announcements. Infrastructure is provided for recording performances in the room. A sound isolated control room is provided at the back of the balcony. Appropriate stage and house lighting are designed to the meet the needs of an acoustical concert setting. Pull-out choral risers and terraces for the orchestra are provided for a wide range of orchestral and choral performance configurations. Overhead stage acoustical reflectors are provided to provide cross-stage communication and reflection to the audience.[33]

The exterior of the McAfee Concert Hall was not changed extensively. However, all exterior doors were restored and the special needs entrance was rebuilt. A new loading entrance was provided near the stage on the south side of the facility. New landscaping and lawn space transformed the setting of the building. Sidewalks to the hall were rebuilt and new lighting brightens and highlights the exterior architecture. Four large urns planted with miniature magnolia trees were placed on pedestals in front of the four columns. The church steeple was totally rebuilt and round windows in the base which had been covered in past years were replaced, bringing architectural interest to the tower. New lighting on the steeple allows this Belmont Boulevard landmark to stand out as a beacon in the night sky on campus.

The Tennessean Introduction to McAfee Concert Hall

The Sunday, September 16 issue of *The Tennessean* included an extensive article by Mary Hance entitled "New McAfee Hall Inspires." The article gave a thorough description of the concert hall, calling it "Schermerhorn junior" with the same architects and acoustical consultants as the downtown venue. The full-page article included an interview with Dean Curtis who gave an overview of the scope of the School of Music and how the new concert hall will showcase the talents of student, faculty and guest artists. Dr. Curtis mentioned that "two treasures" of the space were the wonderful acoustics and the spectacular Aeolian-Skinner organ. The page featured a photograph of the University Symphony Orchestra in rehearsal. A sidebar to the article contained a listing of the major concerts of the fall celebrating the opening of McAfee, while another segment focused on Carolyn McAfee, the major donor for the concert hall.[34]

First Concerts in McAfee Concert Hall

The first School of Music concert in McAfee was the Woods Memorial Piano Concert on September 20 performed by Alexander Kobrin, a young Russian pianist who was the Gold Medal winner of the Twelfth Van Cliburn International Piano Competition in 2005. From the first delicate notes of the Mozart Sonata in B flat (K. 333), it was clear that the acoustics of McAfee were something special, because the round tones of the new Steinway were full and clear even at a low volume level. In contrast, the expressive music of Brahms showed that the hall could be filled with Romantic passion and strength. To end the program Kobrin performed Schumann's brilliant *Carnaval*, Op. 9.[35] Long time listeners to concerts at Belmont were aware that for the first time they had heard something remarkable for Belmont - a great artist playing great music on the finest piano available in a beautiful room with superb acoustics, proving that the goals for McAfee Concert Hall had been achieved.

On September 21 Dr. Richard Shadinger presented the first Music and Discourse lecture in McAfee entitled "Pipe Organ 101." The presentation explained the operation of the pipe organ and the various families of sounds produced. Shadinger played a variety of organ compositions to illustrate how the sounds vary from very quiet sounds to full organ. The numerous students attending the lecture were encouraged to attend the faculty organ concert on October 22 to hear a complete concert on the refurbished Aeolian-Skinner organ.

On October 9 and 11 the first two ensemble concerts were performed in McAfee, giving audiences a chance to hear two new types of sounds in the hall. On October 9 The University Wind Ensemble performed a varied concert (including the Giannini Symphony No. 3 and the impressive "Elsa's Procession to the Cathedral" from Wagner's *Lohengrin*), demonstrating the sound of a large wind group in the room. Since the acoustical volume of the room was increased by one-third, the sound had somewhere to go and the use of the acoustical curtains for the wind ensemble kept the sound from being too harsh or bright.[36]

On October 11 the University Symphony Orchestra began its concert with the Overture to *Russlan and Ludmilla*, followed by the Nashville premiere of Dr. William Pursell's Kaleidoscope, Concerto for Piano and Orchestra, with the composer at the piano. This 1996 work was unusual for Pursell because of its use of a tone row combined with his usual lyrical style. The second half of the concert was Dvorak's colorful Symphony No. 8, Op. 88. The strings of the orchestra found it easy to produce a warm sound without forcing because of the way in which the sound carried. The strings had a naturally good balance with the winds. The hard wood of the stage floor helped to amplify the rich sounds of the cellos and basses.[37] Students from both ensembles remarked how easy it was to make beautiful sounds in such a warm acoustical environment.

The first faculty concert in McAfee on October 22 featured Belmont's two organ teachers, Gregg Bunn and Andrew Risinger in a concert which ranged widely through the organ repertory, showing the immense capabilities of the Aeolian-Skinner pipe organ. Organ works by Bach, Widor, Dupre and Darke revealed the wide variety of warm, soft sounds contrasting with the majestic sound of full organ.[38]

Ribbon-cutting Ceremony for McAfee

At 10:00 on October 5, a Ribbon-cutting ceremony for McAfee Concert Hall was held in front of the building on Belmont Boulevard, where the McAfee family, faculty, students and community friends gathered on this sunny fall morning. Before the ceremony began, the student brass ensemble performed festive music. Attention was given to the lettering above the front portico of the building naming the space "McAfee Concert Hall." In his remarks to the audience President Bob Fisher said "We are incredibly grateful to the McAfee family for their generous gift to make this venue possible. Their commitment to the university has enabled us to build a concert space that matches the high quality of our music programs, and one that will appropriately showcase the amazing talent of our performing arts students. My hope is that the entire Nashville community will be able to enjoy the inspired concerts that will occur in this beautiful new hall." The McAfee family and representative music students joined together in cutting the ribbon in front of the open doors. The attendees were ushered into the hall where various students performed, illustrating the sound in the room with violin, piano and harp music.[39]

Dedicatory Concert for McAfee Concert Hall - A Celebration of Beginnings

One could not envision a more dramatic way to open a new concert hall than the chorus from Vaughan Williams' *Hodie* with the words "Ring out ye Crystal spheres, once bless our human ears." Sung by a huge combined choir with full orchestra, it was an appropriate way to show an opening night crowd the full range of what the hall could accommodate. Following the opening chorus a brass ensemble played a fanfare composed for the concert by Dr. Mark Volker, Associate Professor of Composition. Entitled "To the Trumpeting Place," it included brass and percussion sounding out from the balcony above the audience. Other highlights of the concert were Andrew Risinger playing Widor's *Toccata* (Symphony No. 5) on the organ; Albinoni's *Adagio* in G Minor for the Belmont Strings with organ; Musical Theatre students singing "Do You Hear the People Sing" from *Les Misérables*; and Beethoven's "Hallelujah" from *The Mount of Olives*. There were words of appreciation to the

239

McAfee family from President Fisher and Dean Curtis. At the end of the ceremony the audience joined with the choirs in singing the hymn "When in Our Music God Is Glorified." John Pitcher, a concert reviewer in *Arts Nashville*, was effusive in his praise of the performances and made this observation in his review: "It's no secret that ensembles that routinely play in a great concert hall improve dramatically in quality over time – just think of the strides the Nashville Symphony has made inside the Schermerhorn Symphony Center. Belmont's student and faculty groups will no doubt experience progress in the coming years. Finally, they have a performance space that is worthy of their talents."[40]

The Friends of the Arts at Belmont had raised the $150,000 needed to refurbish the Aeolian-Skinner Organ. At the presentation segment of the concert, Dr. Bob Ikard and Mrs. Ann Lauterbach, representing the FAB board, announced that the organ was to be named "The Cynthia R. Curtis Pipe Organ" in honor of her work as Dean of the School of Music and her leadership in completing the McAfee Concert Hall project. Dean Curtis was totally surprised by the announcement and expressed her appreciation for the honor and the hard work and support of the Friends of the Arts at Belmont. She was presented with a plaque in her honor to be placed in the lobby of the concert hall.

Carolyn Townsend McAfee

Music has always been an essential part of Carolyn Townsend McAfee's life. She graduated from Union University in 1961 with the Bachelor of Music degree with a Major in Organ, and earned a Master of Music in Organ Performance from Vanderbilt University (Peabody College). Mrs. McAfee studied organ under the late Dr. John G. Hughes and the late Dr. Scott Withrow. She has served as organist for Episcopal, Methodist, Presbyterian and Baptist churches. She is a member of the American Guild of Organists, Sigma Alpha Iota and Zeta Tau Alpha. The Visser-Rowland pipe organ at Union University is named in her honor.

Mrs. McAfee has been active in church, children's choirs and civic organizations. She has served on the Board of the Macon (Georgia) Symphony Orchestra and has also served as President of the Macon Symphony Guild. In Macon she is a member of the Morning Music Club. She also served on the Allegro Division of the Atlanta Symphony Associates and currently serves on the Board of the Rome Chamber Music Festival, Rome, Italy.

The Mercer University Board of Trustees named its School of Theology, The James T. and Carolyn McAfee School of Theology in 1997 in honor of Mrs. McAfee and her late husband. In 1995 Union University awarded her a Doctor of Humanities degree. Additionally, Mercer University awarded her the Doctor of Arts degree in 1999.

Mrs. McAfee currently serves on the Board of Trustees for the McAfee Foundation, Belmont University and Mercer University in Macon and Atlanta, Georgia. She and her family have endowed the Townsend School of Music at Mercer University, named in memory of her parents, Raymond Clay and Sophia Malin Townsend. She has been influential in establishing the Townsend-McAfee Institute, a graduate program in church music at Mercer's Townsend School of Music, in conjunction with the McAfee School of Theology.

Mrs. Townsend has one son, Tom McAfee, who is married to the former Julie Crangle of Bolivar, Tennessee. They have two daughters, Zoe and Malin.

It is because of the McAfee family vision for the future of the music programs at Belmont University and their generous commitment to that vision that this great concert Hall stands today.[41]

McAfee Concert Hall Listed in *Nashville Scene's* "Best of Nashville"

The Nashville Scene's annual "Best of Nashville" issue is an anticipated issue because it rates everything from restaurants and performing artists to community leaders and institutions. The McAfee Concert Hall was listed as "Best New Concert Hall." The listing mentioned many of the features of the hall, including the "marvelous acoustics" and the "fabulous 55-rank Aeolian-Skinner pipe organ."[42]

Nashville Symphony Orchestra - A Celebration of Community

As part of the Year of Celebration, the School of Music featured The Nashville Symphony Orchestra on October 28. The free concert brought out a full house, giving the Belmont community and Nashville friends the opportunity to hear the Grammy-Award-Winning orchestra under the direction of Associate Conductor Kelly Corcoran. The concert was a varied one, including short works ranging from Mozart and Wagner to Broadway show tunes. A highlight of the evening was the performance of Guilmant's Introduction and Allegro from Symphony No. 1 for Organ and Orchestra, Op. 42, featuring Belmont's Instructor of Organ and Symphony Organist, Andrew Risinger.[43] The stage of McAfee, roughly the same size as that of the Schermerhorn Symphony Center, easily accommodated the Nashville Symphony. Since the McAfee Hall has about half the seating capacity of the Schermerhorn the listening experience is a much more intimate one than at downtown home of the orchestra. It was observed by some that the Aeolian-Skinner organ seemed to hold its own with orchestra at least as well as the Schermerhorn organ, most likely due to the smaller space the organ sound needs to fill. This concert was the first one with a wider audience of Nashville music lovers, and it was apparent that Nashvillians were becoming aware of the magic of McAfee Concert Hall.

Christmas at Belmont - A Yuletide Celebration

The 2012 version of "Christmas Belmont" had a special quality in the new McAfee Concert Hall. The concert hall with its subtle green colors and wood tones blended perfectly with the huge Christmas floral arrangement behind the organ pipes. The seated risers combined with choir seating on the organ level accommodating huge massed choral groups worked well for the concert which featured a wide range of vocal and instrumental groups. Since McAfee is not a theatre and it lacks large back-stage spaces and elaborate theatrical lighting, the concert presented different challenges of staging compared to Massey Concert Hall and The Schermerhorn Symphony Center. The concert was presented twice on Saturday, December 1 and once on the following day with all three performances full. This yuletide celebration has marked the beginning of the Christmas season of Belmont and much of the Nashville for over a decade.

John Pitcher, writing about the concert in the December 2 issue of *Arts Nashville*, made comments on both the quality of the performances and the venue: "Belmont is celebrating more than just the holidays this weekend. On Saturday night the university presented its annual 'Christmas at Belmont' for the first time in the new McAfee Concert Hall. Every note inside this acoustically marvelous new venue resonated with the clarity of a sleigh bell. Saturday's program served as a showcase of the university's remarkable musical versatility. Belmont's various specialty ensembles performed in every conceivable style – classical, country, bluegrass, pop-rock and Broadway. The performers did justice to every genre." He further commented on the Nashville Children's Choir's "angelic sound," the Belmont Chorale's "polished perfection," the "instrumental virtuosity" of the Belmont strings, and the "the hilarious entertainment" of Company's "Twelve Days of Christmas."[44]

"The Golden Age" of Nashville's Classical Music Scene

The December 6, 2012 issue of the *Nashville Scene's* cover story was intriguingly titled "Nashville Classical Music Scene Enters a Golden Age." The article was a retrospective of 2012 mentioning the performance of Gustav Mahler's "Symphony of a Thousand" by the Nashville Symphony Orchestra and its triumphant concert at Carnegie Hall in New York City. It praised the creative productions of the Nashville Opera and the Nashville Ballet. Among its kudos was a section about the McAfee Concert Hall with the following statement, "Students at Belmont University had a great year, thanks to the opening of the new McAfee Concert Hall. . . . The hall has marvelous acoustics, and the students have a venue worthy of their talents."[45]

Denyce Graves – A Celebration of Unity

Few concerts in the history of The School of Music created more excitement in the Nashville musical community than the "Celebration of Unity" concert on February 15, 2013, featuring Denyce Graves, popular Metropolitan Opera mezzo-soprano. Graves, especially known for title roles in Bizet's *Carmen* and Saint-Saëns' *Samson and Delilah*, has been called by the *USA Today* "an operatic superstar of the 21st Century." Her international accolades are numerous, and her performance at Belmont showed her to be at the top of her vocal ability. The theme for the evening was "A Celebration of Unity," and Graves fit her contributions to the event into that theme. The concert opened with Aaron Copland's majestic *Fanfare for the Common Man*. Music of several cultures was featured including Ginastera's "Malambo" from *Estancia*, Op. 8, performed by the Belmont Symphony Orchestra; "Kyrie" from *A Caribbean Mass* by Glenn McClure, sung by the Belmont Chorale; and The Islamic Call to Prayer sung by Alex Rader, a Musical Theatre Major. Ms. Graves' selections

243

included her signature "Mon Coeur s'ouvre à ta voix" from *Samson and Delilah; the "Habanera" from Carmen; Canto negro* by Montsalvatge; three tradition spirituals; and *Ave Maria* (attributed to Caccini), performed with the Belmont Chorale and the University Symphony Orchestra. The concert ended with the stirring arrangement of "He's Got the Whole World in His Hands" by African-American composer Margaret Bonds.

John Pitcher lauded Ms. Graves in his review of the concert: "One of the Metropolitan Opera's most celebrated stars, Graves is famous not for just singing roles but inhabiting them. Something like that happened in her opening aria. She sang this melody with urgency and determination, as if her life depended on it. She seemingly had become Delilah. Her sound was unforgettable. She opened with dusky notes that emanated from somewhere deep in her chest. As the aria progressed, she seamlessly shifted registers, singing top notes which were pure and creamy. . . . In the "Habanera" she became the fiery gypsy girl, delivering a performance that was at once sensuous, flirtatious and seductive."[46]

Denyce Graves' visit was called an "Artist Residency" because it took place over several days. On the day before the concert she was presented in an open conversation in Massey Concert Hall where she was interviewed by Belmont's Harry Chapman. She spoke to students about her career and encouraged students in the development of their own careers. Students also posed questions in this convocation event. On the day following the "Concert of Unity" Graves worked with Belmont voice students in a vocal master class. Denyce Graves made a big impact on Belmont students and the relationship with Belmont and Graves would become a lasting one, because plans were made for her to appear with Belmont students again in the 2013 performance of "Christmas at Belmont" to be broadcast on PBS in December of 2013.

Richard Taruskin – A Celebration of Learning

Dr. Richard Taruskin, America's most revered musicologist, is known widely for his prolific essays in *The New York Times*. However, in academic circles he is best known for his writing of the six-volume *Oxford History of Western Music*, an opus that took him 13 years to complete. Taruskin is not only known for his writing, but also for interesting and in-depth lectures on all sorts of musical topics. Terry Klefstad, Belmont Coordinator of Musicology Studies, made the following comments about

Belmont's plans to bring Taruskin to Nashville, "We are celebrating all aspects of musical life at Belmont this year. We're bringing in Richard Taruskin as a part of celebrating musical learning." Taruskin's residency at Belmont impacted various groups of students, faculty and community visitors through several events. On the evening of March 24 he met a group of selected music students and faculty for a dinner which included a time for questions and dialogue between students and Taruskin. On the morning of March 25 he presented a lecture entitled "Resisting the Rite" which was open to all students. The same afternoon at a Graduate Research Symposium he spoke on the topic of "Liszt and Bad Taste." That evening in McAfee Concert Hall he presented a lecture open to the public on the topic "Suicide Notes, Faked Memoirs, Toasts to Killers: The Wonderful World of Russian Music." This topic represented his special area of interest, Russian music. Numerous guests from the Nashville academic community attended this open event. On his final morning at Belmont he interacted with several music classes. Taruskin's residency sparked interest among music students because he demonstrated that good academic music research and writing does not have to be impersonal. His goal is to bring issues to the public in order to enrich one's musical experiences.[47]

Piano Faculty Concert – 4 Pianos, 16 Hands

One of the most unique concerts in the first year of McAfee Concert Hall was "4 Pianos – 16 Hands," performed by nine members of the Belmont piano faculty. The concert was designed to showcase the new Steinway pianos in McAfee Concert Hall, but the performers upped the ante by borrowing two extra concert grand pianos from the Steinway Piano Gallery in order to play repertory for four pianos. Only the first and last selections required sixteen hands (Ravel's *Bolero* and Sousa's *Stars and Stripes Forever*), with the other pieces utilizing two pianos or four pianos with one player per piano. While the first and last selections were audience favorites, other highlights were a jazzy version of Mancini's "Days of Wine and Roses" played by Anthony Belfiglio and Bruce Dudley, and David McKay's arrangement of "Theme from Mulholland Falls" played by Belfiglio and McKay. The second half began with a delicate and fanciful arrangement for four pianos of Bach's "Sheep May Safely Graze." An impressive four-piano transcription by Kristian Klefstad of

Stravinsky's *Rite of Spring* part 1, was performed to celebrate the 100th anniversary of the first performance of this iconic work. This unusual concert brought out a large enthusiastic audience who were impressed by the sound of four concert grand pianos in an acoustically live setting. The performers for this event were Anthony Belfiglio, Elena Bennett, Bruce Dudley, Kris Elsberry, Kristian Klefstad, Daniel Landes, Robert Marler, David McKay and Richard Shadinger. It was observed that it is rare for a music school to have such a large and capable piano faculty, especially a faculty who can cooperate fully in order to perform such a complex and wide-ranging program.[48]

President's Concert - Celebration of Achievement

The President's Dinner and Concert on April 20, 2013 capped off a year of impressive concerts in the McAfee Concert Hall. The largest attendance ever for the President's Dinner, preceding the concert, packed the Maddox Grand Atrium, raising substantial funds for scholarships. The concert featured 18 different School of Music ensembles in as many different styles of music. The Applause Award was presented by Dean Curtis and President Fisher to a very deserving Carolyn McAfee, who was given a prolonged standing ovation for the beautiful space around her. With her usual modesty, she thanked the students for their performances and for everyone who had made the evening possible. In honor of Mrs. McAfee the audience sang her favorite hymn "Praise to the Lord, the Almighty." The concert ended with an uplifting arrangement of "Come, Thou Fount of Every Blessing" sung by all the choral ensembles with orchestra and organ.[49]

Framing the Romantic Era - Belmont Camerata Performing Schubert and Schoenberg

On April 22, 2013, the Belmont Camerata completed a successful season of concerts with its first performance in McAfee Concert Hall. The program was entitled "Framing the Romantic Era - Schubert and Schoenberg." The program was unique in that it included landmark works by two young Viennese composers, one at the beginning of the Romantic Era and one at the end of the era. The "Troutt" Quintet by Franz Schubert is one of the most popular chamber works of the century.

Schoenberg's *Verklarte Nacht (Transfigured Night)* was a product of his early period when he was influenced by the music of Wagner. The Schoenberg work is rarely heard in its original version for six players. McAfee Hall had proven that it was well-suited for all varieties of acoustical music from solo performers to the largest of massed groups of choirs with orchestra. With this Camerata outing, the hall revealed that it was also a superb chamber music venue, giving a luminous sound to the strings and a clear, sparkling sound from the Steinway grand. Artistic Director Elisabeth Small was joined on the Schoenberg by Alison Gooding, violin, Sarah Cote and Daniel Reinker, violas, Keith Nicholas and DongDong Zhang, cellos. The intensely chromatic sounds of Schoenberg were enhanced by the friendly McAfee acoustics. The Schubert was performed by Small, violin, Robert Marler, piano, Sarah Cote, viola, Keith Nicholas, cello and Craig Nelson, bass.

On the day before the concert, *The Nashville Tennessean* carried an expansive article about the concert entitled "Romance in the Air" by Amy Stumpfl. Elisabeth Small and Craig Nelson were quoted with their comments on the music. McAfee Hall is given its due with a picture and mention of its strength as a chamber music venue. The publicity prompted a large audience, many of whom had not visited the new concert hall.[50] Thus ended a year of outstanding concerts, unprecedented in their scope and variety in the history of The School of Music.

McAfee Hall – Citation for Excellence

It may seem odd that a building would receive awards, but McAfee Concert Hall received two in the space of a year. In addition to the notice in *The Nashville Scene* "Best of Nashville Issue" (October 23, 2012) as "Best New Concert Hall," the facility received a more prestigious award from the architectural journal *Learning by Design*. The firm of Earl Swensson Associates, Inc. was awarded a Citation for Excellence in the category of Renovation/Adaptive Reuse/Restoration. The journal, praised the aesthetic, acoustical and engineering attributes of the hall, comparing it to the Tonhalle in Zurich, Switzerland. The article describing the building included six photographs of the space. The Citation for Excellence served as an exclamation point to end the busy first year of the McAfee Concert Hall.[51]

The Nation's First University Production of *Les Misérables*

Les Misérables is the one of the most honored musical theatre productions in history. Born in 1980 as a French concept album based on the Victor Hugo novel, it also had a short theatrical run in Paris, closing after three months. In 1985 the London West End production at Queen's Theatre captured the imagination of audiences, becoming the longest-running musical in London history. The following Broadway production became the fourth longest running Broadway show. The Broadway version spawned a series of travelling productions which made their way to major cities across the country. Over time the musical won almost every award possible and broke numerous records for numbers of performances and size of audiences. In 1990 Belmont's own Melissa Davis Austin was chosen to play the role of Cosette for the national touring company. She auditioned for the cast when *Les Misérables* first came to the Tennessee Performing Arts Center, and she was soon called to join the company, later joining the Broadway cast. *Les Misérables* is perhaps the most operatic of all musicals because of its soaring drama and its constantly sung score. Therefore, the work cannot be adequately produced without excellent singers; it was in this aspect that the Belmont students excelled.

By 2012 *Les Mis* had made it to the movie theatre in a blockbuster film which broke all attendance records for a film opening on Christmas Day. The film was nominated for eight Academy Awards. In this atmosphere of renewed enthusiasm for the musical, it was announced that access to the performing rights for productions in college settings was to begin in the fall of 2013. Belmont announced in late fall 2012 that the spring production would be *A Tale of Two Cities* and, in fact, the musical had already been cast. A contact was made with the licensing company for *Les Misérables* asking for permission to become the first university to perform the work; the request was granted. The urgency of the request came because there was hope that Belmont's *Les Misérables* production would become the crowning achievement of Marjorie Halbert's Belmont career, since she was retiring at the end of the school year. Also, the production celebrated the 15th anniversary of the beginning of Belmont's Musical Theatre program.

As rehearsals began in January, 2013 Belmont became a part of the storied history of *Les Misérables*, as the university obtained the rights to perform the work. Excitement grew as the opening date drew nearer and Nashville media began to cover the debut event. A "flashmob" performance of "One Day More" in the Belmont dining hall made it to YouTube and at least two of the local television evening newscasts. The March 1 edition of *Nashville Scene* began its promotion with these words: "Belmont University continues to enhance its reputation as its young theater and music majors make their marks in the world as performers, techies, producers and arts administrators. So it seems wholly appropriate that the school holds the honor of mounting the first-ever university production of *Les Misérables* . . . Tickets will be tough to come by, so act now."[52]

Tickets sold quickly for the ten performances scheduled on two weekends of March 15-17 and March 21-24. Eventually, chairs were added to the back and sides of the theater to allow for more seating capacity in the Troutt Theater, which normally seats about 350.

The cast numbered 44 students, with some of the students cast in smaller roles serving in the ensemble. A few of the roles were double-cast, but overall the students were required to show tremendous physical and vocal stamina to perform five performances over a weekend (and this while keeping up with the heavy class load of music students). In addition to the 44 actors/singers, there was a superb orchestra of 15 players and a production staff of 28.

The four faculty directors for the production came to be known as the "Dream Team," each having their special expertise complementing the others on the team. Marjorie Halbert was Producer of the show. David Shamburger, Director, was responsible for coordinating the complex technical requirements and staging for the production. Jo Lynn Burks served as Musical Director, conducting the pit orchestra with great control and precision. Emily Tello Speck, Assistant Director/Choreographer, planned the intricate stage movement and dance required for the musical. It was evident that this "Dream Team" had the expertise required for such a large production, bringing it off in a way that rivaled many professional companies. The production was enhanced by support from several sponsors: Mike, Nancy, Annie and Becky Flaherty, HCA-TriStar Health, and Marty and Betty Dickens. The increased funding showed in the staging of the production. Sound and lighting were professional in every way, and the sets and scene changes were made with a sense of detail and reality. The Troutt Theater's rigging system was used to its full potential for the numerous scene changes. The battle scenes were particularly well staged, showing the professionalism of the set design and stage management. The orchestra, led by Jo Lynn Burks, provided the emotional background for the heroic story.[53]

The week that *Les Misérables* opened at Belmont was the same week that the Belmont Bruins Men's basketball team was headed to their seventh trip to the NCAA Tournament. ESPN.com carried a story about Belmont entitled "Cinderella Stories: Belmont University." The article was actually about Belmont's notable music alumni and her lively arts environment. The article had these words: ". . .the Christian liberal arts university in Nashville offers much more than a recently successful men's basketball team. Especially if you're into music. . . Allright, one more musical tidbit: on Friday Belmont put on the United States' first college production of *Les Misérables*."[54] Even the sports world was taking notice as Belmont advanced in the world of music as well as the world of sports.

One historical observation can be made in connection with the *Les Misérables* production. The young singer who shared the role of Fantine, Mary Claire Lutz, was the daughter of Belmont music Alumnus Charles Lutz (BM in vocal performance, '82). Mary Claire's grandmother, Barbara Lutz, was a music student at Belmont College in its first year, 1951. She sang in the Belmont Choir of 18 singers her freshman year. The comparison between music of 2013 with music at Belmont 63 years earlier is remarkable. The story of the Lutz family and their connection to Belmont helps tie the history of the School of Music together.

Retirement of Jim Kimmel and Marjorie Halbert

2013 brought the retirements Jim Kimmel and Marjorie Halbert, two long-time faculty members who made important contributions to Belmont University and to the lives of countless students. James Kimmel came to Belmont in 1995 from Millikin University. His teaching duties included directing Belmont's show choir, Company and Belmont Pops. He taught courses in choral music education and supervised Music Education majors in their student teaching Internships. Highly regarded throughout the country as a leader in the field of show choirs, Kimmel raised Company's profile through outstanding singing and choreography. He led Company to performances at national and regional conventions of the American Choral Directors Association. In 2005 Company

250

travelled to Los Angeles where they performed for the National Convention of ACDA and performed in important Los Angeles area high schools. In 1996 he started the annual Music City Showshoppe Show Choir Festival to which outstanding high school show choirs were invited. This well-known regional festival brought Belmont to a place of leadership in the active world of show choirs and helped recruit outstanding singers to Belmont.

Marjorie Halbert came to Belmont as Professor of Voice in 1979. She became the founding director of Company in the fall of 1979, serving as director for 16 years. As a highly regarded voice teacher she was a leader in the National Association of Teachers of Singing (NATS). She was the NATS Mid-South Governor for 1997-2001 and served as the Program Chair for the NATS National Convention in 2008. She was chosen to be a Master Teacher for the NATS Intern Program in 2009. In 1998 she was the founding director of the Belmont Musical Theatre Program, celebrating its 15th year upon her retirement. She spearheaded the founding of Belmont's dance program and was named the Chaney Distinguished Professor for Outstanding Teaching for 2009-2010. In her final year at Belmont she led the Musical Theatre program in its splendid production of *Les Misérables*, the first university performance in the United States of this iconic musical.

Halbert's retirement celebration was held on Sunday afternoon, April 21, 2013. Entitled "Diva . . . Defined: A Celebration of Marjorie Halbert," the event was a surprise performance by many of her former students, all of whom are actively performing on Broadway and other important venues. The program began with a performance of by Frank Raines, Musical Theatre graduate (BM '92) and Halbert son-in-law, of "The Way You Look Tonight." Greg Walter (BM '87) and Garris Wimmer sang "Agony" from *Into the Woods*. Lauren Turner (BM '10), straight from New York, sang "Diva" from *Starmites*. Travis Cottrell (Church Music graduate, BM '92) sang "Forevermore" and "If I Sing." Melissa Austin (BM '95), Belmont's first Broadway performer, sang a medley from *Les Mis*. Kelly Posey (BM '87) sang "We Never Really Say Goodbye" and Ginger Newman sang "Poor Wandering One" from *Pirates of Penzance*. Emily Tello Speck (BM '03, MM '12) and Jake Speck ended the concert with "I'd Give It All for You" (*A New World*). Belmont graduates Katie Zahn (BM '94) and Jeff Slaughter (BM '88) gave spoken tributes to Mrs. Halbert as did Dr. Cynthia Curtis, Dean of the School of Music, Dr.

251

William Troutt, President of Rhodes College, and Dr. Robert Fisher, Belmont President. Several alumni gave their greetings to Mrs. Halbert by way of video presentations. The Belmont dance program presented a tribute to Halbert with two dance numbers on the program.[55] The tribute to Marjorie Halbert was a perfect way to honor one who had affected the lives of so many young musicians. The presentation also served as a showcase of talented Belmont music graduates from the 1980s to the present day.

CHAPTER EIGHTEEN

125 Years
and Counting

As Belmont University hurtled toward the 125th anniversary of educational institutions on the campus (1890-2015), it was clear that the University had come of age in a number ways: enrollment was well over 7,400 and many national indicators showed that Belmont was now a nationally recognized name in academic strength, a leader in the arts, an athletic powerhouse, and a revered Christian institution focusing on meeting the world's needs. Most visibly, two decades of construction had brought major change to the campus. The recent completion of the Baskin Center for the College of Law (2012), the McWhorter Health Sciences Building (2013), The Janet Ayers Academic Center (2014), and Two Oaks Residence Hall (2014), the Johnson Center (2015) and the East Lawn and Fountain (2015) completed what amounted to a new campus beside the old quad. In this context the School of Music continued its trajectory of growth in enrollment, enlargement of faculty, improved facilities and major accomplishments of students and faculty that brought national attention.

New Major in Music Therapy

In the fall of 2014, The School of Music enrolled its first students in the new major in Music Therapy. For several years Belmont had been considering the formation of a program in Music Therapy, since there was not one in Tennessee. Prior to its opening, almost two years of work were required to develop a curriculum to meet the requirements for accreditation by both the National Association of Schools of Music and the American Music Therapists Association. In 2015 Dr. Alejandra Ferrer joined the faculty to serve as Coordinator of the Music Therapy program, by which time the program had quickly grown to over 70 majors. The program was well-suited to Belmont with its focus on careers that meet the needs of the world. The major has daunting requirements because of heavy non-music requirements in Psychology, Biology and Anatomy. In addition, students are expected to be proficient in a number of varied performing areas, including voice, keyboard, guitar and percussion. In the junior and senior years the majors are required to perform 45 hours of Music Therapy Practicum for 4 semesters. Upon completing course requirements, the students must complete a six-month fulltime internship under the leadership of a certified music therapist. When that requirement is completed, the student must pass a national certification exam by the American Music Therapists Association in order to conclude the certification process. Dr. Ferrer mentioned that when students first enter the program they are not totally aware of all the components of the degree. She states that the music therapy major must learn the various components and therapeutic processes of the work of music therapists, which can include work with medical patients, psychiatric patients, special needs children, geriatric patients, and pain management.[56]

Dr. Ferrer led the students to establish Belmont American Music Therapy Association for Students, allowing them to connect with professional music therapists and to plan events which benefit their growth as music therapists. In addition, Dr. Ferrer established a choir for autistic children which began on the Belmont campus in January, 2016. Sponsored by the Rising Star Music Fund, the choir helps autistic students to vocalize and work in a supportive environment of music making. The choir is led by Alejandra Ferrer with assistance from Belmont students.[57]

New Faculty

As the School of Music continued to expand, new faculty members were added to strengthen the instructional program. Dr. Lesley Mann joined the faculty in the fall of 2014 to teach in the area of choral music education. She earned the PhD in Music Education from Florida State University and came to Belmont to teach courses in Music Education, and to supervise student teachers in the Music Education Major. With her strong conducting skills she also conducted Belmont's Women's Choir. Dr. Alejandra Ferrer (PhD, MT-BC, University of Ohio) was appointed to be the Coordinator of the new major in Music Therapy. She came to Belmont in the fall of 2015 to teach courses in Music Therapy, and to oversee the clinical work required of students in the program. Dr. Kelly Garner, a Belmont graduate (BM '92), joined the Belmont faculty in the fall of 2014 as Assistant Professor to teach commercial voice. She had recently completed the DMA degree from the University of Miami, bringing valuable experience as performer, recording artist and song writer. Jo Lynn Burks was appointed in 2015 to a full-time position in Musical Theatre after teaching several years as an adjunct. She teaches in the Musical Theatre program and serves as the Musical Director of productions.

Loss of Beloved Faculty Members

With the passing of time, the School of Music lost three important and beloved professors. Dr. Paul Godwin, who taught at Belmont from 1973 until his retirement in 2009, passed away in the summer of 2014. He was Belmont's first full-time band director and had given strong leadership to the theory and composition areas. He had also served for a number of years as the Associate Dean for Academic Studies. On October 3, 2014 the Belmont Wind Ensemble under the direction of Barry Kraus, dedicated their fall concert to the memory of Paul Godwin.

Mrs. Helen Midkiff Capra, Associate Professor Emerita of Music, passed away at the age of 92 in the summer of 2015. She taught organ, theory, and music history at Belmont from 1957 to 1982. She was responsible for the design of the 1968 Wicks organ in Massey Concert Hall, and taught a generation of church organists who still carry on her legacy. Jeff Binford, (BM '77), one of Mrs. Capra's Belmont students, played the organ for her funeral at the First United Methodist Church in Lebanon, TN.

Dr. Lonnie Bond, long-time Lecturer in voice, passed away in the summer of 2015. He taught voice at Belmont from 1990 to 2015 and was an insightful voice teacher, an experienced bass soloist and a valued colleague. His long career as a church musician and teacher influenced hundreds of students.

Christmas at Belmont, 2013 and 2015

Belmont continued to present "Christmas at Belmont" on the Public Broadcasting System in 2013 and 2015. Each recorded program also aired during the off years when there is not a new production presented. Audiences for the national broadcast continued to grow, bringing national attention to the School of Music. Acclaimed Metropolitan Opera Mezzo-soprano, Denyce Graves was the guest host for the 2013 concert, adding her lustrous voice to the choirs and orchestra of Belmont. In 2015 Kathy Mattea, award-winning country music artist, was the host for the concert, bringing her rich voice and graceful presence to the production. Presented in Nashville's Schermerhorn Symphony Hall, the concert continued to be one of the Nashville's most anticipated Christmas events.

Highlights of School of Music Accomplishments

In March, 2014, the School of Music held a ribbon-cutting to open 16 new state-of-the-art practice rooms in the McAfee Annex. The University allocated funds for this expansion of practice space due to the growing enrollment of the School of Music.

In April, 2014, Belmont hosted the Nashville International Piano Competition, sponsored by the Steinway Society and the Nashville Steinway Gallery. The event brought national attention to Belmont through the presence high-level judges and large number of competitors. McAfee Concert Hall served as a perfect venue for the concerts and competitions.

At the spring Commencement, 2014, the School of Music graduated 136 music majors, a record number of graduates to date.

The Belmont University School of Music was listed as among the nation's "Best Schools of Music" in the October 2014 issue of "InTune" magazine for music educators. The article on Belmont featured an interview with recent graduate Rayvon Owen (BM '14).

On August 31, 2015 the on-line blog *OnStage* posted a list of "The 10 Most Underrated Theatre Colleges" stating that "There is a lot to like about Belmont University's theatre programs." The blog mentions all the degree programs, the strength of the musical theatre major, and the superb productions on campus. The article singled out the Troutt Theatre for its excellent facilities for student productions.[58]

Belmont's Musical Theatre program was named the 2015 winner of the American Prize in Musical Theatre Performance for the fall, 2014 production of "Oklahoma!" conducted by Jo Lynn Burks and led by program coordinator Nancy Allen. The ensemble was selected from applications reviewed from across the United States. The American Prize is a series of new, non-profit, competitions unique in scope and structure, designed to recognize and reward the best performing artists, ensembles and composers in the country based on submitted recordings. The American Prize was founded in 2009 and is awarded annually in many areas of the performing arts. As a part of the entry, Belmont's musical theatre officials noted "This Music Theatre program offers conservatory training in a liberal arts environment. Our students are trained as triple and quadruple threats, ready for New York City by the time they graduate. We have gradates on Broadway, in national tours, originating off-Broadway roles."[59]

Alumni Recognitions

The School of Music continued to honor outstanding alumni in the classical world of music through the awarding of the annual Encore Award. In 2013 the Award was given to Travis Cottrell (BM '92), a well-known, worship pastor, Christian performer and recording artist. The 2014 Encore Award was presented to Greg Walter (BM '87), a successful musical theater performer and professor in musical theatre at the North Carolina School of the Arts. In 2015 Dr. Tina Milhorn Stallard (BM '96), a superb soprano recitalist and Professor of Voice at the University of South Carolina School of Music, was the awardee. The 2016 Encore Award recipient was Meredith Maddox Hicks (BM '92), a violin performance graduate who performs with the Little Rock Symphony Orchestra and teaches violin at the University of Arkansas at Little Rock. During the time these artists were at Belmont to perform concerts, they also met students and worked with them in class settings, sharing their career experience with current students.

Belmont honors outstanding alumni in the commercial music field through the Curtain Call Award. The 2013 award was given to Russell Terrell (BM '87), a first-call background vocalist for Nashville recording artists. The 2014 award went to Danny Wells (BM '83), guitarist and song writer. In 2015 the award was given to Geoff Koch (BM '94), a highly regarded composer for film and television. The 2016 recognition was given to Brandon Fraley (BM '00), vocalist/pianist and composer/arranger, who performs with some of the best-known artists in the music industry.

Lauren Wilkerson Baker (BM '93), music teacher at Clovercroft Elementary School in Williamson County, was named Williamson County Teacher of the Year for 2015-16.

Representative Student Accomplishments

Susan Bay (BM '13) won a prestigious grant from the German Academic Exchange Service for study in Germany for an entire year. She studied musicology, focusing on Baroque opera at the Technical University of Dresden. Her application was strengthened by her writing and research abilities as well as her strong German skills.

Cody Muller, Bass-baritone (BM '14), won second place in the National Association of Teachers of Singing National Singing competition in Boston. Soon thereafter, Muller was awarded a graduate assistantship for graduate study at the Eastman School of Music.

Graduate string student, Briana Murphy (MM '14) wrote an article on Dmitri Shostakovich published by the *Huffington Post* in the spring, 2014.

In the spring, 2015 auditions of the regional National Association of Teachers of Singing, 8 Belmont classical singers were declared winners in the competition held at Vanderbilt University. In addition, 27 Belmont students reached the semi-finals of the auditions.

Sebastian Buhts (BM '13, MM '15) and Josh McClelland (BM '16), percussion students of Chris Norton, were chosen to participate in the summer, 2015 Aspen Summer Music Festival. While there, they performed with the festival orchestras and studied with some of the most respected percussionists in the nation.

Kelly Lenahan (BM '16) and Olivia Richardson (BM '17), piano students of Daniel Landes and Robert Marler respectively, were selected to perform *Carnival of the Animals* by Saint-Saëns with the Nashville Symphony Orchestra in a concert on February 27, 2016.

Faculty Achievements

In August, 2015 Belmont School of Music faculty Elisabeth Small, violin, Dr. Robert Marler, piano and Xiao-fan Zhang, cello, toured China where they presented 10 concerts over a period of 2 weeks. Their performances were presented in the cities of Beijing, Jinan, Nanjing, Shanghai, Guangzhou, Shenzhen and Xining. They performed a culturally diverse program of works by Dvorak, Shostakovich, Corigliano, Debussy, Sibelius, Schubert, Chinese composer Sha Han-kun, and Nashville composer, Carl Marsh. The trio presented 4 masterclasses at Chinese conservatories, and performed on regional Chinese television along with a TV interview. Elisabeth Small made these observations about the China visit, "Instrumental music reaches the human soul, ministering joy and healing where communication is not possible through cultural and language barriers. My teaching will be further informed to nurture the merits of working hard for the sake of meaningfulness and purposeful reward."[60]

Dr. Bill Pursell and his daughter, Laura Pursell, presented a concert with Donny Most at Vitello's in Los Angeles on January 10, 2016. The concert was part of the debut of the duo's new album titled "The Very Last Dance Hall Left in L.A." which was produced by Belmont's arranging instructor Steve Mauldin. An article in *The LA Beat* gave attention to Bill Pursell's illustrious career, his hit recordings, and the many famous performers he has worked with. In connection with the concert, the Pursells were interviewed on local Los Angeles television about the event.[61]

Sandra Dudley, commercial voice professor, performed with the Mike Waldrop Big Band at the National Jazz Educator's Conference, Jan. 9, 2016 in Memphis.

Tammy Rogers King is a member of the bluegrass band SteelDrivers that received a Grammy award for best bluegrass album of the year on January 15, 2016. Rogers is a violin performance graduate of Belmont, as well a current faculty member, and the director of Belmont's Bluegrass Ensemble.

Ensemble Recognitions

Chamber Singers, directed by Dr. Deen Entsminger, presented the world premiere of Marcus Hummon's choral work *The Passion* in a concert on April 4, 2014 at Nashville's Christ Church Cathedral, with a Belmont premiere on March 30, 2015.

The Belmont Musical Theatre program presented a workshop production of the Broadway-bound musical *Over the Rainbow* in May,

2015. Broadway directors led the production which was viewed by Nashville audiences before debuting in New York.

The Belmont Chorale, under the direction of Jeffery Ames and assisted by Jane Warren, made a concert tour to the countries of Latvia and Estonia during May 10-19, 2015. This area of Europe was quite unknown to the students and their comments indicated that they learned much from these tiny freedom-loving countries. According to the students, the high points of the journey were the Chorale concerts at the University of Latvia for a group of appreciative students, a concert in the beautiful acoustics of St. John Church in Riga, and singing for a worship service at St. John's Lutheran Church in Talinn, Estonia. The Belmont Chorale carried their music into a new part of the world in their tradition of overseas tours.[62]

Belmont performing ensembles continued to distinguish themselves through performances at conferences of important professional music organizations. The Belmont Chorale, Jeffery Ames, conductor, performed for the national convention National Association for Music Educators in Nashville in October, 2013. Jazzmin, directed by Kathryn Paradise, performed a concert at the national Jazz Educator's Network Conference on January 9, 2014 in Dallas Texas. The Belmont Wind Ensemble directed by Barry Kraus performed a concert for the Tennessee Music Educators Association in Memphis on April 16, 2015. The Belmont Jazz String Quart, under the direction of Tracy Silverman performed for the National Association for Music Educators on October 25, 2015 in its national convention in Nashville. The Belmont Chorale, Jeffery Ames, director, and the University Symphony Orchestra, conducted by Robert Gregg, performed a Unity Concert for the Southern Division convention of the American Choral Directors' Association on March 11, 2016 in Chattanooga.

On December 10, 2015 Belmont's Musical Theatre production of *White Christmas* prompted a rave review from *Broadway World*. The review by Jeffrey Ellis commented the superb singing and acting, as well the sets and the orchestra. Mention was given to the music conductor as well as the faculty producers of the show. Ellis ended the review that saying that since the production occurred at the end of the semester, it only ran for 4 performances, expressing regret that the show did not have a longer run so more Nashvillians could have seen it.[63]

Dean Cynthia Curtis Announces Retirement

On January 11, 2016 Dean Cynthia Curtis held a called meeting of the College of Visual and Performing Arts faculty for the purpose of announcing her retirement as of May 31, 2016. The announcement brought surprise and shock to many faculty members, but the response was full affirmation for Curtis, represented by long applause and a standing ovation by her colleagues. Dr. Curtis spoke at length about her decision, saying that she felt good about all that had been accomplished over the last 25 years. She also expressed that she thought that nothing was to be gained having a year-long (or more) time in service after she made the decision to retire. She expressed appreciation to faculty for all the hard work and cooperation provided in making the College of Visual and Performing Arts what it had become.

The announcement caught the faculty unawares because everyone realized that the School of Music was in the midst of preparation for an NASM re-evaluation in the fall of 2016. It seemed unlikely that she would retire while that process was underway. Dr. Curtis addressed the issue by saying that she had encouraged all committees working on the NASM document to submit their draft reports quite early, and that she fully planned to have the document completed before her retirement date. She also expressed the willingness to serve as a consultant for the project for part the summer in preparation for the visit by the NASM evaluators in October of 2016.

In a message to the Belmont community (January 13, 2016) Provost Thomas Burns expressed well the accomplishments of Dr. Curtis and Belmont's appreciation for her long and illustrious leadership of the arts at Belmont:

"It is with mixed emotions that I announce to our campus that Dr. Cynthia Curtis, Dean of the College of Visual and Performing Arts (CVPA), will retire from Belmont effective May 31, 2016.

Dr. Curtis has been a part of the Belmont family for 35 years, first as a faculty member in the School of Music and then as Dean of the College of Visual and Performing Arts. In her nearly 25 years as Dean, Dr. Curtis has guided the College through enormous changes and the campus has felt the positive impact of Dr. Curtis' tenure in many ways – whether through the nationally televised performance of Christmas at Belmont from the Schermerhorn Symphony Center or the establishment of highly visible programs like Musical Theatre, Music Therapy and new degrees like the Master of Music, the Bachelor of Fine Arts in Theatre and the Minor in

Dance. Though her achievements as Dean are too numerous to mention here, I do want to highlight a few of the most significant achievements that Dean Curtis has led for CVPA and Belmont:

- Enrollment growth in all areas of the visual and performing arts, including almost tripling the enrollment of the School of Music.
- Facility upgrades and expansions, including the renovation of the Wilson Music Building, the Massey Performing Arts Center, the Troutt Theatre Complex and the McAfee Concert Hall.
- Specialized art's accreditation for the Department of Art (NASAD), the Department of Theatre and Dance (NAST), continued accreditation for the School of Music (NASM) and most recently Music Therapy (AMTA).
- Creating the Friends of the Arts at Belmont to promote and advance the College and to raise scholarship funds.

Dr. Curtis will certainly leave a legacy of a passion for the arts connected to the commitment to student success and program excellence, both in the College and the University. While I recognize that we won't be able to simply "replace" all that Dean Curtis is the University, we will begin a national search for a new Dean very soon and I will be inviting the campus to participate in that search process... For now, though, as the semester continues to move forward, I encourage you to send Dean Curtis well wishes and gratitude. Her passion for our students and the arts will be missed, but not absent, as Dean Curtis has assured me that her retirement does not mean that we won't see her on campus attending many Belmont events. I hope that you will join me in celebrating Dean Curtis' contributions to Belmont and support her as she plans her new adventures in retirement."[64]

In an article from the *Belmont Vision* Cynthia Curtis reflected on her time at Belmont: "I think we often miss the value of going to a place and really investing in it and contributing to it becoming something significant. I'm all for staying in one place, if that place itself is developing in directions that you want it go."

For senior music education major Will Griswold, Curtis became an influence for thinking outside his major and seeing the larger picture when it comes to the arts. Griswold sits on the CVPA Dean's Advisory Council and interacts with Curtis on a regular basis. Curtis challenged him not only to ensure that every voice was heard, but also come up with the best solutions to help the greatest number of people in the CVPA. He said, "She was able to help me step back and say 'When you're dealing with many people you can't please everyone, but you can do your best and take your time to make decisions that affect the greatest number of people for good.'" Madeline Bridges, associate dean for academic studies in the School of Music, spoke about Dean Curtis's mindfulness of all aspects of the arts in her leadership of CVPA. "She's a visionary," she said "it's unusual to find someone who is so competent in daily tasks, but who also sees the big picture and always is moving ahead, thinking about how the school and college can move to the next level." Bridges described Curtis as a hands-on organizer fully attentive to every aspect of the college, remaining so even after her responsibilities increased with the growth of the school over the years. Whether it's planning for Christmas at Belmont at the Schermerhorn, keeping track of the CVPA's finances, guiding ensemble directors, or helping students, Curtis is intimately involved with it all. When she's working with you on whatever it is, it has her full attention and her full support."[65]

In truth, Dr. Curtis' leadership of the School of Music had more influence on its growth and development than any other individual in its history. It is unusual for an administrator to have a long tenure through which can be seen the results of 25 years of vision. When faculty members spoke about Dean Curtis, words often used included "visionary, fair, detailed, dignified and hard-working." In response to Dean Curtis' retirement plans the university announced that Dr. Cynthia Curtis would be honored with the 2016 Applause Award at the annual President's Concert on April 16, 2016.

Coda–and the Beat Goes On

How Does One End a History?

Seniors graduate in May and go on their way, and new freshmen enter in August. Faculty members retire and new faculty join the Belmont family. Facilities change and new ones are added. The music curriculum changes and adapts to meet current challenges. Belmont grows and changes every year with new programs, new buildings and new ideas. Society and its students bring new ideas, attitudes and technology to campus. As a history is being written, new people, events, customs and styles are waiting in the wings to enter the stage for their time in the spotlight. A history has to come to an end at some point, even as the river of events and people continues to flow.

The growth trajectory of Belmont from its beginning in 1890 to the present (2016) is remarkable. Alumni who return after 10 years, 30 years, or even 60 years will find the changes so obvious, that it will at first be difficult to find equilibrium in the large urban university that Belmont has become. However, when one stays on campus for just a short visit, all seems as it should be. The Mansion still stands, looking down the hill as it has for over 160 years. The statues stand as silent sentinels, and the gazebos provide shelter from summer suns as they have for generations of students. The Tower is still there marking the hours with its majestic bells, and remembering a time when it stood in the middle of a great battle. The lawns which stretch down the hill are greener than ever, and Adelicia Acklen would be pleased that the gardens are carefully tended. More significantly, the musical life of the campus is stronger than ever, and its goals clearer and more fully realized. Nashville and the wider world see the Belmont School of Music as a strong school educating young musicians for service in the world. Its concert life, its students and faculty make a profound impact on Nashville's arts community. Over 3,000 music alumni make a positive impact on students, audiences and churches around the world. So, even as things change dramatically, the core values of Belmont remain and returning alumni feel that connection.

The School of Music Profile in 2016

With 734 music majors, the School of Music at Belmont University is one of the largest Schools of Music in a Christian University in the United States. It is a comprehensive School of Music with nine majors under the Bachelor of Music degree: Church Music, Commercial Music, Composition, Music Education, Musical Theatre Performance, Piano Pedagogy, Music Theory, Music Therapy and Music with a minor in another field. The School also offers the BA in Music, the BFA in Musical Theatre, and the Minor in Music. Under the Master of Music degree the School of Music offers Majors in Church Music, Commercial Music, Composition, Music Education, Pedagogy and Performance.

The faculty includes 54 full-time and 86 part-time members. The student faculty ratio is 13:1 with an emphasis on manageable class size. The faculty is an outstanding group of professionals representing best in teaching, musical performance, scholarship and service to the world of music. The faculty is a perfect blend of long-time experienced members combined with the new ideas of young faculty members. Faculty members are dedicated to helping each student achieve their goal to become a well-rounded musician.

Belmont's music majors come from all parts of the country. They are an academically strong group of students with 26.5 average ACT score and average high school GPA of 3.6. Through the careful admissions and audition process, it is assured that they have the talent and academic background to succeed in the rigorous music programs of Belmont. The typical Belmont music major also exhibits a strong work ethic and positive personal ideals, adding to the positive learning environment of the School of Music. Music scholarships amounting to a total of approximately $1,000,000 are awarded to new and returning students each academic year.

Students perform in 14 choral/vocal ensemble ranging from the Belmont Chorale and Oratorio Chorus to pop and jazz ensembles such as Jazzmin and the show choir, Company. Instrumentalists perform in 21 ensembles such as the University Symphony Orchestra and the Wind Ensemble as well as pop ensembles such as the Rock Ensemble, Bluegrass Ensemble, and various Jazz Ensembles. Every ensemble performs at least once a semester and a number of the groups perform more often on and off campus. Several ensembles tour every year and the Belmont Chorale undertakes an overseas tour every few years. Many of the ensembles appear in special events such as The President's Concert in the spring and "Christmas at Belmont" in December which has been broadcast on the Public Broadcasting System every year for over a decade.

The facilities of the School of Music are large enough to handle the instruction, rehearsal and performance done by hundreds of active musicians. The facilities are found in two main locations: The Wilson/Massey complex on the north end of the campus where much of the classroom and studio instruction is done, and the McAfee/Troutt complex on the south side of the campus where most of the instrumental lessons and rehearsals occur. The facilities comprise 17 classrooms/rehearsal spaces, 43 practice rooms, six performance venues and 45 offices/teaching studios. The performance spaces are appropriate for the wide range of performances given, including the intimate Harton Recital Hall, the elegant Belmont Mansion, and the acoustically superb McAfee Concert Hall. Massey Concert Hall has all the sound and lighting equipment necessary for jazz and pop performances. The Troutt Theater is a state-of-the-art venue for opera and musical theater productions. The Curb Café provides an informal setting for small-scale commercial music performances.

The guiding principles of the School of Music are ever-present in the planning and decision-making. The School of Music Vision Statement "is to be one of the nation's leading Schools of Music, preparing talented and aspiring musicians for the 21st Century through embracing artistic standards of the past and exploring musical possibilities for the future." The School's Mission Statement is "to be a stimulating artistic community that fosters the study, performance and creation of music in a context of excellence and respect for diversity in musical styles."

Approximately 3000 music alumni have found their place in communities throughout the country teaching music in schools in elementary, middle and high schools, serving as ministers of music and worship leaders and church organists. Many have earned advanced degrees and serve on college and university music faculties. Belmont music graduates can be found performing on stages of opera theaters, symphony halls and recital halls as singers, pianists, orchestra players, chamber musicians and collaborative pianists. Numerous graduates teach private lessons in all areas of performance. In the world of popular music graduates perform in every imaginable style in venues such as the Grand Ole Opry, jazz clubs, and recording studios. Dozens of musical theater graduates have performed on Broadway, in community theatres and travelling road shows of musical productions. The impact of music graduates across the country is broad and significant. Belmont music alumni offer much more than simply the gift of music, because in their study of music they learn extramusical skills such as hard work, creativity, self-assurance, organization and leadership. In addition, Belmont graduates have a heart for helping others, and they do that every day through their work as musicians.

A Day in the Life

4:00 a.m. -The day starts early for the School of Music. Custodians, who take care of the facilities, arrive long before offices open and classes begin. Trash cans are emptied, floors vacuumed and rooms straightened, ready for a new day of learning.

6:30 a.m. – Daylight is breaking when a lone professor enters the Wilson Building to work on a project that is soon due. Slightly later, a Music Office worker arrives to prepare materials for an important meeting taking place later in the morning.

6:45 a.m. – A solitary piano major waits at the Wilson door, hoping to get to a practice room early. The doors are unlocked at 7:00, but perhaps someone will come along to enter and will let her in. Sure enough, a professor arrives, the student heads to the practice room – scales begin.

7:00 a.m. – the Music Buildings officially open. A few eager students arrive during the hour for early morning practice. The pace picks up as the hour progresses. Students hurriedly arrive, often with breakfast in hand.

8:00 a.m. – The dreaded 8:00 am classes begin. A few students straggle in late yawning as they head to the classrooms. Nine classrooms are humming with activity: music theory, music history, class piano, conducting, and aural skills. A Beethoven Symphony roars from one room. Solfege and takadimi are heard from another. A lively discussion is taking place in another. Slow scales are heard from the piano lab. With no classrooms to spare, 8:00 am classes are plentiful.

9:00 a.m. – The bells in the tower ring the hour for the first time in the day, marking each hour of academic activity. Gradually the private teaching studios become alive with lessons in voice, piano, strings, woodwinds and brass. The percussion studios at the McAfee complex vibrate with energy. A walk through the halls reveals the sounds of Bach, Brubeck, Chopin, Gershwin, Jazz standards, contemporary rock,

Beethoven and country music. Close to 1000 private music lessons will be taught during this week.

10:00 a.m. – The 10:00 hour often provides times for campus events: club meetings, convocation, worship services and lectures. In the School of Music there are meetings of SAI and Phi Music Alpha or the student MENC chapter. A guest musician gives a lecture as part of the Music and Discourse Series. The practice rooms are full with purposeful practice.

Music staff members, representing clerical, admissions, technical and public relations are busily at work. Schedules are set, concert programs are typed and proofed, PR notices are written and sent, questions from prospective students are answered, audition days are planned, student questions and problems are fielded. Clerical support is going full blast in a busy and purposeful office setting.

11:00 a.m. – This hour is probably the busiest classroom time with every classroom filled with students engaged by enthusiastic faculty. Students not in class or practicing find comfortable places to plug in laptop computers or IPads to work on assignments.

At 11:00 prospective students arrive with parents for an information session on the School of Music and its offerings. The visiting high school students seem to be affected by all they see around them – They could be a part of this one day. There is a sense of excitement mixed with a little tension.

Throughout the day students come and go in the Music Library – research questions are answered, books and scores are located. On-line resources are consulted; students listen to CDs in the listening lab or with on-line databases. Some students sit amidst computers and stacks of books, working on term papers or graduate theses.

A Musical Theatre rehearsal goes on in Massey Concert Hall. Blocking is taking place, lines are rehearsed. A group of dancers turns the Massey lobby into an impromptu dance studio.

12:00 – Classes continue at full tilt, but quick lunches are eaten at campus venues or in the Music School atrium. Lively conversations develop, and singing is heard. A violinist and guitarist play jazz in a nearby gazebo.

1:00 p.m. – In the afternoon the pace changes. Everyone is fully awake and engaged. Ensemble rehearsals are heard throughout the Music School. Choral ensembles work on blend and intonation; percussionists conquer incredibly difficult rhythms; a string quartet rehearses Mozart.

2:00 p.m. – Throughout the afternoon performance seminars are held. Vocalists try a song for the first time; a pianist performs a Beethoven Sonata from memory for the first time; ensemble rehearsals continue; in a music education class, a student experiments with a lesson plan with her class.

3:00 p.m. – The teaching in The Belmont Academy of Music begins as pre-college students complete their school day and arrive for their private lessons in the Massey Performing Arts Center.

4:00 p.m. – On Mondays the children in the three choirs of the Nashville Children's Choir program begin to arrive for their weekly rehearsals, taxing the traffic grid of the campus with the arrival of scores of mini-vans and SUVs. The lively pure voices of children are heard throughout the lower level of Massey.

5:00 p.m. – It is late afternoon and classrooms and studios are busy with rehearsals, graduate classes and private lessons. Classes will go on into the evening.

6:00 p.m. – A Junior Commercial Voice Major presents a junior recital in the Curb café. Increasingly, classes are taught in the evening. Students are likely taking class piano, an ensemble, or a general education class during the evening hours.

7:00 p.m. – Final stage preparations are made for the evening's concert in Massey Concert Hall and/or McAfee Concert Hall. The requirements will vary with every concert but a recording crew will set up microphones, sound crews will provide needed sound for the event. Lighting specifications are followed. All equipment and instruments needed are on stage and ready to go. At 7:30 a concert begins, possibly a student ensemble, a choral group, a faculty performance, an opera or musical – the variety is wide.

By 7:30 an audience of students, faculty and community members are in place. An impressive performance takes place, one which is educational as well as an aesthetic experience.

9:00 p.m. – The evening concert is over by now. For many students the evening is still young. Rehearsals of commercial groups fill spaces in Massey until closing time; a pianist rehearses for an upcoming recital in Harton Recital Hall. Practice rooms are full of serious performers and composers. Students work on compositions and music notation in the Computer Lab – music creation seems to come easier at night.

10:00 p.m. – Some students have had enough of study and practice, and go out for the evening, perhaps for something to eat, a movie, or to hear a friend at a showcase performance downtown – there is much music to hear in Nashville.

11:00 p.m. – Practice and study continues – Tomorrow's assignments are uppermost in mind. Sensible students are winding down for the day, hoping to get a good night's rest. Groups of students are headed toward residence halls.

12:30 a.m. – Practice time is over – the practice rooms close at 12:30. Never fear, the Bunch Library is open all night. Students with more study to complete, move in that direction.

1:00 a.m. – The building monitors lock up rooms and shoo the last student out the door. Two students sit beside each other in the atrium, trying out a new song from a recently written lead sheet – a premiere is taking place. A guitar student sits in gazebo strumming chords for a new song.

2:00 a.m. – In the library and residence halls study continues – Readings are completed for tomorrow's classes; written assignments are typed; theory assignments are scribbled onto staff paper; progress is made on term papers.

The Belmont Mansion where it all began sits serenely at the crest of the hill, its lights glowing softly through the red Venetian glass. The campus is quiet, but somewhere music is being created, studied or practiced - the beat goes on.

Sources

Many of the sources used in this document are archival items available only in the Belmont University Archives in the Bunch Library, or items found in files in the School of Music Office. Items of this type include catalogs from Belmont College for Young Women (1891-1913); catalogs from Ward-Belmont College (1913-1950); Ward-Belmont School of Music catalogs (1906-1949); Catalogs from Belmont College and University (1951-2016); Belmont College for Young Women yearbooks *Milady in Brown* (1891-1913); Yearbooks from Ward-Belmont College, *Milestones*, (1914-1951); Belmont College and University yearbook, *The Tower* (1952-1997); Belmont School of Music newsletter, *Belmont Music News* (1980-1992); Belmont University's alumni magazine *The Belmont Circle* (1960-2013); Ward-Belmont's weekly newspaper, *The Hyphen* (1913-1951); Belmont University's student newspaper, *The Vision* (1952-2016). Other items consulted include Nashville newspapers such as *The Banner, The Tennessean, Nashville Scene,* and *Nashville Arts.* Many items come from The Belmont School of Music files, including concert programs, faculty minutes, committee reports, accreditation documents, press releases, and public relations files. These numerous items from Belmont sources are not listed in the bibliography, but are cited when appropriate.

Many individuals were generous with their time for interviews or questions for clarification, and will be cited where appropriate: Jeffery Ames, John Arnn, Maren Bishop, Madeline Bridges, Barbara Redden Burnette, Helen Midkiff Capra, Robert Capra, Jr., Jennifer Coleman, Cynthia Curtis, Sarah Davis, Bruce Dudley, Sandra Dudley, Joan Eakin, Deen Entsminger, Alejandra Ferrer, Lindsay George, Robert Gregg, Sharon Gregg, Tim Gmeiner, Marjorie Halbert, Linda Harmon, James Kimmel, Jeffrey Kirk, Kristian Klefstad, Barry Kraus, Gina Lackore, Virginia LaMothe, Barbara Lutz, Lesley Mann, Keith Mason, Charlie Miller, Keith Moore, Christopher Norton, April Simpkins, Lina Sheahan, Elisabeth Small, Vicky Tarleton, Julie Thomas, Joel Treybig, Jane Warren, Jerry Warren, Mark Whatley, Ted Wylie.

The color photographs on the book cover are used with kind permission of the Belmont University Office of Communications.

Bibliography

Adelicia Acklen Chronology Post-1870, in the archives of the Belmont Mansion.

Adelicia Acklen Chronology Pre-1869, in the archives of the Belmont Mansion.

Barte, Paul. "AGO Convention 2012 Nashville, TN, Convention Reports." *The American Organist* 46, no. 10 (October 2012): 58.

"Belmont Edition," *The Musical Herald,* (October 1908).

Bostick, Alan. "Belmont shapes up as Music City's music school." *Tennessean.* (November 19, 1995): Arts section, 12.

Bradley, Van Allen. *Music for the Millions – The Kimball Piano and Organ Story.* Chicago: Henry Regnery Company, 1957.

Brooks, Candace, Kinsey Oganowski, Anna Stergas, and Liz Timbs. *From Ward Belmont to Belmont College* (DVD 1152). Belmont University, 2005.

Buchanan, Beverly. "The Carillons of Belmont." *The Bulletin of the Guild of Carillonneurs in North America,* 45 (1996):18-44.

"Campus Mourns Sudden Death of Dean Alan Irwin." *Ward-Belmont Hyphen* (December 3, 1949): 1.

Carey, Bill. *Master of the Big Board – The Life, Times and Businesses of Jack C. Massey.* Nashville: Cumberland House, 2005.

Cochran, Heather, Editor. *Celebrating Milestones.* Nashville: Harpeth Hall School, 2001.

Dalton, Sydney, director. *Music at Ward-Belmont.* Ward-Belmont Choir (78 RPM Recording with liner notes), Recorded Publications Co., c. 1950.

DeWitt, John N. "Early Radio Broadcasting in Middle Tennessee." *Tennessee Historical Quarterly*, 30, no. 1 (Spring 1972): 85.

Dorian, Donna and Anne Hall and Mark Brown. *At Home in Tennessee.* Baton Rouge: Louisiana State University Press, 2009.

Duncan, Ivar Lou Myhr. *A History of Belmont College.* Nashville: Belmont College, 1974.

Ellison, Cori. "Stahlman, Sylvia," *Grove Music Online*, Oxford University Press, 2008.

First Presbyterian Church of Nashville: One Hundred Years of Service. Nashville: Foster and Parkes, 1915.

Gabhart, Herbert C. *The Massey-Belmont Story. 2001*

Gabhart, Herbert C. *Work: the Soul of Good Fortune.* Nashville: Broadman Press. 1989.

Gibson, Rhonda. "Friend Claims Music Collection for Belmont," *Belmont Circle* 28, no. 3 (Fall 1989): 19.

Graham, Eleanor. "Belmont – Nashville Home of Adelicia Acklen." *Tennessee Historical Quarterly* 30, no. 4 (Winter 1972): 345-368.

Graul, Karla and Mona Collett. "Shoe merchant makes 'sweet music.'" *Belmont Circle* 32, no. 1 (Spring 1993): 5.

Havighurst, Craig. *Air Castle of the South: WSM and the Making of Music City.* Urbana and Chicago: University of Illinois Press, 2007.

Ikard, Robert W. "Signor de Luca and the Nashville Conservatory of Music." *The Tennessee Historical Quarterly* 60, no. 3 (Fall 2001):176-194.

Ingram, Martha Rivers and D.B. Kellogg. *Apollo's Struggle: A Performing Arts Odyssey in the Athens of the South.* Nashville: Hillsboro Press, 2004.

Innes, Jacqueline Simone. "Belmont Statuary: Four Pieces." *Tennessee Historical Quarterly* 30, no. 4 (Winter 1972): 369-378.

273

Kiser, John W. "Scion of Belmont, Part I." *Tennessee Historical Quarterly* 38, no. 1 (Spring 1979): 34-61.

Kiser, John W. "Scion of Belmont, Part II." *Tennessee Historical Quarterly* 38, no. 2 (Summer 1979):188-203.

Morrison, Louise Douglas. *A Voyage of Faith: The Story of Harpeth Hall.* Nashville: The Harpeth Hall School Auxiliary, 1980.

Nicholas, Louis. *The Louis Nicholas Collection*, Music Special Collection in the Bunch Library at Belmont University. Contains extensive collection of concert programs from Ward-Belmont College.

"Obituaries, Sylvia Stahlman." *Opera News* 63, no. 5 (November 1998): 85.

Pitcher, John. "Belmont Inaugurates McAfee Concert Hall with Gala Concert." *Nashville Arts* (October 8, 2012).

Pitcher, John. "Music Review: Belmont Rings in the Holidays in its New Concert Hall." *Nashville Arts* (December 2, 2012).

Ransom, John Crowe. *Selected Poems.* New York: Alfred A. Knopf, 1964.

Rappaport, Diane. "Music Education for a Changing Job Market." *Keyboard* (January 1982).

Sadie, Stanley. "Wiktor Labunski," *The New Grove Dictionary of Music and Musicians,* (New York: MacMillan Publishers, Limited): 344.

Shadinger, Richard C. "Belmont University Adds Bells to Carillon." *Carillon News* 69 (April 2003): 4-5.

Shadinger, Richard C. "Historic Belmont Tower Undergoes Major Restoration." *Carillon News* 85 (April 2011): 20-21.

Shadinger, Richard C. "The Adelicia Acklen Music Collection: A Glimpse at Piano Pedagogy and Literature on the Tennessee Frontier." Lecture presented at the Tennessee Music Teachers Association, Nashville, TN (June 5, 2000).

Sharp, Tim. *Nashville Music Before Country.* Charleston: Arcadia Publishing Co., 2008.

"TAA History." *Tennessee Arts Academy 25th Anniversary Program,* June 10, 2011.

"The Founding of NAMTA," *Nashville Area Music Teachers Association Membership Directory,* 2011-2012, 3.

Wardin, Albert. *Belmont Mansion: The Home of Joseph and Adelicia Acklen* Nashville: Historic Belmont Association, 1981.

Williams, Wheat. "Belmont: a best-kept secret." *The Nashvillian* (December 5, 1991).

Notes

Part I – The Cultural Legacy of Adelicia Acklen
and the Belmont Mansion

1. Albert Wardin, *Belmont Mansion: The Home of Joseph and Adelicia Acklen* (Nashville: Historic Belmont Association, 1981), 4.
2. Ibid., 4.
3. Information on Adelicia Acklen is drawn from the document "Adelicia Acklen Chronology Pre-1869" in the Belmont Mansion archives.
4. Richard C. Shadinger, "The Adelicia Acklen Music Collection: A Glimpse at Piano Pedagogy and Literature on the Tennessee Frontier" (lecture presented at the Tennessee Music Teachers Association Convention, Nashville, TN, June 5, 2000).
5. Wardin, 15.
6. "Adelicia Acklen Chronology Pre-1869."
7. Marietta Piccolomini [1834-1899] was an Italian soprano, especially known for the role of Violetta in Verdi's *La Traviata*. It is not known what opera the Acklens heard her sing on this visit to New Orleans.
8. Wardin, 20-22.
9. Ibid., 22.
10. "Adelicia Acklen Chronology Pre-1869."
11. Ibid.
12. Jacqueline Simone Innes, "Belmont Statuary: Four Pieces," *Tennessee Historical Quarterly*, 30, no. 4, (Winter 1972): 369-378.
13. Ibid.
14. "Adelicia Acklen Chronology Pre-1869."
15. Wardin, p. 26.
16. Ibid.
17. *The Centenary History of the First Presbyterian Church of Nashville* (Nashville: Foster and Parkes Co., 1915), 69.

18. "Adelicia Acklen Chronology Pre-1869."

19. "Adelicia Acklen Chronology Post-1870." *The Frog Opera*, a popular stage work of the time, was composed by Clarence Miller and published by J.A and R.A. Reid of Providence, RI in 1873.

20. "Adelicia Acklen Chronology Post-1870."

21. Ibid.

22. Ibid.

23. Ibid.

24. Ibid.

25. Wardin, 32.

Part II – Music at Belmont College and Ward-Belmont (1890-1951)

1. Albert Wardin, *Belmont Mansion: The Home of Joseph and Adelicia Acklen* (Nashville: Historic Belmont Association, 1981), 39.

2. *Announcement and Prospectus of Belmont College*, 1891, 9-10.

3. *Announcement and Prospectus of Belmont College*, 1898, 16-17.

4. *Milady in Brown*, 1904.

5. J.L. Ensign, *The Culprit Fay*, Boston: Oliver Ditson and Company, 1872.

6. *Milady in Brown*, 1906.

7. *Belmont School of Music Catalog, 1906.*

8. *Milady in Brown*, 1905.

9. Wesleyan College *Zig-Zag*, Vol. 1, 1902.

10. *Belmont School of Music Catalog*, Summer1906.

11. Van Allen Bradley, *Music for the Millions: The Kimball Piano and Organ Story*. (Chicago: Henry Regnery Company, 1957), 249.

12. "Belmont Edition," *The Musical Herald*, (October 1908).

13. Ibid.

14. *Belmont School of Music Catalog*, 1911-12, 6-7.

15. Ibid.

16. *Belmont School of Music Catalog*, 1906-07, 11-12.

17. Nicolas Slonimsky, *Baker's Biographical Dictionary of Musicians*, 5th ed., s.v. "Hesselberg, Edouard," (New York: G. Schirmer, 1965), 707.

18. *Belmont School of Music Catalog*, 1906-07, 12.

19. Bradley, 249-250.

20. Slonimsky, 707.

21. Melvin Douglas Obituary, *Time* (August 17, 1981).

22. Wardin, 41.

23. *Belmont School of Music Catalog, 1914-15.*

24. *Milestones,* 1915.

25. Programs in the Louis Nicholas Collection in the Music Special Collections, Bunch Library, Belmont University.

26. *Nashville Tennessean,* April 17, 1915.

27. "Nashville Hears Choral Society in *Rose Maiden,*" *Musical America* (June 9, 1917), 21.

28. Edward Potjes, "American Battle Song," (Nashville: Standard Music Co., 1917).

29. *Milestones,* 1918.

30. *Harper's Magazine* (July, 1918), Ad for Ward-Belmont.

31. *Ward-Belmont School of Music Catalog,* 1922.

32. Craig Havighurst, *Air Castle of the South: WSM and the making of Music City.* (Urbana and Chicago: University of Illinois Press, 2007), 3.

33. John N. DeWitt, Jr., "Early Radio Broadcasting In Middle Tennessee," *Tennessee Historical Quarterly,* 31, no. 1, (Spring 1972): 84.

34. John Crowe Ransom, *Selected Poems.* (New York: Alfred A. Knopf, 1964), 37.

35. Ward-Belmont Orchestra program, May, 1923.

36. *Milestones,* 1927.

37. *Milestones,* 1928.

38. *Ward-Belmont Catalog,* 1918-1919, 11.

39. Martha Rivers Ingram and D.B. Kellogg, *Apollo's Struggle: A Performing Arts Odyssey in the Athens of the South,* (Nashville: Hillsboro Press, 2004), 141-143.

40. Robert W. Ikard, "Signor de Luca and the Nashville Conservatory of Music," *Tennessee Historical Quarterly,* 60, no. 3 (Fall 2001): 180.

41. *Nashville Conservatory of Music Catalog,* 1934-1935, 5.

42. Ibid., 5-8.

43. Ibid., preface.

44. Ikard, 182.

45. Stanley Sadie, *The New Grove Dictionary of Music and Musicians,* vol. 10, s.v. "Labunsky, Victor," (New York: MacMillan Publishers, 1980), 344.

46. Beverly Buchanan, "The Carillons of Belmont," *The Bulletin of the Guild of*

Carillonneurs in North America, 45, (1996): 18-26.

47. The original plaque was lost for decades and was later found in storage on campus and returned to the tower in January, 1991.

48. Programs in the Louis Nicholas Collection in the Music Special Collections, Bunch Library, Belmont University.

49. "Belmont Presents Scroll to the Roosevelts on Visit to Campus," *The Ward-Belmont Hyphen*, 23, no. 24 (November 24, 1934): 1.

50. *Good Housekeeping*, (May, 1931): 20. Ad for Ward-Belmont Conservatory of Music.

51. Louis Nicholas, "Tribute to a Teacher," *Nashville Banner*, September 22, 1963.

52. Alvin S. Wiggers, Concert Review, *Nashville Banner*, November 19, 1937.

53. "Belmont Conservatory Receives Accreditation," *The Ward-Belmont Hyphen*, 26, no. 15 (February 8, 1938): 1.

54. Sydney Dalton, Concert Review quoted in: Larry Adams, "The First Nighters: Walter Sharp and the Birth of the Nashville Symphony," *Nashville Scene*, March 7, 1996. (Accessed on-line, July 28, 2011).

55. Information drawn from *Milestones*, 1947-49.

56. Alan Irwin Obituary, *Ward-Belmont Hyphen*, 38, no. 12 (December 3, 1949): 1.

57. *Ward-Belmont Catalog*, 1943-44, 75.

58. *Milestones*, 1941.

59. Information drawn from *Milestones*, 1940-45.

60. Ward-Belmont publicity booklet, n.d. (1940s).

61. Concert program in Belmont University Archives.

62. Concert program in Belmont University Archives.

63. "Belmont Presents French Music Festival," *The Hyphen*, 35, no. 20 (March 8, 1947): 1.

64. Programs in the Louis Nicholas Collection in the Music Special Collections, Bunch Library, Belmont University.

65. "Henry Cowell Lectures and Performs for Ward-Belmont," *Ward-Belmont Hyphen*, 33, no. 20 (March 19, 1947): 1.

66. *Ward-Belmont School of Music Catalog*, 1922-23, 41-42.

67. Fletch Coke, document on the history of music at Christ Church, Nashville, TN.

68. *Milady in Brown*, 1910.

69. Louis Nicholas, "Series of Organ Recitals Feature Program for the Week,"

Tennessean, November 9, 1953.

70. Ingram and Kellogg, 125-127.

71. Buchanan, 25-26.

72. *Milestones,* 1945, 7.

73. Castle Heights Military Academy (1902-1986) was located in Lebanon, TN.

74. *Milestones,* 1943.

75. *Milestones,* 1946-47.

76. *Milestones,* 1948-49.

77. *Music at Ward-Belmont,* Sydney Dalton, Director, c. 1950, 78 RPM recording.

78. "Sylvia Stahlman," *Wikipedia.* (accessed June 9, 2011).

79. *Un Ballo Maschera,* Georg Solti, conductor, London Records, (Liner notes for LP recording, n.d.).

80. Sylvia Stahlman Obituary, *Opera News,* 65, no. 5 (November, 1998): 85.

81. Recordings from Sylvia Stahlman's collection in the Music Special Collections of the Bunch Library of Belmont University.

82. *Milestones,* 1951.

83. *Nashville Tennessean,* February 28, 1951, 1.

84. Louise Douglas Morrison, *A Voyage of Faith: The Story of Harpeth Hall.* (The Harpeth Hall School Auxiliary, 1980), 1-4.

85. *From Ward-Belmont to Belmont College,* Belmont University, 2005 (DVD) in the Belmont University Archives, Bunch Library.

86. Women's schools that closed after World War II include Tennessee College for Women and Tift College (Forsyth, GA). Other schools that became co-educational were Shorter College (Rome, GA), Brenau College (Gainesville, GA), and Women's College of Georgia (Milledgeville, GA).

87. *Ward-Belmont College Catalog,* 1948-49, 87.

Part III – Music at the New Belmont College (1951-1968)

1. The complicated and interesting birth of Belmont College is well chronicled in Chapters 2 and 3 of Herbert Gabhart's book *Work: The Soul of Good Fortune* (Nashville: Broadman Press, 1989).

2. At the writing of this book the enrollment at Belmont University is near 7,800 students. In fact, the School of Music graduated 136 students in the spring, 2014 Commencement, equaling the entire student body of Belmont in 1951.

3. "Bedford Youth First Male to Enroll at Belmont Since Melvyn Douglas," *Nashville Banner*, September 13, 1951.

4. *Belmont College Catalog, 1951-52*, 37.

5. Ibid., 12-13.

6. *The Tower*, 1952, 39. Mrs. Lutz' association with Belmont is a long and close one. As a high school student she studied piano at the Ward-Belmont Conservatory with Amelie Throne. She completed the two-year music program at Belmont College and went on to complete her degree at Baylor University. She is the mother of a Belmont Alumnus Charles Lutz, (BM vocal performance, '83) and the grandmother of Belmont Musical Theater major, Mary Claire Lutz, (BM in Musical Theatre, '13). Her husband, Richard C. Lutz served many years as an Associate Dean in the Massey Business School of Belmont University. She continues to be involved in music in Nashville and sings in the choir of the Immanuel Baptist Church.

7. Barbara Lutz Interview, August 2011.

8. Ibid.

9. Ibid.

10. Ibid.

11. Program for Inauguration of President R. Kelly White, May 18, 1953 in Belmont University Archives.

12. "Sydney Dalton to Begin WSM Series Tonight," *Nashville Tennessean*, August 11, 1952.

13. "Music Instructor Offers Belmont Piano Scholarship," *Nashville Tennessean*, October 31, 1952.

14. Louis Nicholas, "Music Faculty Changes at Belmont," *Nashville Tennessean*, June 7, 1953.

15. Barbara Lutz Interview.

16. Buchanan, "The Carillons of Belmont," *The Bulletin of the Guild of Carillonneurs in North America*, 45 (1996): 26-31.

17. *Belmont College Catalog, 1953-54*, 9-12.

18. Ibid., 36.

19. Ibid., 13.

20. Barbara Redden Burnett interview, August, 2011.

21. *Belmont College Department of Music NASM Self-Evaluation Report*, 1955.

22. Elizabeth Wall interview, August 1980.

23. *Belmont College Catalog, 1955-56*, 9-12.

24. *Belmont College Catalog, 1956-57*, 9-12.

25. *The Tower,* 1957, 64-65.
26. Helen Midkiff Capra interview, June, 2011.
27. *Belmont College Department of Music NASM Self-Evaluation Report,* 1955.
28. Concert Programs in School of Music Files.
29. Gabhart, *Work: The Soul of Good Fortune,* 47.
30. Ibid., 110.
31. Steinway pianos from Ward-Belmont were in use in Hail Hall at the time. Many of these pianos were damaged, but were cleaned, repaired and brought back when renovation was completed. Still, the finish of these pianos acquired a smudged, smoky appearance from the fire. Some of these pianos were in use at Belmont well into the 1990s and the last one was traded in 2008 when Belmont started its initiative to become an "All-Steinway School."
32. *The Tower,* 1962-1964.
33. Information from organ builder Robert Capra.
34. *The Tower,* 1968, 52.
35. Gabhart, *Work: The Soul of Good Fortune,* 107.
36. Louis Nicholas, *Thor Johnson: American Conductor,* 269.
37. Gabhart, *Work: The Soul of Good Fortune,* 130.
38. Herbert Gabhart, *The Massey-Belmont Story,* 108-109.
39. Information from the charter documents of the two organizations in The Belmont University School of Music Office.

Part IV – Belmont Music under Jerry Warren (1969-1991):
A Firm Foundation

1. In future years three of Jerry Warren's former students from Shorter, Dr. David Bridges, Dr. Madeline Bridges and Dr. Richard Shadinger, would join the music faculty of Belmont.
2. Jerry Warren interview, June, 2010.
3. Ibid.
4. *Belmont College Catalog,* 1972-1979.
5. Jerry Warren interview.
6. In 2012 the School of Music began planning for a Major in Music Therapy to begin in the Fall of 2014, 37 years later.
7. *National Association of Schools of Music Self Study Documents,* 1977.
8. Jerry Warren interview.

9. In the 1970s and 80s, the Turnley Studio was a destination for Nashville tour companies – a place to demonstrate recording techniques to Nashville visitors. For a time it was a revenue-producing enterprise that provided summer work for music business majors.

10. Gabhart, *Work: The Soul of Good Fortune*, 224-225.

11. Program from "PraiSing," March 10-13, 1975.

12. Program from dedicatory concert for the Joyce Bush Grand Piano, August 7, 1973. The Joyce Bush Steinway Grand was used in Harton Concert Hall for many years and was later moved to the Belmont Mansion for concerts. Eventually, it was moved to a classroom, where it was used for piano and vocal seminars and rehearsals. After more than 30 years of service, this piano was traded in for a new Steinway concert grand when Belmont became an "All-Steinway School" in 2007.

13. Jerry Warren relates this account: with the increased number of piano students, piano faculty members had discovered that they could roll practice pianos out into the hallway and teach a makeshift piano class. One morning Professor Elizabeth Wall was teaching a group of about six students in this manner when Dr. Gabhart came through the building with a guest. He was aghast at the sound of the pianos and the fact that the hall was blocked. Dr. Warren explained to him that, without a piano lab, this was the only way to teach multiple students without placing them all in private lessons, which was, of course, more costly for the college. Dr. Gabhart immediately began seeking a donor for the piano lab, resulting in the gift from Tree International.

14. Statistics from Music Department documents.

15. Jerry Warren interview.

16. *Belmont College Catalog*, 1978-1984.

17. Charlie Miller interview, June, 2011.

18. Diane Rappaport, "Music Education for a Changing Job Market," *Keyboard* (January, 1982).

19. "Company Wins Third Place in National Competition," *Belmont Circle* (September, 1982) 21, no. 2, 6.

20. Program from memorial service for Dr. Richard LaMar, October 26, 1978.

21. "Festival of Music This Week at Belmont," *Tennessean*, November 30, 1978.

22. Programs in the School of Music files.

23. "The Founding of NAMTA," *Nashville Area Music Teachers Association Membership Directory*, 2011-2012, 3.

24. "Belmont Music Foundation Organized," *Belmont Music News* (Spring,

1981): 1.

25. *Belmont Music News*, (Fall, 1981): p. 2.

26. "Belmont College Pi Kappa Lambda is Installed," *Belmont Music News* (Fall, 1982): 1.

27. Program for Inaugural Concert for Dr. William E. Troutt, October 28, 1982.

28. Program for the Inauguration of Dr. William E. Troutt, October 29, 1982.

29. Faculty minutes from Music Faculty Retreat, January 18-19, 1983.

30. *Belmont Music News*, (Spring, 1983): 1.

31. Ibid., 2.

32. "Belmont Divided into Four Schools," *Belmont Circle* (January-March, 1983), 22, no. 1, 4.

33. *Belmont Music News*, (Fall, 1983): 1.

34. Jerry Warren interview.

35. *Belmont Music News*, (Fall, 1983): 2.

36. *Belmont College Catalog*, 1980-1989.

37. "Belmont's Orchestral Program a Promising Addition," *Belmont Circle*, 24, no. 2, (Spring-Summer, 1985): 10; and Programs of the Belmont Orchestra concerts, 1984-1986.

38. "Master of Music Education Degree Offered at Belmont," *Belmont Music News*, (Spring, 1987): p. 1.

39. "The Tennessee Arts Academy History," *Tennessee Arts Academy, 25th Year*, (July 10-15, 2011): 21.

40. *Belmont Music News*, 1984-1985.

41. Recording Reviews, *Fanfare* (January/February, 1986).

42. "More than Music," *Belmont Music News* (August-September, 1989): p. 1.

43. *National Association of Schools of Music Self-Study Report, Belmont College*, 1986.

44. Beverly Buchanan, "The Carillons of Belmont," *The Bulletin of the Guild of Carillonneurs in North America*, 35, (1996) 31-44.

45. Rhonda Gibson, "John Robinson Named Fulbright Scholar," *Belmont Music News*, (October 1987): p. 1. As of writing of the book, John Robinson is Team leader for The Celtic Languages Team, an evangelical mission group in Cymru, Wales, which works with churches in a variety of Celtic languages. He is now fluent in Welsh, as well as other Celtic languages.

46. Camerata concert program, February 18, 1988, in program files in the School of Music .

47. Information from Camerata files in the School of Music.

48. "SAI Awards 'Ring of Excellence' to Elizabeth Wall," *Belmont Music News,* (December-January, 1987-88): 1.

49. "Cheekwood Music Series Scheduled," *Belmont Music News,* (November, 1987).

50. "Jazz Ensemble to Play at TMEA Convention," *Belmont Music News,* (March, 1988): 1.

51. *National Association of Schools of Music Commission on Graduate Studies Plan Approval Document,* Belmont College, 1988.

52. *Belmont Music News,* (April, 1988): 2.

53. Ibid., 1.

54. "Kodaly Certification Program Initiated," *Belmont Music News,* (August-September, 1988): 3.

55. Rhonda Gibson, "Friend Claims Music Collection for Belmont," *Belmont Circle,* 28, no. 3, (Fall, 1989): 19.

56. "Pursell Work Premieres February 22," *Belmont Music News,* (February, 1988): 1.

57. Commercial Music Showcase programs in the files of the School of Music.

58. Mona Collett, "Belmont's Covenant for Quality," *Belmont Circle,* 30, no. 1, (Spring, 1991): 5-7.

59. TAG Team files in School of Music office.

60. See Appendix 4 for list of recipients of the Applause Award.

61. President's Concert programs in School of Music files.

62. Madeline Bridges and Marilyn Shadinger interviews, October, 2012.

63. Karla Graul, "From Belmont to Broadway," *Belmont Circle,* 30, no. 2, (Fall, 1991): 22.

64. Jerome Reed, "Music of Les Six Captured in Belmont College Festival," *Tennessean,* February 1, 1990, 5-D.

65. Program for String Quartets in School of Music files.

66. "Chorale to Celebrate 20th-Year Reunion," *Belmont Music News,* (February, 1990): 1.

67. "What's New ... in the SOM," *Belmont Music News,* (August/September, 1990): 1.

68. "Karla Graul Named to New Position as Public Relations Assistant," *Belmont Music News,* (February, 1991): 1.

69. "Personnel Changes Affect Academic Administration," *Belmont Circle,* Vol. 30, No. 2, (Fall, 1991): 20.

70. Ibid.

71. "Belmont University: A New Beginning," *Belmont Circle*, Vol. 30, No. 2, (Fall, 1991): 5.

Part V – The School of Music under Cynthia Curtis (1991-1999)

1. Cynthia Curtis interview, July 7, 2011; "Kraft General Foods Sponsors Series," *Belmont Music News*, (Fall, 1991): 1.

2. "Belmont Camerata Chosen for Television," *Belmont Music News*, (September, 1991): 1.

3. "Billboard Chooses Belmont to Judge Annual Song Contest," *Belmont Music News*, (Winter, 1992): 1.

4. Karla Graul and Mona Collett, "Shoe Merchant Makes 'Sweet Music,'" *Belmont Circle*, Vol. 32, No. 1, (Spring, 1991): 5.

5. Program from dedication of the Wilson Music Building.

6. "Belmont Announces new Dean of Music," *Nashville Banner*, June 21, 1993, B-3.

7. Wheat Williams, "Belmont: a best-kept secret," *The Nashvillian*, December 5, 1991.

8. Cynthia Curtis interview, July 7, 2011.

9. *Belmont Music News*, 1991-1993.

10. Notes of meetings held at Belmont, March 21-22, 1993.

11. Ted Wylie, "To Russia . . .For Music," *Belmont Music News* (Fall, 1993): 1; Jerry Warren Interview and journal from the trip by Richard Shadinger.

12. Ibid.

13. Misha Stefanuk, "My Opening of America," *Belmont Circle*, Vol. 33, No. 1, (Spring, 1994): 4.

14. Vocal Institute files in the School of Music.

15. Jennifer Coleman Interview.

16. Program for 25th Anniversary Chorale Concert, March 25, 1995, in School of Music program files.

17. Music Faculty Minutes, August, 1995.

18. Alan Bostic, "Belmont Sharpens Up as Music City's Music School," *Tennessean*, November 19, 1995, 12.

19. The painting by Ron York now hangs in the Conference Room in the Wilson Music Building.

20. Music Public Relation files, 1996-2000.

21. Minutes for Friends of the School of Music, 1995.

22. See Appendix 3 for list of all Friends of the School of Music Presidents.

23. Interview with Sarah Davis, August, 2012.

24. "New Scholarship Funds Established," *Belmont Music News* (Fall, 1996): 5.

25. Interview with Sarah Davis.

26. Curtain Call Award Programs, School of Music Files.

27. See Appendix 5 for list of all Curtain Award recipients.

28. Program for Louis Nicholas Tribute, February 13, 1996, in School of Music program files.

29. National Association of Schools of Music, 1996 Self-study Belmont University School of Music.

30. *Belmont University Graduate Bulletin*, 1999-2000, 65-75.

31. *World Church Music Symposium Agenda* and journal of Richard Shadinger.

32. Belmont Academy documents in the School of Music files.

33. Brad Schmitt, "Stars Raise $75,000 for Belmont," *Tennessean*, September 10, 1996, D-1.

34. *Christmas at Belmont*, Acklen Records, Belmont University, November 20, 1996 (Compact Disc recording).

35. Massey Concert Hall renovation files in the School of Music.

36. Program for "When in Our Music ...," October 6, 1997, in School of Music program files.

37. Program from President's Concert, October 11, 1997, in the School of Music program files.

38. Program from the organ rededication concert, March 6, 2000, in the School of Music files and files on the reconstruction of the Wicks organ.

39. Programs from the John Rutter Choral Festival, October 29-31, 1998, in the School of Music program files.

40. "Christmas at Belmont" Programs (1997-2000) in the School of Music files.

41. Keith Mason interview.

42. Programs from Ballet performance at Belmont in the School of Music files.

43. Program from *Pierrot Lunaire* performance, May 3, 1999, in School of Music files.

44. Jerry Warren interview; Programs from Belle Voci in School of Music files.

Part VI – A New Millennium:
The School of Music Comes of Age (2000-2012)

1. *Belmont University Bulletin*, 1999 -2000, 3.

2. Statistics in the School of Music files.

3. Oratorio Chorus concert program in the School of Music program files.

4. Richard Speight, "Pomp and Ceremony: Belmont Inaugurates its Fourth President," *Belmont Circle*, 38, no. 1, (Fall, 2000): 2.

5. Jared Porter, "Recording Artist Surprised by Turn of Events," *Belmont Circle*, Vol. 38, No. 1 (Fall, 2000): 23.

6. Josh Turner Recital program, October 6, 2000, in the School of Music program files.

7. Alan Bostic, "Weill, Weill, Weill," *Tennessean*, October 8, 2000.

8. Program from the David Willcocks Festival, October 26-27, 2000, in School of Music program files.

9. "Belmont Offers New Degree in Musical Theater," *Belmont Circle*, 37, no. 2, (Winter, 1999): 14. Programs from Musical Theater performances; Marjorie Halbert interview.

10. *Belmont University Bulletin*, "General Education".

11. Information from the Compensation Committee of the College of Visual and Performing Arts.

12. Richard Hoffman interview.

13. "Alumnus Researches Bulgarian Maestro's Music," *The Belmont Circle*, Vol. 40, No. 2 (Spring, 2003): 25.

14. From programs of "Christmas at Belmont" in School of Music files.

15. James Kimmel interview.

16. Elisabeth Small interview.

17. Kristian Klefstad interview.

18. Barry Kraus interview.

19. Richard Hoffman interview.

20. Jane Warren interview.

21. Robert Gregg interview.

22. Program from Symphony Orchestra Concert, Feb. 28, 2009 in School of Music program files.

23. Sarah Davis interview.

24. School of Music files on endowed scholarships.

25. School of Music Scholarship Committee documents.

26. Files on piano replacement in the School of Music.

27. Program in School of Music program files.

28. Information from Vicky Tarleton, Belmont University Department of Advancement.

29. National Association of Schools of Music 1996 Self-Study Document, Belmont University School of Music.

30. Program for Retirement Celebration for Dr. Jerry Warren, April 13, 2007 in School of Music files.

31. Program from the Guild of Carrillonneurs in North America (June 19-22, 2007).

32. "Clifton Forbis," quoted on website for Columbia Management.

33. Encore Award Committee files in the School of Music Office.

34. Concert programs in School of Music Office.

35. Concert program for Woods Memorial Concert, September 10, 2010, in School of Music files.

36. Meg Tully, "Towering Tradition: Belmont's Historic Bell Tower Undergoes Restoration," *The Belmont Circle* (Fall, 2010): 12-13.

37. "Belmont Announces New Concert Hall," Belmont Office of Communications Press Release, August 20, 2010.

38. Information from School of Music files on MM in Commercial Music.

39. School of Music concert brochures for Fall 2010 and Spring 2011.

40. *In Concert,* Nashville Symphony program (January, 2011).

41. Program from the concert, January 22, 2011.

42. Program from the 40th Anniversary Chorale Concert, May 7, 2011.

43. Journal by Richard Shadinger, May 15-25, 2011.

44. Program for the Belmont String Chamber Orchestra in School of Music files.

45. Timothy Gmeiner interview; library statistics from Bunch Music Library.

VII – Projections for the Future (2012-2014)

1. Lina Tergesen Sheahan interview.

2. Encore Award Program, February 14, 2012, in School of Music program files.

3. Program from Graduate Hooding Ceremony, May 4, 2012, in School of Music program files.

4. Jessica Bliss, "Nashville Proves Itself at Carnegie" *Tennessean,* May 13, 2012, 1, 6A.

5. "From Bedroom to Business: How to Make a Living as a Working Musician with Roy Vogt," *Bass Music Magazine* (February, 2012).

6. Mark Patton "DODD's honor band, chorus make great music together," *Stars and Stripes* (March 31, 2011).

7. Madeline Bridges and John Feierabend, *The Book of Church Songs and Spirituals*, Chicago: GIA Publications, 2011.

8. Opera review, *Tennessean*, April 13, 2012.

9. Elisabeth Small interview.

10. Zoro, *The Big Gig: Big-Picture Thinking for Success*, Van Nuys: Alfred Publishing Co., 2012.

11. Michael Brantley, "Tammy Rogers: Taking the Lead," *Fiddler Magazine*, 19, no.1, (Spring 2012): 9.

12. John Pitcher, "String Theory," *Nashville Scene*, 31, no. 14, (May 3, 2012): 15-22.

13. Letter to Joel Treybig from the International Trumpet Guild, February 20, 2012.

14. *In Concert*, Nashville Symphony Orchestra program magazine, 2011-2012 issues.

15. Christopher Norton interview.

16. Terry Klefstad, "A Soviet Opera in America," In *Contemplating Shostakovich* by Alexander Ivaskin and Andrew Kirkman. Burlington: Ashgate Publishing Company, 2012.

17. Terry Klefstad, "Shostakovich and the Peace Conference," *Music and Politics*, 6, no. 2 (Spring, 2012).

18. Virginia Lamothe, "Dancing at the Wedding: Some Thoughts on Performance Issues in Claudio Monteverdi's 'Lasciate I monti' (*Orfeo*, 1607)," *Early Music* (November, 2008).

19. Virginia Lamothe, "Fanning the Flames of Love: Hidden Performance Solutions for Claudio Monteverdi's *Ballo delle ingrate* found in Renaissance Dance," (Ann Arbor: Steglein Publishing, Inc.), 2007.

20. Sandra Dudley interview.

21. Lindsay George interview.

22. School of Music faculty meeting minutes, August, 2012.

23. Joan Eakin interview.

24. Figures derived from program files in the School of Music.

25. Program for Colman lecture, September 6, 2012, in School of Music program files.

26. Program for Alumni concert, September 8, 2012, in School of Music program files.

27. Program from McAfee Dedication Concert, October 6, 2012, in School of

Music files.

28. Press release from Belmont Office of Communications, August 1, 2011.

29. Celebration Planning Committee files, Spring 2011.

30. Sarah Davis interview.

31. Information from The Milnar Organ Company.

32. "Nashville Chamber Singers/Matthew Dirst and Friends," *The American Organist*, 46, no. 10, (October, 2012): 58.

33. Email from C. Russell Todd, Akustiks, sent to Cynthia Curtis, September 10, 2012.

34. Mary Hance, "New McAfee Hall Inspires," *Tennessean*, September 16, 2012, 20D.

35. Program from Kobrin Recital, September 20, 2012, in School of Music program files.

36. Program from Wind Ensemble Concert, October 9, 2012, in School of Music program files.

37. Program from Belmont Symphony Orchestra Concert, October 11, 2012, in School of Music program files.

38. Program from Organ Recital, October 22, 2012, in School of Music program files.

39. "Belmont University Celebrates Grand Opening of McAfee Concert Hall," Press release from Belmont Office of Communications, October 5, 2012.

40. John Pitcher, "Belmont Inaugurates McAfee Concert Hall with Gala Concert," *Nashville Arts*, October 8, 2012.

41. Biographical information from Dedicatory Concert program in School of Music program files.

42. "Best of Nashville," *Nashville Scene*, 31, no. 37, October 11, 2012.

43. Program from the Nashville Symphony Orchestra Concert program, October 23, 2012 in School of Music program files.

44. John Pitcher, "Music Review: Belmont Rings in the Holidays in its New Concert Hall," *Nashville Arts*, December 2, 2012.

45. John Pitcher, "Nashville's Classical Scene Enters a Golden Age," *Nashville Scene, 31, no. 45.*

46. John Pitcher, "Classical Review: Denyce Graves Hits All the Right Notes at Belmont," *Nashville Arts*, February 18, 2013.

47. John Pitcher, "Famed Music Historian Richard Taruskin Will Visit Belmont," *Nashville Arts*, March 22, 2013.

48. "4 Pianos-16 Hands- Belmont University School of Music Piano Faculty:

McAfee Concert Hall, April 13, 2013" *Music City Mike,* Music Review, April 14, 2013.

49. John Pitcher, "Belmont 24th Annual President's Concert Honors Carolyn Townsend McAfee," *Nashville Arts,* April 22, 2013.

50. Amy Stumpfl, "Romance in the Air: Belmont Camerata celebrates Schubert, Schoenberg," *Tennessean,* April 21, 2013.

51. "Citation for Excellence - Renovation/Adaptive Reuse/Restoration: Belmont University – McAfee Concert Hall," *Learning by Design,* Spring 2013, 74-75.

52. "Making History – Les Misérables," *Nashville Scene,* March 14, 2013, 46.

53. Program for *Les Misérables* in School of Music program files.

54. Patrick Dorsey, "Cinderella Stories: Belmont University," *ESPN Playbook,* online, (Accessed March 20, 2013).

55. Program from Marjorie Halbert Retirement Celebration, April 21, 2013, in School of Music program files.

56. Alejandra Ferrer interview.

57. Rau, Nate. "Belmont launches choir for children with autism." *Tennessean,* December 16, 2015.

58. "The 10 Most Underrated Theatre Colleges." *Onstageblog,* August 31, 2015.

59. "Musical Theatre Wins American Prize for 'Oklahoma' Production." *Belmont FYI,* January 15, 2016.

60. "School of Music Faculty Complete Chinese Tour." *Belmont FYI,* August 13, 2015.

61. "Father Daughter Duo Bill and Laura Pursell to Storm the Stage at Vitello's January 10." *The LA Beat,* January 10, 2016.

62. Jeffery Ames interview.

63. "BWW Review: Belmont University Theatre's *White Christmas.*" *Broadwayworld.com/Nashville.* December 10, 2015.

64. Provost Thomas Burns' Email message to Belmont University Faculty, January 13, 2016.

65. "A look back on CVPA Dean Cynthia Curtis's 35 years at Belmont." *The Belmont Vision,* February 4, 2016.

Appendix 1
Ward-Belmont Music Faculty

Clements, Mrs. M.S.	1891	Guitar, Mandolin, Banjo
Dismukes, Mattie L.	1891	Piano
McCandless, Kate L.	1891	Piano
Sloane, Grace Gardner	1891	Voice
Wendel, Annie F.	1891	Piano
Geary, Mamie	1895	Violin
LeBarge, L.E.	1895	Guitar, Mandolin, Banjo
Leftwich, Alice K.	1895	Piano/Theory
Macgruder, Fannie	1895	Voice
Guest, J.H.	1903	Violin
Hartzell, E.W.	1903	Guitar, Mandolin, Banjo
Powell, Mrs. Douglas	1903	Piano
Schuler, Lura	1903	Piano
Taliaferro, Julia	1903	Voice/Music History
Gieske-Berry, Sophi M.	1904	Piano
Corum, May	1905	Practice Superintendent
Duncan, Katherine S.	1905	Piano
Hesselberg, Edouard	1905	Piano/Director of School of Music
Skidmore-Conner, Marie L.	1905	Violin
Sutherland, Ida H.	1905	Voice
Washburn, Charles C.	1905	Voice
Corley, Virginia	1906	Practice Superintendent
Buckner, Cuthbert	1907	Voice
Chandler, Susie	1907	Practice Superintendent
Heilman, Louise Elisabeth	1907	Voice
Hequembourg, Florence Dillard	1907	Violin
Webb, Florence	1907	Organ/Piano
Zarbell, Meda	1907	Piano
Bogengrief, Marie Louise	1908	Piano
Parker, Nina Dale	1908	Cello
Wheeler, Lelia Lewis	1908	Voice
Whipplinger, Johanna	1908	Voice
Merson, Elise D.	1909	Voice

Nance, Louise	1909	Superintendent of Practice
Osborne, Mabel Collins	1909	Theory
Valtinee, Paul	1909	Violin
Harris, Bessie	1910	Superintendent of Practice
Heinrich, Madame Franziska	1910	Piano
Henkel, Arthur	1910	Organ/Piano
Moory, Helen T.	1910	Piano
Mudroch, Gabriela	1910	Voice
Mudroch, Vratislov	1910	Violin
Parmalee, Mabel L.	1910	Theory and History
Maxwell, Buda Love	1911	Piano
Ross, Harry A.	1911	Violin
Townsend, Pauline Sherwood	1911	Concert Ettiquette
Forrest, Marguerite Palmiter	1912	Voice
Randegger, Aldo	1912	Piano/Director of School of Music
Graziani, Madame Elise	1913	Voice
Blythe, Venable	1914	Practice Superintendent/Theory
Boyer, Florence	1914	Voice
Koelker, Ida Stark	1914	Piano
Martin, James Browne	1914	Theory/History
Massey, Eva	1914	Piano
Schmitz, Estell Roy	1914	Piano
Schmitz, Fritz	1914	Violin
Throne, Amelie	1914	Piano
Winkler, Emil	1914	Piano/Director of School of Music
Winkler, Mary Falconer	1914	Piano
Potjes, Edouard	1917	Piano/Director of School of Music
De Luca, Gaetano Salvatore	1918	Voice
Dunn, Dorothy Isabel	1918	Musical Sciences
Rose, Kenneth D.	1918	Violin
Goodman, Lawrence	1919	Piano/Director of School of Music
Rose, Hazel Coate	1919	Piano
Kirkman, Katherine	1920	Assistant in Musical Science
Ransom, Annie Phillips	1920	Piano
Sloan, Helen Todd	1920	Piano
Mead, Edward Gould	1921	Musical Sciences
Best, Louise	1922	Piano
Fentress, Allene	1922	Violin Accompanist

Reeves, Alberta	1922	Voice Accompanist
Strick Alfred Hoskin	1922	Musical Sciences
Owsley, Mattie Buckner	1923	Practice Superintendent
Paschall, Hattie Thula	1923	Voice Accompanist
Webster, George Allen	1923	Musical Sciences/Glee Club
Barnes, Henry W.B.	1924	Musical Sciences
Wesson, Henry	1925	Musical Sciences/Organ
Baber, Elizabeth Gwatkin	1926	Harp
Douthit, Mary	1927	Piano
Harper, Claire	1927	Violin Accompanist
Shannon, Marguerite	1927	Voice Accompanist
Sullivan Adrienne F.	1927	Musical Sciences
Humphrey, Stetson	1928	Voice
Humphrey, Ida Crance	1930	Voice
Riggs, Lawrence H.	1930	Musical Sciences
Thuss, Clemence	1930	Piano
Dorris, Mildred	1932	Practice Superintendent
Jackson, Frances Helen	1932	Harp
Oman, Nell Godwin	1932	Violin Assistant
Thompson, Lavelle	1932	Practice Superintendent
Cavert, Annie	1933	Practice Superintendent
Dalton, Sydney	1933	Voice
Underwood, Roy	1934	Piano/Director of School of Music
Brackinreed, Verna	1937	Piano
Faxon, Nancy Plummer	1941	Voice
Irwin, Alan	1941	Piano/Dean of the Conservatory
Myers, Lady Corinne	1941	Practice Supervisor/Secretary
Olson, Vivienne	1941	Cello
Salisbury, Rosamond	1942	Cello/Theory
Wall, Elizabeth	1942	Piano
Adams, Elizabeth Albee	1943	Voice
Dann, Mary G.	1943	Cello/Theory
Irwin, Florence	1943	Piano
Malone, Mary Cornelia	1943	Voice
Rose, Katherine	1944	Piano
Van Sickle, Marilyn Redinger	1945	Voice
Benton, Maribel	1947	Piano
Schneck, Grace	1947	Theory
Sefton, Jane	1947	Piano
Davis, Marjorie	1948	Theory
Zepernick, Werner	1950	Piano/Dean of the Conservatory
McFarland, Nancy Elliott	1950	Piano

Appendix 2

School of Music Full-Time Faculty

Dalton, Sydney (WB)*	1951	Voice
Henkel, Arthur (WB)*	1951	Organ
Irwin, Florence (WB)*	1951	Piano
Rose, Kenneth (WB)*	1951	Violin
Throne, Amalie (WB)*	1951	Voice
Van Sickle, Marilyn (WB)*	1951	Voice
Wall, Elizabeth (WB)*	1951	Music History/Piano/Music Librarian
Harper, Josephine Cook*	1953	Piano
Mathis, William S.*	1953	Organ/Department Chair
Stephens, Genter*	1953	Voice
Turman, Peggy Jo Tapp	1953	Piano
Turbeville, Nyra	1954	Piano
White, Dee Wayne	1954	Voice/Choral Ensembles
Lawson, Betty	1955	Voice
Sawyer, Robert B.	1955	Theory
Sebren, Herbert L.	1955	
Daniel, Cyrus C.	1956	Theory
Pearson, Fred, B., Jr.	1956	Voice/Choral Ensembles
Koonts, Cortlandt Morpor	1957	Piano
Midkiff, Helen*	1958	Organ/Theory
Mulloy, Robert*	1961	Voice/Choral Ensembles
Burgin, John C.	1963	Voice
Hartley, Kenneth*	1964	Choral Ensembles/Chair of Department
Thompson, J. William	1965	Voice
Archie Kliewer*	1966	Classical Voice
Lyall, Max*	1966	Piano/Theory
Thompson, E.D.	1967	Band
Warren, Jerry	1969	Voice, Conducting, Choral Ensembles/Dean
LaMar, Richard*	1970	Piano
Godwin, Paul*	1973	Theory/Composition/Concert Band/Associate Dean

Martin, Boyd	1974	Music Education/Ensembles
Shadinger, Richard	1974	Music History/Piano/Church Music/Associate Dean
Kelly, Sherry	1975	Classical Voice/Choral Ensembles
Collins, Newton Jaye*	1976	Percussion/Theory
Ford, Linda	1976	Piano/Piano Pedagogy/ Theory
Wood, Albert	1976	Music Education
Collins, Diane	1977	Classical Voice/Opera
Fern, Terry	1978	Classical Voice
Ford, Randall	1979	Concert Band/Clarinet
Gmeiner, Timothy	1979	Music Librarian
Halbert, Marjorie	1979	Classical Voice/ Choral Ensembles/Musical Theater
Lebon, Rachel	1979	Commercial Voice
Marler, Robert	1979	Piano
Pell, John	1980	Guitar
Curtis, Cynthia	1980	Music Education/Music History/Dean
Moore, Keith	1980	Voice/Vocal Literature and Diction
Pursell, William	1980	Composition/Orchestration/Music History
Arnn, John	1981	Commercial Piano
Elsberry, Kristie	1981	Theory/Piano/Associate Dean
Ferguson, James	1981	Commercial Voice
Thomas, John Baker	1981	Voice/Church Music
Landes, Daniel	1984	Piano/Church Music
Gregg, Robert	1984	Orchestra/Music History/Associate Dean
Zielinski, Shirley	1984	Voice/Opera
Harrington, Michael	1985	Theory/Music History/Commercial Music
Kenyon, Janet	1985	Commercial Voice
Wylie, Ted	1985	Voice/International Studies
Ellis, Keith*	1986	Trumpet/Music Education/Concert Band
Ford, Karrin	1986	Theory/Organ
Walker, Jeannine	1986	Commercial Voice/Choral Ensemble
Binkley, Carolyn	1987	Commercial Voice
Entsminger, Deen	1988	Music Education/Choral Ensemble/Composition
Kirk, Jeffrey	1994	Saxophone/Commercial Arranging/Associate Dean

297

Lewis, Donald	1994	Music Education
Murphy, Kevin	1994	Commercial Voice/Choral Ensemble
Dudley, Sandra	1995	Commercial Voice
Kimmel, James	1995	Music Education/Choral Ensembles
Sharp, Timothy	1996	Choral Ensembles/Church Music
Bridges, Madeline	1998	Music Education/Associate Dean
Mason, Keith	1998	Music Technology
Smiley, Henry	1998	Commercial Voice/Vocal Ensemble
Bullock, Emily	1999	Classical Voice/Opera
Hoffman, Richard	2000	Theory
Scruggs, Edgar	2000	Choral Ensembles/Conducting
Norton, Christopher	2001	Percussion/Percussion Ensemble
Whitten, Kristi	2001	Voice/ Opera
McLeod, Kenneth	2002	Musicology
Warren, Jane	2003	Choral Ensembles/Conducting/ Theory
Small, Elisabeth	2003	Violin/Camerata
Garner, Kelly	2004	Commercial Voice
Bennett, Bruce	2004	Commercial Voice
Schallert, Gary	2004	Music Education/Concert Band
Coleman, Jennifer	2004	Voice/Vocal Pedagogy
Manwarren, Mathew	2005	Piano
Treybig, Joel	2005	Trumpet/Belmont Brass/Theory
Belfiglio, Anthony	2006	Commercial Piano
Dudley, Bruce	2006	Commercial Piano/Theory
Klefstad, Kristian	2006	Piano/Piano Pedagogy
Klefstad, Terry	2006	Musicology
Paradise, Kathryn	2007	Commercial Voice/Vocal Ensemble
Ames, Jeffery	2008	Choral Ensembles/Conducting
Kraus, Barry	2008	Wind Ensemble/Music Education
Lamothe, Peter	2008	Musicology
Shamburger, David	2008	Voice/Musical Theater
Volker, Mark	2009	Composition
Eng, Clare	2011	Theory
Whatley, Mark	2011	Voice
Graham, Alex	2011	Saxophone
Allen, Nancy	2014	Voice/Musical Theater
Mann, Lesley	2014	Choral Music Education
Ferrer, Alejandra	2015	Music Therapy
Eaves, Stephen	2016	Dean, College of Visual and Performing Arts

*deceased

298

Appendix 3

Presidents of Friends of the School of Music

1995-96 – Ronn Huff
1996-97 – Michael Omartian
1997-98 – Ronn Huff
1998-99 – Jamie Dunham
1999-2000 – Patricia Bullard
2000-2001 – Patricia Bullard
2001-2002 – Sigourney Cheek
2002-2003 – Ann Lauterbach
2003-2004 – Ann Lauterbach
Becomes Friends of the Arts at Belmont (FAB)
2004-2005 – Rick Hart
2005-2006 – Anne Shepherd
2006-2007 – Andy Valentine
2007-2008 – Arlyn Cheney
2008-2009 - Samuel Allen
2009-2010 – Ann Bumstead
2010-2011 – Anne Knestrick
2011-2012 – Sharon Sheriff
2012-2013 – Dr. Robert Ikard
2013-2014 – James Aderhold
2014-2015 – Chris Simonsen
2015-2016 – Dr. James Perry
2016-2017 – X Lucas

Appendix 4

Applause Award Recipients
at President's Concerts

1992 - Donna Hilley (Release of the SOM Cassette "Kaleidoscope")
1993 – Sam A. Wilson
1994 – Jerry L. Warren
1995 – James A. Cotham IV (Posthumously)
1996 - Friends of the School of Music
1997 - Barbara Massey Rogers
1999 – Chet Atkins
2000 – Ronn Huff
2001 – Patricia Taylor Bullard; In Memory of Margaret Maddox
2002 – Vince Gill/Amy Grant
2003 – Kenneth Schermerhorn
2004 – Cheekwood Botanical Garden and Museum of Art, Frist Center for the
      Visual Arts, Nashville Ballet, Nashville Opera, Nashville Symphony,
      Tennessee Repertory Theatre
2005 – ASCAP, BMI, SESAC
2006 – Eddy Arnold
2007 – Martha Ingram
2008 – Steinway Piano Company
2009 - Beaman Family Foundation
2010 – The Grand Ole Opry
2011 – Earl Swensson and Associates, Architect
2012 – CeCe Wynans
2013 – Carolyn McAfee
2014 – Ricky Skaggs
2015 – Michael W. Smith
2016 – Cynthia R. Curtis

Appendix 5
School of Music Curtain Call Award

1995 – Chris Rodriguez (1983), guitarist, recording artist

1996 – Tammy Rogers (1987), violinist/fiddler, recording artist, member of Steel Drivers

1997 – Gordon Mote (1993), pianist, recording artist

1998 – Jozef Nuyens (1996), guitarist, producer; owner, Castle Studio

1999 – Melodie Crittenden (1992), singer, recording artist

2000 – Fleming McWilliams, pop singer, recording artist

2001 – Will Denton (1992), drummer, recording artist

2002 – Jill Phillips Gullahorn (1998), singer, recording artist

2003 – Ginny Owens (1997), award-winning Christian singer/songwriter

2004 – Josh Turner (2001), award-winning country artist

2005 – Denver Bierman (1999), trumpeter and leader of Denver and the Mile High Orchestra

2006 – Dan Muckala (1993), pianist, producer, songwriter

2007 – Melinda Doolittle (1999), performer and recording artist, American Idol finalist

2009 – Bernie Herms (1995), pianist, recording artist

2010 – Chester Thompson (2010), drummer for Phil Collins; faculty, Belmont University

2011 – Tim Lauer (1990), pianist, band leader, arranger

2012 – Tad Wilson (1992), Broadway performer, pop singer and recording artist

2013 - Russell Terrell (1987), first-call background singer for recording sessions

2014 – Danny Wells (1983), guitarist, award-winning song writer

2015 – Geoffrey Koch (1994), Composer, arranger for film and television

2016 – Brandon Fraley (2000), Song writer, pianist,

Appendix 6
School of Music Curtain Call Award

2009 – Clifton Forbis (1985), Tenor, performer with the Metropolitan Opera and opera companies in Europe; Chair, Department of voice, Southern Methodist University

2009 – Daniel Weeks (1989), Tenor, voice faculty at the Cincinnati College Conservatory of Music; frequent performer with opera companies and orchestras around the country

2010 – Dr. Sharon Lawhon (1979), Soprano and Dr. Daniel Lawhon (1983), Organist. Sharon Lawhon, Professor of Voice at Samford University and a concert vocalist; Dan Lawhon, Organist-Choirmaster at the Church of the Covenant in Birmingham and Instructor in Organ at Samford University

2012 – Maestra Teresa Cheung (1988), Conductor of the Altoona (PA) Symphony Orchestra

2012 – Dr. Alfredo Colman (1993), Assistant Professor of Musicology/Ethnomusicology at Baylor, author, lecturer and specialist in South American music

2013 – Travis Cottrell (1992), composer, singer, church musician

2014 – Gregg Walter (1987), musical theatre performer, Faculty, North Carolina School of the Arts

2015 – Tina Milhorn Stallard (1996), Soprano concert artist, Faculty, School of Music, University of North Carolina

2016 – Meredith Maddox Hicks (1993), Concert violinist, player, with the Little Rock Symphony Orchestra and instructor in violin, University of Arkansas, Little Rock

About the Author

Richard Shadinger received the BM degree in piano from Shorter University, and the MM and DMA from the School of Church Music of the Southern Baptist Theological Seminary. He began his teaching career at Belmont in 1974. During his years on the faculty he taught musicology, piano and church music, and served for over 25 years as an Associate Dean for the School of Music.

He often performs at Belmont and in the Nashville community as a pianist, harpsichordist and organist. In addition, he plays the 43-bell carillon in Belmont's historic tower.

Shadinger has written numerous articles on subjects related to church music and piano literature. He has served as organist at Nashville's Immanuel Baptist Church since 1982. In *Music on the Beautiful Mountain* he chronicles the history of music on the Belmont campus from the time of Adelicia Acklen until 2016, including Belmont College for Young Women (1890), Ward-Belmont College (1914), Belmont College (1951), and Belmont University (1991).

This publication is limited to 500 copies from which this is number *99*.